Larrie Benton Zacharie (Ed.)

Alpha 21164

Larrie Benton Zacharie (Ed.)

Alpha 21164

Microprocessor, Digital Equipment Corporation, DEC Alpha

VerPublishing

Imprint

All parts of this book are extracted from Wikipedia, the free encyclopedia (www.wikipedia.org).

You can get detailed informations about the authors of this collection of articles at the end of this book. The editors (Ed.) of this book are no authors. They have not modified or extended the original texts.

Pictures published in this book can be under different licences than the GNU Free Documentation License. You can get detailed informations about the authors and licences of pictures at the end of this book.

The content of this book was generated collaboratively by volunteers. Please be advised that nothing found here has necessarily been reviewed by people with the expertise required to provide you with complete, accurate or reliable information. Some information in this book maybe misleading or wrong. The Publisher does not guarantee the validity of the information found here. If you need specific advice (f.e. in fields of medical, legal, financial, or risk management questions) please contact a professional who is licensed or knowledgeable in that area.

Cover image: www.ingimage.com
Concerning the licence of the cover image please contact ingimage.

Publisher:
VerPublishing is a trademark of
International Book Market Service Ltd., 17 Rue Meldrum, Beau Bassin, 1713-01 Mauritius
Email: info@bookmarketservice.com
Website: www.bookmarketservice.com

Published in 2012

Printed in: U.S.A., U.K., Germany. This book was not produced in Mauritius.

ISBN: 978-620-1-56496-1

Contents

Articles

References

Alpha_21164

The **Alpha 21164**, also known by its code name, **EV5**, is a microprocessor developed and fabricated by Digital Equipment Corporation that implemented the Alpha instruction set architecture (ISA). It was introduced in January 1995, succeeding the Alpha 21064A as Digital's flagship microprocessor. It was succeeded by the Alpha 21264 in 1998.

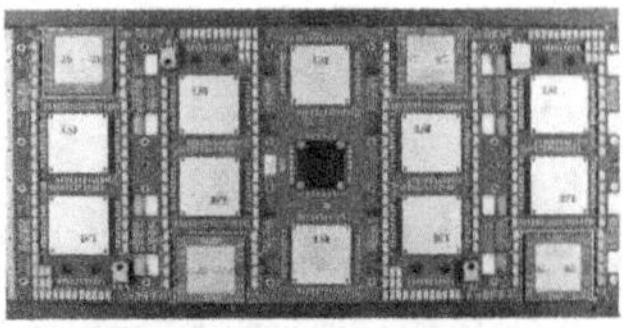

Four 300 MHz Alpha 21164 microprocessors on a Cray T3E-600 processor board.

History

First silicon of the Alpha 21164 was produced in February 1994, and the OpenVMS, Digital UNIX and Windows NT operating systems were successfully booted on it. It was sampled in late 1994 and was introduced in January 1995 at 266 MHz. A 300 MHz version was introduced in March 1995. The final Alpha 21164, a 333 MHz version, was announced on 2 October 1995, available in sample quantities. The Alpha 21164 was replaced by the Alpha 21164A as Digital's flagship microprocessor in 1996 when a 400 MHz version became available in volume quantities.

Users

Digital used the Alpha 21164 operating at various clock frequencies in their AlphaServer servers, AlphaStation workstations. Digital also used the Alpha 21164 in their Alpha VME 5/352 and Alpha VME 5/480 single board computers and AlphaPC 164 and AlphaPC 164LX motherboards. Alpha partner Cray Research used a 300 MHz Alpha 21164 in their T3E-600 supercomputer. Third parties such as DeskStation also built workstations using the Alpha 21164.

Performance

The 21164 continued the performance lead from the 275 MHz Alpha 21064A until the introduction of the Intel Pentium Pro in November 1995, when a 200 MHz version outperformed the 300 MHz 21164 on the SPECint95_base benchmark suite. The 21164 retained its floating-point performance lead. The 333 MHz 21164 introduce the following year outperformed the Pentium Pro, but it was later surpassed by the MIPS Technologies R10000 and then by the Hewlett-Packard PA-8000 in the same year.[1]

Description

The Alpha 21164 is a four-issue superscalar microprocessor capable of issuing a maximum of four instructions per clock cycle to four execution units: two integer and two floating-point. The integer pipeline is seven stages long, and the floating-point pipeline is ten stages long. The 21164 implemented a 43-bit virtual address and a 40-bit physical address. It was therefore capable of addressing 8 TB of virtual memory and 1 TB of physical memory.

Integer unit

The integer unit consisted of two integer pipelines and the integer register file. The two pipelines, the add pipeline and the multiply pipeline are not identical, each are responsible for executing different instructions, although both are capable of executing common add, logical, load, compare, and conditional move instructions. The multiply pipeline exclusively executes shift, store, and multiply instructions (in a non-pipelined multiplier). The add pipeline exclusively executes branch instructions.

Except for branch, conditional move, and multiply instructions, all other instructions begin and finish execution during stage five for a one cycle latency. Branch and conditional move instructions are executed during stage six so they can be issued with a compare instruction whose result they depend on.

The integer register file contained forty 64-bit registers, of which thirty-two are specified by the Alpha Architecture and eight are for use by PALcode as scratchpad memory. The register file has four read ports and two write ports evenly divided between the two integer pipelines.[2]

Floating-point unit

The floating-point unit consisted of two floating-point pipelines and the floating point register file. The two pipelines are not identical, one executed all floating-point instructions except for multiply, and the other executed only multiply instructions. Both pipelines have four stages. A non-pipelined floating-point divider is connected to the add pipeline. All floating-point instructions except for divide have four-cycle latency. Divides have variable latency that depends on whether the operation is being performed on single or on double precision floating-point numbers and numbers. Including overhead, single precision divides have a 15- to 31-cycle latency, whereas double precision divides have a 22- to 60-cycle latency.

Cache

The 21164 has three levels of cache, two on-die and one external and optional. The caches and the associated logic consisted of 7.2 million transistors.[3]

The primary cache is split into separate caches for instructions and data, referred to as the I-cache and D-cache respectively. They are 8 KB in size, direct-mapped and have a cache line size of 32 bytes. The D-cache is dual-ported, to improve performance, and is implemented by duplicating the cache twice. It uses a write-through write policy and an on-read allocation policy.

The secondary cache, known as the S-cache, is on-die and has a capacity of 96 KB. An on-die secondary cache was required as the 21164 required more bandwidth than an external secondary cache could supply in order to provide it with enough instructions and data.[4] The cache required two cycles to access due to its large area. To improve performance, the cache is pipelined. Another benefit of an on-die secondary cache was that it could be easily implemented as a multi-way cache, and as a result, the cache is three-way set associative, offering improved hit rates than direct-mapped caches.[5] The S-cache, due to the large physical area required, was implemented in two halves which flank the I-box, E-box, F-box and M-box. This was done so the cache could return data in two cycles.

The tertiary cache, known as the B-cache, is implemented with external SRAMs. The B-cache was optional and some systems using the Alpha 21164 did not have any. The B-cache could have a capacity of 1 to 64 MB, smaller capacities were not supported as they were rendered useless by the on-die S-cache.[6] It is direct-mapped, uses a write-back write policy and a on-write allocation policy. The B-cache is controlled by on-die external interface logic, unlike the 21064, which required an external cache controller. The B-cache could be built with asynchronous or synchronous SRAMs. The B-cache is accessed via the system bus.

External interface

The external interface is a 128-bit system bus. The system bus operates at a clock frequency that is 3 to 15 times lower than the internal clock frequency, or 20 to 100 MHz with an internal clock frequency 300 MHz. The system bus' clock signal is generated by the microprocessor.

Clock

The internal clock frequency is generated by dividing an external clock signal by two. The Alpha 21164 therefore requires an external clock signal of 600 MHz for a 300 MHz Alpha 21164.

Fabrication

The Alpha 21164 contains 9.3 million transistors on a die measuring 16.5 by 18.1 mm (299 mm^2), which was close to the maximum limits of the process. The die was fabricated in Digital's fifth-generation complementary metal–oxide–semiconductor (CMOS) process, CMOS-5, a 0.50 µm process with four levels of aluminium interconnect.[7] The 21164 used a 3.3-volt (V) power supply. It dissipated 46 W at 266 MHz, 51 W at 300 MHz, 56 W at 333 MHz.

Package

The Alpha 21164 is packaged in a 499-pin ceramic interstitial pin grid array (IPGA) measuring 57.40 by 57.40 mm. The package had a heat spreader with two studs to which the heat sink was bolted to.

Derivatives

Alpha 21164 (EV56)

The Alpha 21164 was the basis of a further development code-named **EV56**. It was introduced as the Alpha 21164, but was originally known as the **Alpha 21164A**. It operated at clock frequencies of 366, 433, 500, 533, 600 and 666 MHz.[8] [9]

A 500 MHz Alpha 21164 (EV56) microprocessor

History

It was first described in October 1995 at the Microprocessor Forum. On 13 November 1995, Digital announced that samples would ship later in the month. The first version, operating at 366 MHz, was introduced in 1996. On 8 July 1996, Digital announced that a 433 MHz version was available and a 500 MHz version was sampling with volume quantities due in September 1996. The 433 MHz version was priced at $1,492 per unit in quantities of 1,000. The 600 MHz version was introduced on 31 March 1997, shipping in volume quantities. Samsung Electronics signed a deal with Digital in June 1996 to second source the Alpha 21164A and the company was the only one to fabricate the 666 MHz model. 366 to 500 MHz samples were introduced on 11 November 1996 with volume availability in 1997. The Alpha 21164A was fabricated at Digital's Hudson, Massachusetts and Samsung's Kihueng, South Korea fabrication plants.

Users of the Alpha 21164A included Cray Research, Digital, Network Appliance (now NetApp), and DeskStation. Cray Research used 450, 600 and 675 MHz Alpha 21164As in later models of their T3E supercomputer. Digital used the Alpha 21164A operating at various clock frequencies in their AlphaServers, AlphaStations, Celebris XL workstations and Digital Personal Workstations. NetApp used 400, 500 and 600 MHz Alpha 21164As in their storage systems. DeskStation used the Alpha 21164A in their Raptor Reflex workstations.

Description

The most notable change was the inclusion of Byte Word Extensions (BWX), an extension to the Alpha Architecture designed to improve byte and word accesses. These instructions are executed by the multiply pipeline. The Alpha 21164A contained 9.66 million transistors on a die measuring 14.4 mm by 14.5 mm, for a die area of 209 mm^2.[10] Digital fabricated the die in their sixth generation CMOS process, CMOS-6, a 0.35 μm process with four layers of interconnect. Samsung fabricated the die in their 0.35 μm process with four layers of interconnect based on a 0.3 μm process they developed in early 1996. The Alpha 21164A used a 3.3 V power supply, dissipating 31.0 W at 366 MHz, 36.0 W at 433 MHz, 41.0 W at 500 MHz, 43.5 W at 533 MHz and 48.5 W at 600 MHz.

Alpha 21164PC (PCA56)

The **Alpha 21164PC**, also known as the **PCA56**, is a low-cost version of the Alpha 21164A introduced on 17 March 1997. The microprocessor was jointly developed by Digital and Mitsubishi Electric Corporation, and both companies fabricated the design. Mitsubishi later suspended the joint development agreement for future Alpha microprocessors with Digital in early 1998 and ceased to fabricate the Alpha 21164PC in mid-1998, exited the Alpha market because the economic conditions in the company's markets.[11] [12]

The Alpha 21164PC operated at clock frequencies of 400, 466 and 533 MHz. Major changes are the omission of the S-cache, a larger I-cache, and the inclusion of Motion Video Instructions (MVI), an extension to the Alpha Architecture which introduced single instruction multiple data (SIMD) instructions for improving the performance of MPEG encoding. The S-cache was removed to reduce the transistor count, which reduced the die size and in turn, cost. The I-cache was doubled in capacity to 16 KB from 8 KB to compensate for the lack of S-cache, as the Alpha 21164 relied on the S-cache to complement the I-cache in order to provide enough bandwidth to achieve adequate performance. The amount of B-cache was limited to 512 KB to 4 MB, with 1 and 2 MB capacities also supported. The microprocessor uses a 43-bit virtual address and 33-bit physical address.

The Alpha 21164PC contained 3.5 million transistors on a die measuring 8.65 by 16.28 mm, for a die area of 141 mm^2. Digital fabricated the die in the same process as the Alpha 21164, CMOS-5. The Alpha 21164PC was packaged in 413-pin IPGA measuring 49.78 by 49.78 mm. It used a 3.3 V power supply, dissipating 26.5 W at 400 MHz, 30.5 W at 466 MHz and 35.0 W at 533 MHz.

The Alpha 21164PC was used by Digital in their AlphaPC 164SX motherboard.

Alpha 21164PC (PCA57)

A derivative of the PCA56, the **PCA57** was designed and fabricated by Samsung Electronics in a 0.28 μm CMOS process. The PCA57 was introduced in late 1998 and operated at clock frequencies of 533, 600 and 666 MHz. Improvements to the PCA56 microarchitecture included doubled I-cache and D-cache capacities: 32 KB and 16 KB respectively. The PCA57 contained 5.7 million transistors on a die measuring 6.7 mm by 15 mm, for a die area of 101 mm^2. It operated on a 2.5 V power supply and dissipated 18 W at 533 MHz, 20 W at 600 MHz and 23 W at 666 MHz.

The PCA57 was used by Digital in its AlphaPC 164RX motherboard.

Chipsets

Digital and VLSI Technology developed chipsets for the 21164 and its derivatives. Digital also developed custom application-specific integrated circuit (ASICs) for use in the high-end models of their AlphaServer family such as the AlphaServer 8200 and 8400.

21171

The 21171, also known as Alcor, was the first chipset for the 21164, introduced in January 1995 alongside the microprocessor it supports. It was developed and fabricated by Digital. The 21171 is an upgraded DECchip 21071 modified to support the new system bus protocol the 21164 uses. It consisted of a control chip that contained the memory and PCI controllers, and four data slice chips that interfaced the 256-bit memory bus and PCI bus to the system bus. The 21171 provides a 64-bit wide PCI bus that runs at 33 MHz.

21172

The 21172, also known as Alcor2, was an updated 21171 that supported the 21164A.

Pyxis

The Pyxis chipset, also known as the 21174, supported the 21164A and 21164PC microprocessors. Unlike previous chipsets, it was designed for low-cost systems. As a result, it was a single-chip design packaged in a 474-contact ceramic ball grid array (CBGA) instead of multiple packages.[13] It was subsequently used in cost-sensitive applications such as entry-level workstations (Digital Personal Workstation a-Series) and motherboards such as the AlphaPC 164LX and 164SX. When it was introduced, the 21174 was priced at US$142 in quantities of 1,000.[14]

The 21174 contains a memory controller and PCI controller. The memory controller supported up to 512 MB of synchronous dynamic random access memory (SDRAM) and accesses it via a 128-bit memory bus. The memory can be either ECC or parity protected. The PCI controller provided a PCI or PCI-X bus.

Polaris

Polaris is a system controller developed by VLSI Technology for personal computers that supports the 21164A and 21164PC microprocessors. Polaris was announced on 16 June 1997.[15] It supports up to 768 MB of EDO DRAM or up to 512 MB of SDRAM. The memory is accessed via a 128-bit bus. It provides a 32-bit, 33 MHz PCI bus for I/O.

Users of Polaris included Digital, for its AlphaPC 164RX motherboard.

Notes

[1] Gwennap 1996
[2] Bowhill et al., "Circuit implementation of a 300-MHz 64-bit second-generation CMOS Alpha CPU", p. 124.
[3] Bowhill et al., "Circuit implementation of a 300-MHz 64-bit second-generation CMOS Alpha CPU", p. 111.
[4] Gwennap, "Digital Leads the Pack with 21164", p. 1.
[5] Gwennap, "Digital Leads the Pack with 21164", pp. 1–2.
[6] Gwennap, "Digital Leads the Pack with 21164".
[7] Bowhill, et al., "Circuit implementation of a 300-MHz 64-bit second-generation CMOS Alpha CPU", pp. 100–101.
[8] *Alpha 21164 Microprocessor Data Sheet, August 1998*, p. 113.
[9] *Digital Semiconductor 21164 Alpha Microprocessor Product Brief, 31 March 1997*, p. 2.
[10] Bouchard, "Design objectives of the 0.35 µm Alpha 21164 Microprocessor", p. 3, 5.
[11] Foremski, "Mitsubishi steps back from Alpha".
[12] Foremski, "Mitsubishi Electric stops Alpha microprocessor manufacture".
[13] Schumann 1997
[14] Gwennap 1997
[15] VLSI Technology 1997

References

- Bouchard, Gregg. "Design objectives of the 0.35 μm Alpha 21164 Microprocessor" (http://www.hotchips.org/archives/hc8/2_Mon/HC8.S1/HC8.1.2.pdf). IEEE Hot Chips Symposium, August 1996, IEEE Computer Society.
- Bowhill, William J. et al. (1995). "Circuit Implementation of a 300-MHz 64-bit Second-generation CMOS Alpha CPU". *Digital Technical Journal*, Volume 7, Number 1, pp. 100–118.
- Edmondson, John H. et al. (1995). "Internal Organization of the Alpha 21164, a 300-MHz 64-bit Quad-issue CMOS RISC Microprocessor". *Digital Technical Journal*, Volume 7, Number 1, 1995. pp. 119–135.
- Edmondson, John H. et al. (1995). "Superscalar Instruction Execution in the 21164 Alpha Microprocessor". *IEEE Micro*. pp. 33–43.
- Foremski, Tom (10 February 1998). "Mitsubishi steps back from Alpha" (http://www.electronicsweekly.com/Articles/1998/02/10/6285/mitsubishi-steps-back-from-alpha.htm). *Electronics Weekly*.
- Foremski, Tom (10 July 1998). "Mitsubishi Electric stops Alpha microprocessor manufacture" (http://www.electronicsweekly.com/Articles/1998/07/10/8039/mitsubishi-electric-stops-alpha-microprocessor-manufacture.htm). *Electronics Weekly*.
- Gwennap, Linley (12 September 1994). "Digital Leads the Pack with 21164". *Microprocessor Report*, Volume 8, Number 12.
- Gwennap, Linley (8 July 1996). "Digital's 21164 Reaches 500 MHz". *Microprocessor Report*, Volume 10, Number 9.
- Gwennap, Linley (31 March 1997). "Digital's 21164PC Aimed at PC Market". *Microprocessor Report*, Volume 11, Number 4.
- Ryan, Bob (October 1994). "Alpha Rides High". *Byte*.
- Samsung Semiconductor, Inc. (11 November 1996). " Samsung Introduces 500MHz Alpha 21164 Microprocessor; First product resulting from the Digital/Samsung licensing agreement to begin mass production by Q2 1997 (http://www.thefreelibrary.com/Samsung+Introduces+500MHz+Alpha+21164+Microprocessor;+First+product...-a018845426)". Press release.
- Schumann, Reinhard C. (1997). "Design of the 21174 memory controller for Digital Personal Workstations" (http://www.hpl.hp.com/hpjournal/dtj/vol9num2/vol9num2art5.pdf). *Digital Technical Journal* **9** (2): 57–70.
- VLSI Technology (16 June 1997). "Polaris, VLSI's New Alpha System Controller, Breaks the Gigabyte/Second Memory Transfer Barrier. End-Users Gain Full Performance on Alpha Systems". Press release.

Further reading

- Bannon, P., Saito, Y. (1997). "The Alpha 21164PC microprocessor" (http://ieeexplore.ieee.org/xpls/abs_all.jsp?arnumber=584665). *Proceedings of Compcon '97*, pp. 20–27.
- Bhandarkar, Dileep P. (1995). *Alpha Architecture and Implementations*. Digital Press.
- Carlson, D. et al. (1998). "A 667 MHz RISC microprocessor containing a 6.0 ns 64 b integer multiplier". *ISSCC Digest of Technical Papers*, pp. 294–295.
- Carlson, D.A.; Castelino, R.W.; Mueller, R.O. (November 1997). "Multimedia extensions for a 550-MHz RISC microprocessor" (http://ieeexplore.ieee.org/xpls/abs_all.jsp?arnumber=641681). *IEEE Journal of Solid-State Circuits* **32** (11): pp. 1618–1624.
- Jain, A.K. et al. (1997). "1.38 cm^2 550 MHz microprocessor with multimedia extensions". *ISSCC Digest of Technical Papers*, pp. 174–175, 451.
- Gronowski, Paul E. et al. (May 1998). "High-performance microprocessor design". *IEEE Journal of Solid-State Circuits* **33** (5): pp. 676–686.

- Kobayashi, S. et al. (1997). "A 550 MHz Alpha microprocessor targeted at PC applications" (http://ieeexplore.ieee.org/xpls/abs_all.jsp?arnumber=614758). *Proceedings of the 1997 International Symposium on VLSI Technology, Systems, and Applications*, pp. 203–207.

Microprocessor

Intel 4004, the first general-purpose, commercial microprocessor

A **microprocessor** incorporates the functions of a computer's central processing unit (CPU) on a single integrated circuit (IC),[1] or at most a few integrated circuits.[2] It is a multipurpose, programmable device that accepts digital data as input, processes it according to instructions stored in its memory, and provides results as output. It is an example of sequential digital logic, as it has internal memory. Microprocessors operate on numbers and symbols represented in the binary numeral system.

The advent of low-cost computers on integrated circuits has transformed modern society. General-purpose microprocessors in personal computers are used for computation, text editing, multimedia display, and communication over the Internet. Many more microprocessors are part of embedded systems, providing digital control of a myriad of objects from appliances to automobiles to cellular phones and industrial process control.

Origins

During the 1960s, computer processors were constructed out of small and medium-scale ICs each containing from tens to a few hundred transistors. For each computer built, all of these had to be placed and soldered onto printed circuit boards, and often multiple boards would have to be interconnected in a chassis. The large number of discrete logic gates used more electrical power—and therefore, produced more heat—than a more integrated design with fewer ICs. The distance that signals had to travel between ICs on the boards limited the speed at which a computer could operate.

In the NASA Apollo space missions to the moon in the 1960s and 1970s, all onboard computations for primary guidance, navigation and control were provided by a small custom processor called "The Apollo Guidance Computer". It used a primitive gate array whose only logic elements were three-input NOR gates.[3]

The integration of a whole CPU onto a single chip or on a few chips greatly reduced the cost of processing power. The integrated circuit processor was produced in large numbers by highly automated processes, so unit cost was low. Single-chip processors increase reliability as there were many fewer electrical connections to fail. As microprocessor designs get faster, the cost of manufacturing a chip (with smaller components built on a semiconductor chip the same size) generally stays the same.

Microprocessors integrated into one or a few large-scale ICs the architectures that had previously been implemented using many medium- and small-scale integrated circuits. Continued increases in microprocessor capacity have rendered other forms of computers almost completely obsolete (see history of computing hardware), with one or more microprocessors used in everything from the smallest embedded systems and handheld devices to the largest mainframes and supercomputers.

The first microprocessors emerged in the early 1970s and were used for electronic calculators, using binary-coded decimal (BCD) arithmetic on 4-bit words. Other embedded uses of 4-bit and 8-bit microprocessors, such as terminals, printers, various kinds of automation etc., followed soon after. Affordable 8-bit microprocessors with

16-bit addressing also led to the first general-purpose microcomputers from the mid-1970s on.

Since the early 1970s, the increase in capacity of microprocessors has followed Moore's law; this originally suggested that the number of transistors that can be fitted onto a chip doubles every year,[4] though Moore later refined the period to two years.[5]

Embedded applications

Thousands of items that were traditionally not computer-related include microprocessors. These include large and small household appliances, cars (and their accessory equipment units), car keys, tools and test instruments, toys, light switches/dimmers and electrical circuit breakers, smoke alarms, battery packs, and hi-fi audio/visual components (from DVD players to phonograph turntables.) Such products as cellular telephones, DVD video system and ATSC HDTV broadcast system fundamentally require consumer devices with powerful, low-cost, microprocessors. Increasingly stringent pollution control standards effectively require automobile manufacturers to use microprocessor engine management systems, to allow optimal control of emissions over widely varying operating conditions of an automobile. Non-programmable controls would require complex, bulky, or costly implementation to achieve the results possible with a microprocessor.

A microprocessor control program can be easily tailored to different needs of a product line, allowing upgrades in performance with minimal redesign of the product. Different features can be implemented in different models of a product line at negligible production cost.

Microprocessor control of a system can provide control strategies that would be impractical to implement using electromechanical controls or purpose-built electronic controls. For example, an engine control system in an automobile can adjust ignition timing based on engine speed, load on the engine, ambient temperature, and any observed tendency for knocking - allowing an automobile to operate on a range of fuel grades.

Structure

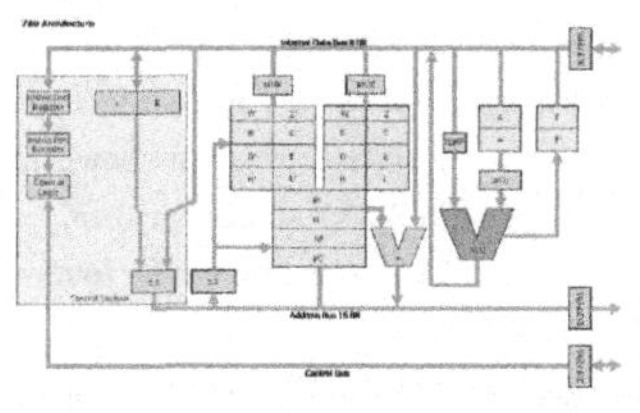

A block diagram of the internal architecture of the Z80 microprocessor, showing the arithmetic and logic section, register file, control logic section, and buffers to external address and data lines

The internal arrangement of a microprocessor varies depending on the age of the design and the intended purposes of the processor. The complexity of an integrated circuit is bounded by physical limitations of the number of transistors that can be put onto one chip, the number of package terminations that can connect the processor to other parts of the system, the number of interconnections it is possible to make on the chip, and the heat that the chip can dissipate. Advancing technology makes more complex and powerful chips feasible to manufacture.

A minimal hypothetical microprocessor might only include an arithmetic logic unit (ALU) and a control logic section. The ALU performs operations such as addition, subtraction, and operations such as AND or OR. Each operation of the ALU sets one or more flags in a status register, which indicate the results of the last operation (zero value, negative number, overflow. or others). The logic section retrieves instruction operation codes from memory, and initiates whatever sequence of operations of the ALU required to carry out the instruction. A single operation code might affect many individual data paths, registers, and other elements of the processor.

As integrated circuit technology advanced, it was feasible to manufacture more and more complex processors on a single chip. The size of data objects became larger; allowing more transistors on a chip allowed word sizes to increase from 4- and 8-bit words up to today's 64-bit words. Additional features were added to the processor architecture; more on-chip registers speeded up programs, and complex instructions could be used to make more compact programs. Floating-point arithmetic, for example, was often not available on 8-bit microprocessors, but had to be carried out in software. Integration of the floating point unit first as a separate integrated circuit and then as part of the same microprocessor chip, speeded up floating point calculations.

Occasionally the physical limitations of integrated circuits made such practices as a bit slice approach necessary. Instead of processing all of a long word on one integrated circuit, multiple circuits in parallel processed subsets of each data word. While this required extra logic to handle, for example, carry and overflow within each slice, the result was a system that could handle, say, 32-bit words using integrated circuits with a capacity for only 4 bits each.

With the ability to put large numbers of transistors on one chip, it becomes feasible to integrate memory on the same die as the processor. This CPU cache has the advantage of faster access than off-chip memory, and increases the processing speed of the system for many applications. Generally, processor speed has increased more rapidly than external memory speed, so cache memory is necessary if the processor is not to be delayed by slower external memory.

Firsts

Three projects delivered a microprocessor at about the same time: Garrett AiResearch's Central Air Data Computer (CADC) (1968), Texas Instruments (TI) TMS 1000 (1971 September), and Intel's 4004 (1971 November).

Intel 4004

The 4004 with cover removed (left) and as actually used (right)

The Intel 4004 is generally regarded as the first commercially available microprocessor,[6] [7] and cost $60.[8] The first known advertisement for the 4004 is dated November 15, 1971 and appeared in Electronic News.[9] The project that produced the 4004 originated in 1969, when Busicom, a Japanese calculator manufacturer, asked Intel to build a chipset for high-performance desktop calculators. Busicom's original design called for a programmable chip set consisting of seven different chips. Three of the chips were to make a special-purpose CPU with its program stored in ROM and its data stored in shift register read-write memory. Ted Hoff, the Intel engineer assigned to evaluate the project, believed the Busicom design could be simplified by using dynamic RAM storage for data, rather than shift register memory, and a more traditional general-purpose CPU architecture. Hoff came up with a four–chip architectural proposal: a ROM chip for storing the programs, a dynamic RAM chip for storing data, a simple I/O device and a 4-bit central processing unit (CPU). Although not a chip designer, he felt the CPU could be integrated into a single chip, but as he lacked the technical know-how the idea remained just a wish for the time being.

While the architecture and specifications of the MCS-4 came from the interaction of Hoff with Stanley Mazor, a software engineer reporting to him, and with Busicom engineer Masatoshi Shima, during 1969, Mazor and Hoff moved on to other projects while in April 1970, Intel hired Federico Faggin as project leader, a move that ultimately made the single-chip CPU final design a reality (Shima instead designed the Busicom calculator firmware and assisted Faggin during the first six months of the implementation). Faggin, who originally developed the silicon gate technology (SGT) in 1968 at Fairchild Semiconductor[10] and designed the world's first commercial integrated circuit using SGT, the Fairchild 3708, had the correct background to lead the project into what would become the first commercial general purpose microprocessor, since it was his very own invention, SGT in addition to his new methodology for random logic design, that made it possible to implement a single-chip CPU with the proper speed, power dissipation and cost. The manager of Intel's MOS Design Department was Leslie L. Vadász. at the time of the MCS-4 development, but Vadasz's attention was completely focused on the mainstream business of semiconductor memories and he left the leadership and the management of the MCS-4 project to Faggin, which was ultimately responsible for leading the 4004 project to its outcome. Production units of the 4004 were first delivered to Busicom in March 1971 and shipped to other customers in late 1971.

TMS 1000

The Smithsonian Institution says TI engineers Gary Boone and Michael Cochran succeeded in creating the first microcontroller (also called a microcomputer) in 1971. The result of their work was the TMS 1000, which went commercial in 1974.[11]

TI developed the 4-bit TMS 1000 and stressed pre-programmed embedded applications, introducing a version called the TMS1802NC on September 17, 1971 which implemented a calculator on a chip.

TI filed for the patent on the microprocessor. Gary Boone was awarded U.S. Patent 3757306 [12] for the single-chip microprocessor architecture on September 4, 1973. It may never be known which company actually had the first working microprocessor running on the lab bench. In both 1971 and 1976, Intel and TI entered into broad patent cross-licensing agreements, with Intel paying royalties to TI for the microprocessor patent. A history of these events is contained in court documentation from a legal dispute between Cyrix and Intel, with TI as intervenor and owner of the microprocessor patent.

A computer-on-a-chip combines the microprocessor core (CPU), memory, and I/O (input/output) lines onto one chip. The computer-on-a-chip patent, called the "microcomputer patent" at the time, U.S. Patent 4074351 [13], was awarded to Gary Boone and Michael J. Cochran of TI. Aside from this patent, the standard meaning of microcomputer is a computer using one or more microprocessors as its CPU(s), while the concept defined in the patent is more akin to a microcontroller.

Pico/General Instrument

In 1971 Pico Electronics[14] and General Instrument (GI) introduced their first collaboration in ICs, a complete single chip calculator IC for the Monroe/Litton Royal Digital III calculator. This chip could also arguably lay claim to be one of the first microprocessors or microcontrollers having ROM, RAM and a RISC instruction set on-chip. The layout for the four layers of the PMOS process was hand drawn at x500 scale on mylar film, a significant task at the time given the complexity of the chip.

The PICO1/GI250 chip introduced in 1971. This was designed by Pico Electronics (Glenrothes, Scotland) and manufactured by General Instrument of Hicksville NY

Pico was a spinout by five GI design engineers whose vision was to create single chip calculator ICs. They had significant previous design experience on multiple calculator chipsets with both GI and Marconi-Elliott.[15] The key team members had originally been tasked by Elliott Automation to create an 8 bit computer in MOS and had helped establish a MOS Research Laboratory in Glenrothes, Scotland in 1967.

Calculators were becoming the largest single market for semiconductors and Pico and GI went on to have significant success in this burgeoning market. GI continued to innovate in microprocessors and microcontrollers with products including the CP1600, IOB1680 and PIC1650.[16] In 1987 the GI Microelectronics business was spun out into the Microchip PIC microcontroller business.

CADC

In 1968, Garrett AiResearch (which employed designers Ray Holt and Steve Geller) was invited to produce a digital computer to compete with electromechanical systems then under development for the main flight control computer in the US Navy's new F-14 Tomcat fighter. The design was complete by 1970, and used a MOS-based chipset as the core CPU. The design was significantly (approximately 20 times) smaller and much more reliable than the mechanical systems it competed against, and was used in all of the early Tomcat models. This system contained "a 20-bit, pipelined, parallel multi-microprocessor". The Navy refused to allow publication of the design until 1997. For this reason the CADC, and the MP944 chipset it used, are fairly unknown.[17] Ray Holt graduated California Polytechnic University in 1968, and began his computer design career with the CADC. From its inception, it was shrouded in secrecy until 1998 when at Holt's request, the US Navy allowed the documents into the public domain. Since then several have debated if this was the first microprocessor. Holt has stated that no one has compared this microprocessor with those that came later.[18] According to Parab et al. (2007), *"The scientific papers and literature published around 1971 reveal that the MP944 digital processor used for the F-14 Tomcat aircraft of the US Navy qualifies as the first microprocessor. Although interesting, it was not a single-chip processor, and was not general purpose – it was more like a set of parallel building blocks you could use to make a special-purpose DSP form. It indicates that today's industry theme of converging DSP-microcontroller architectures was started in 1971."*[19] This convergence of DSP and microcontroller architectures is known as a Digital Signal Controller.

Gilbert Hyatt

Gilbert Hyatt was awarded a patent claiming an invention pre-dating both TI and Intel, describing a "microcontroller".[20] The patent was later invalidated, but not before substantial royalties were paid out.[21] [22]

Four-Phase Systems AL1

The Four-Phase Systems AL1 was an 8-bit bit slice chip containing eight registers and an ALU.[23] It was designed by Lee Boysel in 1969.[24] [25] [26] At the time, it formed part of a nine-chip, 24-bit CPU with three AL1s, but it was later called a microprocessor when, in response to 1990s litigation by Texas Instruments, a demonstration system was constructed where a single AL1 formed part of a courtroom demonstration computer system, together with RAM, ROM, and an input-output device.[27]

8-bit designs

The Intel 4004 was followed in 1972 by the Intel 8008, the world's first 8-bit microprocessor. The 8008 was not, however, an extension of the 4004 design, but instead the culmination of a separate design project at Intel, arising from a contract with Computer Terminals Corporation, of San Antonio TX, for a chip for a terminal they were designing,[28] the Datapoint 2200 — fundamental aspects of the design came not from Intel but from CTC. In 1968, CTC's Austin O. "Gus" Roche developed the original design for the instruction set and operation of the processor. In 1969, CTC contracted two companies, Intel and Texas Instruments, to make a single-chip implementation, known as the CTC 1201.[29] In late 1970 or early 1971, TI dropped out being unable to make a reliable part. In 1970, with Intel yet to deliver the part, CTC opted to use their own implementation in the Datapoint 3300, using traditional TTL logic instead (thus the first machine to run "8008 code" was not in fact a microprocessor at all). Intel's version of the 1201 microprocessor arrived in late 1971, but was too late, slow, and required a number of additional support chips. CTC had no interest in using it. CTC had originally contracted Intel for the chip, and would have owed them $50,000 for their design work.[29] To avoid paying for a chip they did not want (and could not use), CTC released Intel from their contract and allowed them free use of the design.[29] Intel marketed it as the 8008 in April, 1972, as the world's first 8-bit microprocessor. It was the basis for the famous "Mark-8" computer kit advertised in the magazine *Radio-Electronics* in 1974.

The 8008 was the precursor to the very successful Intel 8080 (1974), which offered much improved performance over the 8008 and required fewer support chips, Zilog Z80 (1976), and derivative Intel 8-bit processors. The competing Motorola 6800 was released August 1974 and the similar MOS Technology 6502 in 1975 (both designed largely by the same people). The 6502 family rivaled the Z80 in popularity during the 1980s.

A low overall cost, small packaging, simple computer bus requirements, and sometimes the integration of extra circuitry (e.g. the Z80's built-in memory refresh circuitry) allowed the home computer "revolution" to accelerate sharply in the early 1980s. This delivered such inexpensive machines as the Sinclair ZX-81, which sold for US$99. A variation of the 6502, the MOS Technology 6510 was used in the Commodore 64 and yet another variant, the 8502, powered the Commodore 128.

The Western Design Center, Inc (WDC) introduced the CMOS 65C02 in 1982 and licensed the design to several firms. It was used as the CPU in the Apple IIe and IIc personal computers as well as in medical implantable grade pacemakers and defibrillators, automotive, industrial and consumer devices. WDC pioneered the licensing of microprocessor designs, later followed by ARM and other microprocessor Intellectual Property (IP) providers in the 1990s.

Motorola introduced the MC6809 in 1978, an ambitious and thought-through 8-bit design source compatible with the 6800 and implemented using purely hard-wired logic. (Subsequent 16-bit microprocessors typically used microcode to some extent, as CISC design requirements were getting too complex for purely hard-wired logic only.)

Another early 8-bit microprocessor was the Signetics 2650, which enjoyed a brief surge of interest due to its innovative and powerful instruction set architecture.

A seminal microprocessor in the world of spaceflight was RCA's RCA 1802 (aka CDP1802, RCA COSMAC) (introduced in 1976), which was used onboard the Galileo probe to Jupiter (launched 1989, arrived 1995). RCA COSMAC was the first to implement CMOS technology. The CDP1802 was used because it could be run at very low power, and because a variant was available fabricated using a special production process (Silicon on Sapphire), providing much better protection against cosmic radiation and electrostatic discharges than that of any other processor of the era. Thus, the SOS version of the 1802 was said to be the first radiation-hardened microprocessor.

The RCA 1802 had what is called a *static design*, meaning that the clock frequency could be made arbitrarily low, even to 0 Hz, a total stop condition. This let the Galileo spacecraft use minimum electric power for long uneventful stretches of a voyage. Timers and/or sensors would awaken/improve the performance of the processor in time for important tasks, such as navigation updates, attitude control, data acquisition, and radio communication. Current versions of the Western Design Center 65C02 and 65C816 have static cores and thus will retain data even when the clock is completely halted.

12-bit designs

The Intersil 6100 family consisted of a 12-bit microprocessor (the 6100) and a range of peripheral support and memory ICs. The microprocessor recognised the DEC PDP-8 minicomputer instruction set. As such it was sometimes referred to as the **CMOS-PDP8**. Since it was also produced by Harris Corporation, it was also known as the **Harris HM-6100**. By virtue of its CMOS technology and associated benefits, the 6100 was being incorporated into some military designs until the early 1980s.

16-bit designs

The first multi-chip 16-bit microprocessor was the National Semiconductor IMP-16, introduced in early 1973. An 8-bit version of the chipset was introduced in 1974 as the IMP-8.

Other early multi-chip 16-bit microprocessors include one used by Digital Equipment Corporation (DEC) in the LSI-11 OEM board set and the packaged PDP 11/03 minicomputer, and the Fairchild Semiconductor MicroFlame 9440, both of which were introduced in the 1975 to 1976 timeframe.

In 1975, National introduced the first 16-bit single-chip microprocessor, the National Semiconductor PACE, which was later followed by an NMOS version, the INS8900.

Another early single-chip 16-bit microprocessor was TI's TMS 9900, which was also compatible with their TI-990 line of minicomputers. The 9900 was used in the TI 990/4 minicomputer, the TI-99/4A home computer, and the TM990 line of OEM microcomputer boards. The chip was packaged in a large ceramic 64-pin DIP package, while most 8-bit microprocessors such as the Intel 8080 used the more common, smaller, and less expensive plastic 40-pin DIP. A follow-on chip, the TMS 9980, was designed to compete with the Intel 8080, had the full TI 990 16-bit instruction set, used a plastic 40-pin package, moved data 8 bits at a time, but could only address 16 KB. A third chip, the TMS 9995, was a new design. The family later expanded to include the 99105 and 99110.

The Western Design Center (WDC) introduced the CMOS 65816 16-bit upgrade of the WDC CMOS 65C02 in 1984. The 65816 16-bit microprocessor was the core of the Apple IIgs and later the Super Nintendo Entertainment System, making it one of the most popular 16-bit designs of all time.

Intel "upsized" their 8080 design into the 16-bit Intel 8086, the first member of the x86 family, which powers most modern PC type computers. Intel introduced the 8086 as a cost effective way of porting software from the 8080 lines, and succeeded in winning much business on that premise. The 8088, a version of the 8086 that used an 8-bit external data bus, was the microprocessor in the first IBM PC. Intel then released the 80186 and 80188, the 80286 and, in 1985, the 32-bit 80386, cementing their PC market dominance with the processor family's backwards compatibility. The 80186 and 80188 were essentially versions of the 8086 and 8088, enhanced with some onboard peripherals and a few new instructions; they were not used in IBM-compatible PCs because the built-in perpherals and their locations in the memory map were incompatible with the IBM design. The 8086 and successors had an innovative but limited method of memory segmentation, while the 80286 introduced a full-featured segmented memory management unit (MMU). The 80386 introduced a flat 32-bit memory model with paged memory management.

The Intel x86 processors up to and including the 80386 do not include floating-point units (FPUs). Intel introduced the 8087, 80287, and 80387 math coprocessors to add hardware floating-point and transcendental function capabilities to the 8086 through 80386 CPUs. The 8087 works with the 8086/8088 and 80186/80188,[30] the 80187 works with the 80186/80188, the 80287 works with the 80286 and 80386,[31] and the 80387 works with the 80386 (yielding better performance than the 80287). The combination of an x86 CPU and an x87 coprocessor forms a single multi-chip microprocessor; the two chips are programmed as a unit using a single integrated instruction set.[32] Though the 8087 coprocessor is interfaced to the CPU through I/O ports in the CPU's address space, this is transparent to the program, which does not need to know about or access these I/O ports directly; the program accesses the coprocessor and its registers through normal instruction opcodes. Starting with the successor to the 80386, the 80486, the FPU was integrated with the control unit, MMU, and integer ALU in a pipelined design on a single chip (in the 80486DX version), or the FPU was eliminated entirely (in the 80486SX version). An ostensible coprocessor for the 80486SX, the 80487, was actually a complete 80486DX which disabled and replaced the coprocessorless 80486SX that it was installed to upgrade.

32-bit designs

16-bit designs had only been on the market briefly when 32-bit implementations started to appear.

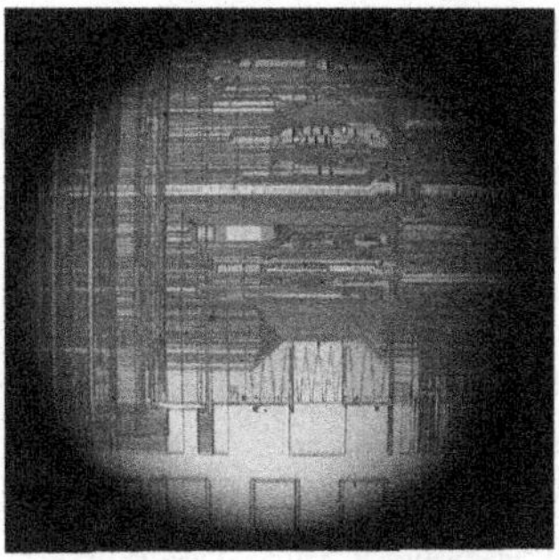

Upper interconnect layers on an Intel 80486DX2 die

The most significant of the 32-bit designs is the MC68000, introduced in 1979. The 68K, as it was widely known, had 32-bit registers in its programming model but used 16-bit internal data paths, 3 16-bit Arithmetic Logic Units, and a 16-bit external data bus (to reduce pin count), and externally supported only 24-bit addresses (internally it worked with full 32 bit addresses). In PC-based IBM-compatible mainframes the MC68000 internal microcode was modified to emulate the 32-bit System/370 IBM mainframe.[33] Motorola generally described it as a 16-bit processor, though it clearly has 32-bit capable architecture. The combination of high performance, large (16 megabytes or 2^{24} bytes) memory space and fairly low cost made it the most popular CPU design of its class. The Apple Lisa and Macintosh designs made use of the 68000, as did a host of other designs in the mid-1980s, including the Atari ST and Commodore Amiga.

The world's first single-chip fully 32-bit microprocessor, with 32-bit data paths, 32-bit buses, and 32-bit addresses, was the AT&T Bell Labs BELLMAC-32A, with first samples in 1980, and general production in 1982[34] [35] After the divestiture of AT&T in 1984, it was renamed the WE 32000 (WE for Western Electric), and had two follow-on generations, the WE 32100 and WE 32200. These microprocessors were used in the AT&T 3B5 and 3B15 minicomputers; in the 3B2, the world's first desktop supermicrocomputer; in the "Companion", the world's first 32-bit laptop computer; and in "Alexander", the world's first book-sized supermicrocomputer, featuring ROM-pack memory cartridges similar to today's gaming consoles. All these systems ran the UNIX System V operating system.

Intel's first 32-bit microprocessor was the iAPX 432, which was introduced in 1981 but was not a commercial success. It had an advanced capability-based object-oriented architecture, but poor performance compared to contemporary architectures such as Intel's own 80286 (introduced 1982), which was almost four times as fast on typical benchmark tests. However, the results for the iAPX432 was partly due to a rushed and therefore suboptimal Ada compiler.

The ARM first appeared in 1985. This is a RISC processor design, which has since come to dominate the 32-bit embedded systems processor space due in large part to its power efficiency, its licensing model, and its wide selection of system development tools. Semiconductor manufacturers generally license cores such as the ARM11 and integrate them into their own system on a chip products; only a few such vendors are licensed to modify the ARM cores. Most cell phones include an ARM processor, as do a wide variety of other products. There are microcontroller-oriented ARM cores without virtual memory support, as well as SMP applications processors with virtual memory.

Motorola's success with the 68000 led to the MC68010, which added virtual memory support. The MC68020, introduced in 1985 added full 32-bit data and address buses. The 68020 became hugely popular in the Unix supermicrocomputer market, and many small companies (e.g., Altos, Charles River Data Systems) produced desktop-size systems. The MC68030 was introduced next, improving upon the previous design by integrating the MMU into the chip. The continued success led to the MC68040, which included an FPU for better math performance. A 68050 failed to achieve its performance goals and was not released, and the follow-up MC68060 was released into a market saturated by much faster RISC designs. The 68K family faded from the desktop in the early 1990s.

Other large companies designed the 68020 and follow-ons into embedded equipment. At one point, there were more 68020s in embedded equipment than there were Intel Pentiums in PCs.[36] The ColdFire processor cores are derivatives of the venerable 68020.

During this time (early to mid-1980s), National Semiconductor introduced a very similar 16-bit pinout, 32-bit internal microprocessor called the NS 16032 (later renamed 32016), the full 32-bit version named the NS 32032. Later the NS 32132 was introduced which allowed two CPUs to reside on the same memory bus, with built in arbitration. The NS32016/32 outperformed the MC68000/10 but the NS32332 which arrived at approximately the same time the MC68020 did not have enough performance. The third generation chip, the NS32532 was different. It had about double the performance of the MC68030 which was released around the same time. The appearance of RISC processors like the AM29000 and MC88000 (now both dead) influenced the architecture of the final core, the NS32764. Technically advanced, using a superscalar RISC core, internally overclocked, with a 64 bit bus, it was still capable of executing Series 32000 instructions through real time translation.

When National Semiconductor decided to leave the Unix market, the chip was redesigned into the Swordfish Embedded processor with a set of on chip peripherals. The chip turned out to be too expensive for the laser printer market and was killed. The design team went to Intel and there designed the Pentium processor, which is very similar to the NS32764 core internally. The big success of the Series 32000 was in the laser printer market, where the NS32CG16 with microcoded BitBlt instructions had very good price/performance and was adopted by large companies like Canon. By the mid-1980s, Sequent introduced the first symmetric multiprocessor (SMP) server-class computer using the NS 32032. This was one of the design's few wins, and it disappeared in the late 1980s. The MIPS R2000 (1984) and R3000 (1989) were highly successful 32-bit RISC microprocessors. They were used in high-end workstations and servers by SGI, among others. Other designs included the interesting Zilog Z80000, which arrived too late to market to stand a chance and disappeared quickly.

In the late 1980s, "microprocessor wars" started killing off some of the microprocessors. Apparently, with only one major design win, Sequent, the NS 32032 just faded out of existence, and Sequent switched to Intel microprocessors.

From 1985 to 2003, the 32-bit x86 architectures became increasingly dominant in desktop, laptop, and server markets, and these microprocessors became faster and more capable. Intel had licensed early versions of the architecture to other companies, but declined to license the Pentium, so AMD and Cyrix built later versions of the architecture based on their own designs. During this span, these processors increased in complexity (transistor count) and capability (instructions/second) by at least three orders of magnitude. Intel's Pentium line is probably the most famous and recognizable 32-bit processor model, at least with the public at large.

64-bit designs in personal computers

While 64-bit microprocessor designs have been in use in several markets since the early 1990s, the early 2000s saw the introduction of 64-bit microprocessors targeted at the PC market.

With AMD's introduction of a 64-bit architecture backwards-compatible with x86, x86-64 (also called **AMD64**), in September 2003, followed by Intel's near fully compatible 64-bit extensions (first called IA-32e or EM64T, later renamed **Intel 64**), the 64-bit desktop era began. Both versions can run 32-bit legacy applications without any performance penalty as well as new 64-bit software. With operating systems Windows XP x64, Windows Vista x64, Windows 7 x64, Linux, BSD and Mac OS X that run 64-bit native, the software is also geared to fully utilize the capabilities of such processors. The move to 64 bits is more than just an increase in register size from the IA-32 as it also doubles the number of general-purpose registers.

The move to 64 bits by PowerPC processors had been intended since the processors' design in the early 90s and was not a major cause of incompatibility. Existing integer registers are extended as are all related data pathways, but, as was the case with IA-32, both floating point and vector units had been operating at or above 64 bits for several years. Unlike what happened when IA-32 was extended to x86-64, no new general purpose registers were added in 64-bit PowerPC, so any performance gained when using the 64-bit mode for applications making no use of the larger address space is minimal.

Multicore designs

A different approach to improving a computer's performance is to add extra processors, as in symmetric multiprocessing designs, which have been popular in servers and workstations since the early 1990s. Keeping up with Moore's Law is becoming increasingly challenging as chip-making technologies approach their physical limits.

In response, microprocessor manufacturers look for other ways to improve performance in order to hold on to the momentum of constant upgrades in the market.

A multi-core processor is simply a single chip containing more than one microprocessor core. This effectively multiplies the processor's potential performance by the number of cores (as long as the operating system and software is designed to take advantage of more than one processor core). Some components, such as bus interface and cache, may be shared between cores. Because the cores are physically very close to each other, they can communicate with each other much faster than separate processors in a multiprocessor system, which improves overall system performance.

In 2005, the first personal computer dual-core processors were announced. As of 2012, dual-core and quad-core processors are widely used in home PCs and laptops while quad, six, eight, ten, twelve, and sixteen-core processors are common in the professional and enterprise markets with workstations and servers.

Sun Microsystems has released the Niagara and Niagara 2 chips, both of which feature an eight-core design. The Niagara 2 supports more threads and operates at 1.6 GHz.

High-end Intel Xeon processors that are on the LGA 771, LGA1336, and LGA 2011 sockets and high-end AMD Opteron processors that are on the C32 and G34 sockets are DP (dual processor) capable, as well as the older Intel Core 2 Extreme QX9775 also used in an older Mac Pro by Apple and the Intel Skulltrail motherboard. AMD's G34 motherboards can support up to four CPUs and Intel's LGA 1567 motherboards can support up to eight CPUs.

The modern desktop sockets do not support systems with multiple CPUs but very few applications outside of the professional market can make good use of more than four cores and both Intel and AMD currently offer fast quad and six core desktop CPUs so this is generally a moot point anyway. AMD also offers the first and still currently the only eight core desktop CPUs with the FX-8xxx line but anything with more than four cores is generally not very useful in home desktops. As of January 24 of 2012, these FX processors are generally inferior to similarly priced and some times cheaper Intel quad core Sandy Bridge models.

The desktop market has been in a transition towards quad core CPUs since Intel's Core 2 Quads were released and now are quite common although dual core CPUs are still more prevalent. This is largely because of people using older or mobile computers, both of which have a much lower chance of having more than two cores than newer desktops and because of how most computer users are not heavy users. AMD offers CPUs with more cores for a given amount of money than similarly priced Intel CPUs but the AMD cores are somewhat slower than Intel cores so the two will trade blows in different applications depending on how well threaded the programs being used are.

For example, Intel's cheapest Sandy Bridge quad core CPUs often cost almost twice as much as AMD's cheapest Athlon II, Phenom II, and FX quad core CPUs but Intel has dual core CPUs in the same price ranges as AMD's cheaper quad core CPUs. In an application that uses one or two threads the Intel dual cores will out-perform AMD's similarly priced quad core CPUs and if a program supports three or four threads the cheap AMD quad core CPUs will out-perform the similarly priced Intel dual-core CPUs.

Historically AMD and Intel have switched places as the company with the fastest CPU several times. Intel is currently winning on the desktop side of the computer CPU market with their Sandy Bridge and upcoming Ivy Bridge series. In servers AMD's new Opterons seem to have superior performance for their price points. This means that AMD is currently more competitive in low to mid end servers and workstations where more cores and threads are more effectively utilized since professional software often uses more, if not all available threads.

RISC

In the mid-1980s to early-1990s, a crop of new high-performance Reduced Instruction Set Computer (RISC) microprocessors appeared, influenced by discrete RISC-like CPU designs such as the IBM 801 and others. RISC microprocessors were initially used in special-purpose machines and Unix workstations, but then gained wide acceptance in other roles.

In 1986, HP released its first system with a PA-RISC CPU. The first commercial RISC microprocessor design was released either by MIPS Computer Systems, the 32-bit R2000 (the R1000 was not released) or by Acorn computers, the 32-bit ARM2 in 1987. The R3000 made the design truly practical, and the R4000 introduced the world's first commercially available 64-bit RISC microprocessor. Competing projects would result in the IBM POWER and Sun SPARC architectures. Soon every major vendor was releasing a RISC design, including the AT&T CRISP, AMD 29000, Intel i860 and Intel i960, Motorola 88000, DEC Alpha.

As of 2007, two 64-bit RISC architectures are still produced in volume for non-embedded applications: SPARC and Power ISA.

Special-purpose designs

A microprocessor is a general purpose system. Several specialized processing devices have followed from the technology. Microcontrollers integrate a microprocessor with periphal devices for control of embedded system. A digital signal processor (DSP) is specialized for signal processing. Graphics processing units may have no, limited, or general programming facilities. For example, GPUs through the 1990s were mostly non-programmable and have only recently gained limited facilities like programmable vertex shaders.

Market statistics

In 2003, about $44 billion (USD) worth of microprocessors were manufactured and sold.[37] Although about half of that money was spent on CPUs used in desktop or laptop personal computers, those count for only about 2% of all CPUs sold.[38]

About 55% of all CPUs sold in the world are 8-bit microcontrollers, over two billion of which were sold in 1997.[39]

As of 2002, less than 10% of all the CPUs sold in the world are 32-bit or more. Of all the 32-bit CPUs sold, about 2% are used in desktop or laptop personal computers. Most microprocessors are used in embedded control applications such as household appliances, automobiles, and computer peripherals. Taken as a whole, the average price for a microprocessor, microcontroller, or DSP is just over $6.[38]

About ten billion CPUs were manufactured in 2008. About 98% of new CPUs produced each year are embedded.[40]

See also

- Arithmetic logic unit
- Central processing unit
- Comparison of CPU architectures
- Computer architecture
- Computer engineering
- CPU design
- Floating point unit
- Instruction set
- List of instruction sets
- List of microprocessors
- Microarchitecture

- Microcode
- Microprocessor chronology

Notes

[1] Osborne, Adam (1980). *An Introduction to Microcomputers*. **Volume 1: Basic Concepts** (2nd ed.). Berkely, California: Osborne-McGraw Hill. ISBN 0-931988-34-9.

[2] Krishna Kant *Microprocessors And Microcontrollers: Architecture Programming And System Design*PHI Learning Pvt. Ltd., 2007 ISBN 81-203-3191-5 page 61, describing the iAPX 432

[3] Back to the Moon: The Verification of a Small Microprocessor's Logic Design (http://klabs.org/richcontent/verification/80k85_verification/index.htm) - NASA Office of Logic Design

[4] Moore, Gordon (19 April 1965). "Cramming more components onto integrated circuits" (ftp://download.intel.com/museum/Moores_Law/Articles-Press_Releases/Gordon_Moore_1965_Article.pdf) (PDF). *Electronics* **38** (8). . Retrieved 2009-12-23.

[5] (PDF) *Excerpts from A Conversation with Gordon Moore: Moore's Law* (ftp://download.intel.com/museum/Moores_Law/Video-Transcripts/Excepts_A_Conversation_with_Gordon_Moore.pdf). Intel. 2005. . Retrieved 2009-12-23.

[6] Mack, Pamela E. (30 November 2005). "The Microcomputer Revolution" (http://www.clemson.edu/caah/history/FacultyPages/PamMack/lec122/micro.htm). . Retrieved 2009-12-23.

[7] (PDF) *History in the Computing Curriculum* (http://www.hofstra.edu/pdf/CompHist_9812tla6.PDF). . Retrieved 2009-12-23.

[8] Halfhill, Tom, "The Intel 4004's 35th Anniversary", Microprocessor Report, Dec. 18, 2006, www.MPRonline.com

[9] Faggin, Federico; Hoff, Marcian E., Jr.; Mazor, Stanley; Shima, Masatoshi (December 1996). "The History of the 4004" (http://ieeexplore.ieee.org/xpl/freeabs_all.jsp?arnumber=546561). *IEEE Micro* **16** (6): 10–20. .

[10] Faggin, F.; Klein, T.; L. (23 October 1968). "Insulated Gate Field Effect Transistor Integrated Circuits with Silicon Gates" (http://www.intel4004.com/images/iedm_covart.jpg) (JPEG image). International Electronic Devices Meeting. IEEE Electron Devices Group. . Retrieved 2009-12-23.

[11] Augarten, Stan (1983). *The Most Widely Used Computer on a Chip: The TMS 1000* (http://smithsonianchips.si.edu/augarten/p38.htm). New Haven and New York: Ticknor & Fields. ISBN 0-89919-195-9. . Retrieved 2009-12-23.

[12] http://www.google.com/patents?vid=3757306

[13] http://www.google.com/patents?vid=4074351

[14] McGonigal, James (20 September 2006). "Microprocessor History: Foundations in Glenrothes, Scotland" (http://www.spingal.plus.com/micro). *McGonigal personal website* accessdate=2009-12-23. .

[15] Tout, Nigel. "ANITA at its Zenith" (http://anita-calculators.info/html/anita_at_its_zenith.html). *Bell Punch Company and the ANITA calculators*. . Retrieved 2010-07-25.

[16] 16 Bit Microprocessor Handbook by Gerry Kane, Adam Osborne ISBN 0-07-931043-5 (0-07-931043-5)

[17] Holt, Ray M.. "World's First Microprocessor Chip Set" (http://web.archive.org/web/20100725060322/http://www.microcomputerhistory.com/index.php). Ray M. Holt website. Archived from the original (http://www.microcomputerhistory.com) on 2010-07-25. . Retrieved 2010-07-25.

[18] Holt, Ray (27 September 2001). *Lecture: Microprocessor Design and Development for the US Navy F14 FighterJet* (http://www.pdl.cmu.edu/SDI/2001/092701.html) (Speech). Room 8220, Wean Hall, Carnegie Mellon University, Pittsburgh, PA, US. . Retrieved 2010-07-25.

[19] Parab, Jivan S.; Shelake, Vinod G.; Kamat, Rajanish K.; Naik, Gourish M. (2007) (PDF). *Exploring C for Microcontrollers: A Hands on Approach* (http://ee.sharif.edu/~sakhtar3/books/Exploring C for Microcontrollers.pdf). Springer. p. 4. ISBN 978-1-4020-6067-0. . Retrieved 2010-07-25.

[20] Hyatt, Gilbert P., "Single chip integrated circuit computer architecture", Patent 4942516 (http://www.google.com/patents/about?id=cNcbAAAAEBAJ), issued July 17, 1990

[21] "The Gilbert Hyatt Patent" (http://www.intel4004.com/hyatt.htm). *intel4004.com*. Federico Faggin. . Retrieved 2009-12-23.

[22] Crouch, Dennis (1 July 2007). "Written Description: CAFC Finds Prima Facie Rejection(Hyatt v. Dudas (Fed. Cir. 2007)" (http://www.patentlyo.com/patent/2007/07/hyatt-v-dudas-f.html). *Patently-O blog*. . Retrieved 2009-12-23.

[23] Basset, Ross (2003). "When is a Microprocessor not a Microprocessor? The Industrial Construction of Semiconductor Innovation" (http://books.google.com/books?id=rsRJTiu1h9MC). In Finn, Bernard. *Exposing Electronics*. Michigan State University Press. p. 121. ISBN 0-87013-658-5. .

[24] "1971 - Microprocessor Integrates CPU Function onto a Single Chip" (http://www.computerhistory.org/semiconductor/timeline/1971-MPU.html). *The Silicon Engine*. Computer History Museum. . Retrieved 2010-07-25.

[25] Shaller, Robert R. (15 April 2004). "Dissertation: Technological Innovation in the Semiconductor Industry: A Case Study of the International Technology Roadmap for Semiconductors" (http://web.archive.org/web/20061219012629/http://home.comcast.net/~gordonepeterson2/schaller_dissertation_2004.pdf) (PDF). George Mason University. Archived from the original (http://home.comcast.net/~gordonepeterson2/schaller_dissertation_2004.pdf) on 2006-12-19. . Retrieved 2010-07-25.

[26] RW (3 March 1995). "Interview with Gordon E. Moore" (http://www-sul.stanford.edu/depts/hasrg/histsci/silicongenesis/moore-ntb.html). *LAIR History of Science and Technology Collections*. Los Altos Hills, California: Stanford University. .

[27] Bassett 2003. pp. 115, 122.

[28] Ceruzzi, Paul E. (May 2003). *A History of Modern Computing* (2nd ed.). MIT Press. pp. 220–221. ISBN 0-262-53203-4.

[29] Wood, Lamont (August 2008). "Forgotten history: the true origins of the PC" (http://www.webcitation.org/5vZKtCs1r). Computerworld. Archived from the original (http://www.computerworld.com/s/article/9111341/ Forgotten_PC_history_The_true_origins_of_the_personal_computer) on 2011-01-07. . Retrieved 2011-01-07.

[30] Intel 8087 datasheet, pg. 1

[31] Intel387 DX MATH COPROCESSOR datasheet, pg. 1, March 1992 (Order Number: 240448-005)

[32] "Essentially, the 80C187 can be treated as an additional resource or an extension to the CPU. The 80C186 CPU together with an 80C187 can be used as a single unified system." Intel 80C187 datasheet, p. 3, November 1992 (Order Number: 270640-004).

[33] Priorartdatabase.com (http://priorartdatabase.com/IPCOM/000059679#)

[34] "Shoji, M. Bibliography" (http://cm.bell-labs.com/cm/cs/bib/shoji.bib). Bell Laboratories. 7 October 1998. . Retrieved 2009-12-23.

[35] "Timeline: 1982–1984" (http://www.bell-labs.com/org/physicalsciences/timeline/span23.html). *Physical Sciences & Communications at Bell Labs*. Bell Labs, Alcatel-Lucent. 17 January 2001. . Retrieved 2009-12-23.

[36] Turley, Jim (July 1998). "MCore: Does Motorola Need Another Processor Family?" (http://web.archive.org/web/19980702003323/ http://www.embedded.com/98/9807sr.htm). *Embedded Systems Design*. TechInsights (United Business Media). Archived from the original (http://www.embedded.com/98/9807sr.htm) on 1998-07-02. . Retrieved 2009-12-23.

[37] WSTS Board Of Directors. "WSTS Semiconductor Market Forecast World Release Date: 1 June 2004 - 6:00 UTC" (http://web.archive.org/web/20041207091926/http://www.wsts.org/press.html) (Press release). World Semiconductor Trade Statistics. Archived from the original (http://www.wsts.org/press.html) on 2004-12-07. .

[38] Turley, Jim (18 December 2002). "The Two Percent Solution" (http://www.embedded.com/shared/printableArticle.jhtml?articleID=9900861). *Embedded Systems Design*. TechInsights (United Business Media). . Retrieved 2009-12-23.

[39] Cantrell, Tom (1998). "Microchip on the March" (http://web.archive.org/web/20070220134759/http://www.circuitcellar.com/library/designforum/silicon_update/3/index.asp). Archived from the original (http://www.circuitcellar.com/library/designforum/silicon_update/3/) on 2007-02-20. .

[40] Barr, Michael (1 August 2009). "Real men program in C" (http://www.embedded.com/columns/barrcode/218600142?pgno=2). *Embedded Systems Design*. TechInsights (United Business Media). p. 2. . Retrieved 2009-12-23.

References

- Ray, A. K.; Bhurchand, K.M.. *Advanced Microprocessors and Peripherals*. India: Tata McGraw-Hill.

External links

- Dirk Oppelt. "The CPU Collection" (http://www.cpu-collection.de/). Retrieved 2009-12-23.
- Gennadiy Shvets. "CPU-World" (http://www.cpu-world.com/). Retrieved 2009-12-23.
- Jérôme Cremet. "The Cecko's CPU Library" (http://gecko54000.free.fr/). Retrieved 2009-12-23.
- "How Microprocessors Work" (http://computer.howstuffworks.com/microprocessor.htm). Retrieved 2009-12-23.
- William Blair. "IC Die Photography" (http://diephotos.blogspot.com/). Retrieved 2009-12-23.
- John Bayko (December 2003). "Great Microprocessors of the Past and Present" (http://jbayko.sasktelwebsite.net/cpu.html). Retrieved 2009-12-23.
- Wade Warner (22 December 2004). "Great moments in microprocessor history" (http://www-106.ibm.com/developerworks/library/pa-microhist.html?ca=dgr-mw08MicroHistory). IBM. Retrieved 2009-12-23.
- Ray M. Holt. "theDocuments" (http://firstmicroprocessor.com/?page_id=17). *World's First Microprocessor*. Retrieved 2009-12-23.

Digital_Equipment_Corporation

Industry	Computer manufacturing
Fate	Assets were sold to various companies. What remained was sold to Compaq.
Successor(s)	Hewlett-Packard (2002 – present) Compaq (1998–2002)
Founded	1957
Defunct	1998
Headquarters	Maynard, Massachusetts, United States
Key people	Ken Olsen (founder, president, and chairman) Harlan Anderson (co-founder) C. Gordon Bell (VP Engineering, 1972-1983)
Products	PDP minicomputers VAX minicomputers Alpha servers and workstations DECnet VT100 terminal StrongARM microprocessors Digital Linear Tape
Employees	over 140,000 (1987)

Digital Equipment Corporation was a major American company in the computer industry and a leading vendor of computer systems, software and peripherals from the 1960s to the 1990s. Also known as **DEC**[1] and using the trademark **DIGITAL**, its PDP and VAX products were the most successful (in terms of sales) minicomputers.

From 1957 until 1992 its headquarters was located in a former wool mill at Clock Tower Place, Maynard, Massachusetts. DEC was acquired in June 1998 by Compaq, which subsequently merged with Hewlett-Packard in May 2002. Some parts of DEC, notably the compiler business and the Hudson, Massachusetts facility, were sold to Intel.

Digital Equipment Corporation should not be confused with the unrelated companies Digital Research, Inc or Western Digital (despite the latter manufacturing the LSI-11 chipsets used in DEC's low end PDP-11/03 computers).

Overview

Initially focusing on the small-end of the computer market allowed DEC to grow without its potential competitors making serious efforts to compete with them. Their PDP series of machines became popular in the 1960s, especially the PDP-8, widely considered to be the first successful minicomputer. Looking to simplify and update their line, DEC replaced most of their smaller machines with the PDP-11 in 1970, eventually selling over 600,000 units and cementing DECs position in the industry. Originally designed as a follow-on to the PDP-11, DEC's VAX-11 series was the first widely used 32-bit minicomputer, sometimes referred to as "superminis". These were able to compete in many roles with larger mainframe computers, such as the IBM System/370. The VAX was a best-seller, with over 400,000 sold, and its sales through the 1980s propelled the company into the second largest in the industry. At its peak, DEC was the second largest employer in Massachusetts, second only to the state government.

The rapid rise of the business microcomputer in the late 1980s, and especially the introduction of powerful 32-bit systems in the 1990s, quickly eroded the value of DEC's systems. DEC's last major attempt to find a space in the rapidly changing market was the DEC Alpha 64-bit RISC processor architecture. DEC initially started work on Alpha as a way to re-implement their VAX series, but also employed it in a range of high-performance workstations. Although the Alpha processor family met both of these goals, and, for most of its lifetime, was the fastest processor family on the market, it did little to affect the bottom line or repair the company's status.

The company was acquired in June 1998 by Compaq, in what was at that time the largest merger in the history of the computer industry. At the time, Compaq was focused on the enterprise market and had recently purchased several other large vendors. DEC was a major player overseas where Compaq had less presence. However, Compaq had little idea what to do with its acquisitions, and soon found itself in financial difficulty of its own. The company subsequently merged with Hewlett-Packard in May 2002. As of 2007 some of DEC's product lines were still produced under the HP name.

History

Origins

Ken Olsen and Harlan Anderson were two engineers who had been working at MIT Lincoln Laboratory on the lab's various computer projects. The Lab is best known for their work on what would today be known as "interactivity", and their machines were among the first where operators had direct control over programs running in real-time. These had started in 1944 with the famed Whirlwind which was originally developed to make a flight simulator for the US Navy, although this was never completed.[2] Instead, this effort evolved into the SAGE system for the US Air Force, which used large screens and light guns to allow operators to interact with radar data stored in the computer.[3]

DEC was headquartered at a former wool mill at Clock Tower Place, Maynard MA from 1957 until 1992

When the Air Force project wound down, the Lab turned their attention to an effort to build a version of the Whirlwind using transistors in place of vacuum tubes. In order to test their new circuitry, they first built a small 18-bit machine known as TX-0 which first ran in 1956.[4] When the TX-0 successfully proved the basic concepts, attention turned to a much larger system, the 36-bit TX-2 with a then-enormous 64 kWords of core memory. Core was so expensive that parts of TX-0's memory were stripped for the TX-2, and what remained of the TX-0 was then given to MIT on permanent loan.[5]

At MIT, Olsen and Anderson noticed something odd: students would line up for hours to get a turn to use the stripped-down TX-0, while largely ignoring a faster IBM machine that was also available. The two decided that the draw of interactive computing was so strong that they felt there was a market for a small machine dedicated to this role, essentially a commercialized TX-0. They could sell this to users where graphical output or realtime operation would be more important than outright performance. Additionally, as the machine would cost much less than the larger systems then available, it would also be able to serve users that needed a lower-cost solution dedicated to a specific task, where a larger 36-bit machine wouldn't be needed.[6]

In 1957 when the pair and Ken's brother Stan went looking for capital, they found that the American business community was hostile to investing in computer companies. Many smaller computer companies had come and gone in the 1950s, wiped out when new technical developments rendered their platforms obsolete, and even large companies like RCA and General Electric were failing to make a profit in the market. The only serious expression of interest came from Georges Doriot and his American Research and Development Corporation (AR&D). Worried that a new computer company would find it difficult to arrange further financing, Doriot suggested the fledgling company change its business plan to focus less on computers, and even change their name from "Digital Computer Corporation".[6]

The pair returned with an updated business plan that outlined two-phases for the company's development. They would start by selling computer modules as stand-alone devices that could be purchased separately and wired together to produce a number of different digital systems for lab use. Then, if these "digital modules" were able to build a self-sustaining business, the company would be free to use them to develop a complete computer in their Phase II.[7] The newly christened DEC received $70,000 from AR&D for a 70% share of the company,[6] and began operations in a Civil War era textile mill in Maynard, Massachusetts, where plenty of inexpensive manufacturing space was available.

Digital modules

System Building Blocks 1103 hex-inverter card (both sides)

In early 1958 DEC shipped its first products, the "Digital Laboratory Module" line. The Modules consisted of a number of individual electronic components and germanium transistors mounted to a circuit board, the actual circuits being based on those from the TX-2.[8]

The Laboratory Modules were packaged in an extruded aluminum housing,[9] intended to sit on an engineer's workbench. They were then connected together using banana plug patch cords inserted at the front of the modules. Three versions were offered, running at 5 MHz (1957), 500 kHz (1959), or 10 MHz (1960).[8] The Modules proved to be in high demand in other computer companies, who used them to build equipment to test their own systems. Despite the recession of the late 1950s, the company sold $94,000 worth of these modules during 1958 alone, turning a profit at the end of its first year.[6]

The original Laboratory Modules were soon supplemented with the "Digital Systems Module" line, which were identical internally but packaged differently. The Systems Modules were designed with all of the connections at the back of the module using 22-pin Amphenol connectors, and were attached to each other by inserting them into a custom 19-inch rack. These versions allowed 25 modules be to inserted into a single 5-1/4 inch section of racking, and allowed the high densities needed to build a computer.[8] DEC used the Systems Modules to build their "Memory Test" machine for testing core memory systems, selling about 50 of these pre-packaged units over the next eight years.[10]

Modules were part of DEC's product line into the 1970s, although they went through several evolutions during this time as technology changed. The same circuits were then packaged as the first "R" (red) series "Flip-Chip" modules. Later, other module series provided additional speed, much higher logic density, and industrial I/O capabilities.[11] Digital published extensive data about the modules in free catalogs that became very popular.

PDP-1 family

A PDP-1 system, with Steve Russell, developer of Spacewar! at the console. This is a canonical example of the PDP-1, with the console typewriter on the left, CPU and main control panel in the center, the Type 30 display on the right.

With the company established and a successful product on the market, DEC turned its attention to the computer market once again as part of its planned "Phase II".[7] In August 1959, Ben Gurley started design of the company's first computer, the PDP-1. In keeping with Doriot's instructions, the name was an initialism for "Programmable Data Processor", leaving off the term "computer". As Gurley put it, "We aren't building computers, we're building 'Programmable Data Processors'." The prototype was first shown publicly at the Joint Computer Conference in Boston in December 1959.[12] The first PDP-1 was delivered to Bolt, Beranek and Newman in November 1960,[13] and formally accepted the next April.[14] The PDP-1 sold in basic form for $120,000, or about $900,000 in 2011 US dollars.[15] By the time production ended in 1969, 53 PDP-1s had been delivered.[10] [16]

The PDP-1 was supplied standard with 4096 words of core memory, 18-bits per word, and ran at a basic speed of 100,000 operations per second. It was constructed using many System Building Blocks that were packaged into several 19-inch racks. The racks were themselves packaged into a single large mainframe case, with a hexagonal control panel containing switches and lights mounted to lay at table-top height at one end of the mainframe. Above the control panel was the system's standard input/output solution, a punch tape reader and writer. Most systems were purchased with two peripherals, the Type 30 vector graphics display, and a Soroban Engineering modified IBM Model B Electric typewriter that was used as a printer. The Soroban system was notoriously unreliable, and often replaced with a modified Friden Flexowriter, which also contained its own punch tape system. A variety of more-expensive add-ons followed, including magnetic tape systems, punched card readers and punches, and faster punch tape and printer systems.

When DEC introduced the PDP-1, they also mentioned larger machines at 24, 30 and 36-bits, based on the same design.[17] During construction of the prototype PDP-1, some design work was carried out on a 24-bit PDP-2, and the 36-bit PDP-3. Although the PDP-2 never proceeded beyond the initial design, the PDP-3 found some interest and was designed in full.[18] Only one PDP-3 appears to have been built, in 1960, by the CIA's Scientific Engineering Institute (SEI) in Waltham, Massachusetts. According to the limited information available, they used it to process radar cross section data for the Lockheed A-12 reconnaissance aircraft. Gordon Bell remembered that it was being used in Oregon some time later, but could not recall who was using it.[19]

In November 1962 DEC introduced the $65,000 PDP-4. The PDP-4 was similar to the PDP-1 and used a similar instruction set, but used slower memory and different packaging to lower the price. Like the PDP-1, about 54 PDP-4's were eventually sold, most to a customer base similar to the original PDP-1.[20]

In 1964 DEC introduced its new Flip Chip module design, and used it to re-implement the PDP-4 as the PDP-7. The PDP-7 was introduced in December 1964, and about 120 were eventually produced.[21] An upgrade to the Flip Chip led to the R series, which in turn led to the PDP-7A in 1965.[22] The PDP-7 is most famous as the original machine for the Unix operating system.[23]

A more dramatic upgrade to the PDP-1 series was introduced in August 1966, the PDP-9.[24] The PDP-9 was instruction compatible with the PDP-4 and –7, but ran about twice as fast as the –7 and was intended to be used in larger deployments. At only $19,900 in 1968,[25] the PDP-9 was a big seller, eventually selling 445 machines, more than all of the earlier models combined.[26]

Even while the PDP-9 was being introduced, its replacement was being designed, and was introduced as 1969's PDP-15, which re-implemented the PDP-9 using integrated circuits in place of modules. Much faster than the PDP-9 even in basic form, the PDP-15 also included a floating point unit and a separate input/output processor for further performance gains. Over 400 PDP-15's were ordered in the first eight months of production, and production eventually amounted to 790 examples in 12 basic models.[26] However, by this time other machines in DEC's lineup could fill the same niche at even lower price points, and the PDP-15 would be the last of the 18-bit series.

PDP-8 family

In 1962, Lincoln Laboratory used a selection of System Building Blocks to implement a small 12-bit machine, and attached it to a variety of analog-to-digital (A to D) input/output (I/O) devices that made it easy to interface with various analog lab equipment. The LINC proved to attract intense interest in the scientific community, and has since been referred to as the first real minicomputer,[27] a machine that was small and inexpensive enough to be dedicated to a single task even in a small lab.

A PDP-8 on display at the Smithsonian's National Museum of American History in Washington, D.C.. This example is from the first generation of PDP-8s, built with discrete transistors and later known as the *Straight 8*.

Seeing the success of the LINC, in 1963 DEC took the basic logic design but stripped away the extensive A to D systems to produce the PDP-5. The new machine, the first outside the PDP-1 mould, was introduced at WESTCON on 11 August 1963. A 1964 ad expressed the main advantage of the PDP-5, "Now you can own the PDP-5 computer for what a core memory alone used to cost: $27,000"[28] 116 PDP-5s were produced until the lines were shut down in early 1967. Like the PDP-1 before it, the PDP-5 inspired a series of newer models based on the same basic design that would go on to be more famous than its parent.

On 22 March 1965, DEC introduced the PDP-8, which replaced the PDP-5's modules with the new R-series modules using Flip Chips. The machine was re-packaged into a small tabletop case, which remains distinctive for its use of smoked plastic over the CPU which allowed one to easily see the wire-wrapped internals of the CPU. Sold standard with 4 kWords of 12-bit core memory and a Teletype Model 33 ASR for basic input/output, the machine listed for only $18,000. The PDP-8 is referred to as the first *real* minicomputer because of its sub-$25,000 price.[29] [30] Sales were, unsurprisingly, very strong, and helped by the fact that several competitors had just entered the market with machines aimed directly at the PDP-5's market space, which the PDP-8 trounced. This gave the company two years of unrestricted leadership,[31] and eventually 1450 "straight eight" machines were produced before it was replaced by newer implementations of the same basic design.[28]

DEC hit an even lower price-point with the PDP-8/S, the S for "serial". As the name implies the /S used a serial arithmetic unit, which was much slower but reduced costs so much that the system sold for under $10,000.[32] DEC then used the new PDP-8 design as the basis for a new LINC, the two-processor LINC-8. The LINC-8 used one PDP-8 CPU and a separate LINC CPU, and included instructions to switch from one to the other. This allowed customers to run their existing LINC programs, or "upgrade" to the PDP-8, all in software. Although not a huge seller, 142 LINK-8s were sold starting at $38,500.[28] Like the original LINC to PDP-5 evolution, the LINC-8 was then modified into the single-processor PDP-12, adding another 1000 machines to the 12-bit family.[28] [33] Newer circuitry designs led to the PDP-8/I and PDP-8/L in 1968.[11] In 1975, one year after an agreement between Digital and Intersil, the Intersil 6100 chip was launched, effectively a PDP-8 on a chip. This was a way to allow PDP-8 software to be run even after the official end-of-life announcement for the Digital PDP-8 product line.

PDP-10 family

A "B" (blue) series Flip Chip module containing nine transistors, 1971

While the PDP-5 introduced a lower-cost line, 1963's PDP-6 was intended to take DEC into the mainframe market with a 36-bit machine. However, the PDP-6 proved to be a "hard sell" with customers, as it offered few advantages over similar machines from the better established vendors like IBM or Honeywell, in spite of its low cost around $300,000. Only 23 were sold,[34] or 26 depending on the source,[35] and unlike earlier models the low sales meant the PDP-6 was not improved with intermediate versions. However, the PDP-6 is historically important as the platform that introduced "Monitor", an early time-sharing operating system that would evolve into the widely used TOPS-10.[36]

In spite of the PDP-6's limited commercial success, it introduced many features that clearly had commercial benefit. When the Flip Chip packaging allowed the PDP-6 to be re-implemented at a much lower cost, DEC took the opportunity to carry out a similar evolution of their 36-bit design and introduced the PDP-10 in 1968. The PDP-10 was as much a success as the PDP-6 was a failure; during its lifetime about 700 mainframe PDP-10s were sold before production ended in 1984.[34] The PDP-10 was widely used in university settings, and thus was the basis of many advances in computing and operating system design during the 1970s. DEC later re-branded all of the models in the 36-bit series as the "DECsystem-10", and PDP-10s are generally referred to by the model of their CPU, like "KA10". Later upgrades produced the compatible DECSYSTEM-20, along with TOPS-20 that included virtual memory.

DECtape

One of the most unusual peripherals produced for the PDP-10 was the DECtape. The DECtape was a length of special 3/4-inch wide magnetic tape wound on 5-inch reels. The recording format was a 10-track approach using fixed-length numbered 'blocks' organized into a standard file structure, including a directory. Files could be written, read, changed, and deleted on a DECtape as though it were a disk drive. For greater efficiency, the DECtape drive could read and write to a DECtape in both directions.

In fact, some PDP-10 systems had no disks at all, using DECtapes alone for their primary data storage. The DECtape was also widely used on other PDP models, since it was much easier to use than hand-loading multiple paper tapes. Primitive early time-sharing systems could use DECtapes as system devices and swapping devices. Although superior to paper tape, DECtapes were relatively slow, and were supplanted as reliable disk drives became affordable.

PDP-11

In 1968, DEC was developing a PDP machine that would be based on 8-bit bytes instead of 6-bit characters. Known as the "PDP-X", the project was eventually cancelled. Several team members decamped and set up Data General in May 1968, and rapidly brought the 16-bit NOVA minicomputer to market. DEC immediately found itself behind in the industry transition to 8-bit bytes, and soon lost its crown as the largest minicomputer vendor.

The PDP-11 16-bit computer was designed in a crash program by Harold McFarland, Gordon Bell, Roger Cady, and others.[37] The project was able to leap forward in design with the arrival of Harold McFarland, who had been researching 16-bit designs at Carnegie Mellon University. One of his simpler designs became the PDP-11, although when they first viewed the proposal, management was not impressed and almost cancelled it.[37]

In particular, the new design did not include many of the addressing modes that were intended to make programs smaller in memory, a technique that was widely used on other DEC machines and CISC designs in general. This would mean the machine would spend more time accessing memory, which would slow it down. However, the machine also extended the idea of multiple "General Purpose Registers" (GPRs), which gave the programmer flexibility to use these high-speed memory caches as they needed, potentially addressing the performance issues.

A major advance in the PDP-11 design was Digital's Unibus, which supported all peripherals through memory mapping. This allowed a new device to be added easily, generally only requiring plugging a hardware interface board into the backplane, and then installing software that read and wrote to the mapped memory to control it. The relative ease of interfacing spawned a huge market of third party add-ons for the PDP-11, which made the machine even more useful.

The combination of architectural innovations proved superior to competitors and the "11" architecture was soon the industry leader, propelling DEC back to a strong market position. The design was later expanded to allow paged physical memory and memory protection features, useful for multitasking and time-sharing. Some models supported separate instruction and data spaces for an effective virtual address size of 128 kB within a physical address size of up to 4 MB. Smaller PDP-11s, implemented as single-chip CPUs, continued to be produced until 1996, by which time over 600,000 had been sold.[26]

The PDP-11 supported several operating systems, including Bell Labs' new Unix operating system as well as DEC's DOS-11, RSX-11, IAS, RT-11, DSM-11, and RSTS/E. Many early PDP-11 applications were developed using standalone paper-tape utilities. DOS-11 was the PDP-11's first disk operating system, but was soon supplanted by more capable systems. RSX provided a general-purpose multitasking environment and supported a wide variety of programming languages. IAS was a time-sharing version of RSX-11D. Both RSTS and Unix were time-sharing systems available to educational institutions at little or no cost, and these PDP-11 systems were destined to be the "sandbox" for a rising generation of engineers and computer scientists. Large numbers of PDP-11/70s were deployed in telecommunications and industrial control applications. AT&T became DEC's largest customer.

RT-11 provided a practical real-time operating system in minimal memory, allowing the PDP-11 to continue Digital's critical role as a computer supplier for embedded systems. Historically, RT-11 also served as the inspiration for many microcomputer OS's, as these were generally being written by programmers who cut their teeth on one of the many PDP-11 models. For example, CP/M used a command syntax similar to RT-11's, and even retained the awkward PIP program used to copy data from one computer device to another. As another historical footnote, DEC's use of "/" for "switches" (command-line options) would lead to the adoption of "\" for pathnames in MS-DOS and Microsoft Windows as opposed to "/" in Unix.[38]

The evolution of the PDP-11 followed earlier systems, eventually including a single-user deskside personal computer form, the MicroPDP-11. In total, around 600,000 PDP-11's of all models were sold. and a wide variety of third-party peripheral vendors had also entered the computer product ecosystem.

Many PDP-11-like machines were also introduced by competitors. The PDP-11 series was cloned in COMECON countries as the SM EVM series, and was produced in quantities comparable to original PDP-11 production.

VAX

In 1976, DEC decided to extend the PDP-11 architecture to 32-bits while adding a complete virtual memory system to the simple paging and memory protection of the PDP-11. The result was the VAX architecture. The first computer to use a VAX CPU was the VAX-11/780, which DEC referred to as a *superminicomputer*. Although it was not the first 32-bit minicomputer, the VAX-11/780's combination of features, price, and marketing almost immediately propelled it to a leadership position in the market after it was released in 1978. VAX systems were so successful that in 1983, DEC canceled its Jupiter project, which had been intended to build a successor to the PDP-10 mainframe, and instead focused on promoting the VAX as the single computer architecture for the company.[39]

Supporting the VAX's success was the VT52, one of the most successful smart terminals. Building on earlier less successful models (the VT05 and VT50), the VT52 was the first terminal that did everything one might want in a single chassis. The VT52 was followed by the even more successful VT100 and its follow-ons, making DEC one of the largest terminal vendors in the industry. With the VT series, DEC could now offer a complete top-to-bottom system from computer to all peripherals, which formerly required collecting the required devices from different suppliers.

The VAX processor architecture and family of systems evolved and expanded through several generations during the 1980s, culminating in the NVAX microprocessor implementation and VAX 7000/10000 series in the early 1990s.[40]

Early microcomputers

The introduction of the first general purpose microprocessors inevitably led to the first microcomputers around 1975. At the time these systems were of limited utility, and Ken Olsen famously derided them in 1977, stating "There is no reason for any individual to have a computer in his home."[41] Unsurprisingly, DEC did not put much effort into the microcomputer area in the early days of the market. At the beginning of the 1980s, DEC built the VT180 (codenamed "Robin"), which was a VT100 terminal with an added Z80-based microcomputer running CP/M, but this product was initially available only to DEC employees.[42]

It was only after IBM had successfully launched the IBM PC in 1981 that DEC responded with their own systems. In 1982, Digital introduced not one, but three incompatible machines which were each tied to different proprietary architectures. The first, the DEC Professional, was based on the PDP-11/23 (and later, the 11/73) running the RSX-11M+ derived, but menu-driven, P/OS ("Professional Operating System"). This DEC machine easily outperformed the PC, but was more expensive than, and completely incompatible with IBM PC hardware and software, offering far fewer options for customizing a system. In addition, a new user would have to learn an awkward, slow, and inflexible menu-based user interface which appeared to be radically different from PC-DOS or CP/M, which were more commonly used on the 8080 and 8088 based microcomputers of the time. A second offering, the DECmate II was the latest version of the PDP-8 based word processors, but not really suited to general computing, nor competitive with Wang Laboratories' popular word processing equipment.

The best known of DEC's early microcomputers was the dual-processor (Z80 and 8088) Rainbow 100, which ran the 8-bit CP/M operating system on the Z80 and the 16-bit CP/M-86 operating system on the Intel 8086 processor. It could also run a UNIX System III implementation called VENIX. Applications from standard CP/M could be re-compiled for the Rainbow, but by this time users were expecting custom-built (pre-compiled binary) applications such as Lotus 1-2-3, which was eventually ported along with MS-DOS 2.0 and introduced in late 1983. Although the Rainbow generated some press, it was unsuccessful due to its high price and lack of marketing and sales support.[43]

The way the DEC standard RX50[44] floppy disk drive supported DEC's initial offerings seemed to encapsulate their approach to the personal computer market. Although the mechanical drive hardware was nearly identical to other 5.25" floppy disk drives available on competing systems,[45] DEC sought to differentiate their product by using a proprietary disk format for the data written on the disk. The DEC format had a higher capacity for data, but the RX50 drives were incompatible with other PC floppy drives. This required DEC owners to buy higher-priced, specially-formatted floppy media, which was harder to obtain through standard distribution channels. DEC attempted to enforce exclusive control over its floppy media sales by copyrighting its proprietary disk format, and requiring a negotiated license agreement and royalty payments from anybody selling compatible media. The proprietary data format meant that RX50 floppies were not interchangeable with other PC floppies, further isolating DEC products from the developing de facto standard PC market. Hardware hackers and DEC enthusiasts eventually reverse-engineered the RX50 format,[44] [46] but the damage had already been done, in terms of market confusion and isolation.

A further system was introduced in 1986 as the VAXmate, which included Microsoft Windows 1.0 and used VAX/VMS-based file and print servers along with integration into DEC's own DECnet-family, providing LAN/WAN connection from PC to mainframe or supermini. The VAXmate replaced the Rainbow, and in its standard form was the first widely marketed diskless workstation.

Networking and clusters

In 1984, DEC launched its first 10 Mbit/s Ethernet. Ethernet allowed scalable networking, and VAXcluster allowed scalable computing. Combined with DECnet and Ethernet-based terminal servers (LAT), DEC had produced a networked storage architecture which allowed them to compete directly with IBM. Ethernet replaced token ring, and went on to become the dominant networking model in use today.

In September 1985, DEC became the fifth company to register a .com domain name (dec.com).

Along with the hardware and protocols, DEC also introduced the VAXcluster concept, which allowed several VAX machines to be tied together into a single larger storage system. VAXclusters allowed a DEC-based company to scale their services by adding new machines to the cluster at any time, as opposed to buying a faster machine and using that to replace a slower one. The flexibility this offered was compelling, and allowed DEC to attack high-end markets formerly out of their reach.

Diversification

Although their microcomputer efforts were eventually considered failures, the PDP-11 and VAX lines continued to sell in record numbers. Better yet, DEC was competing very well against the market leader, IBM, taking an estimated $2 billion away from them in the mid-80s. In 1986, Digital's profits rose 38 percent when the rest of the computer industry experienced a downturn, and by 1987 the company was threatening IBM's number one position in the computer industry.[6]

At its peak, Digital was the second-largest computer company in the world, with over 100,000 employees. It was during this time that the company branched out development into a wide variety of projects that were far from its core business in computer equipment. The company invested heavily in custom software. In the 1970s and earlier most software was custom-written to serve a specific task, but by the 1980s the introduction of relational databases and similar systems allowed powerful software to be built in a modular fashion, potentially saving enormous amounts of development time. Software companies like Oracle became the new darlings of the industry, and DEC started their own efforts in every "hot" niche, in some cases several projects for the same niche. Some of these products competed with DEC's own partners, notably Rdb which competed with Oracle's products on the VAX, part of a major partnership only a few years earlier.

Although many of these products were well designed, most of them were DEC-only or DEC-centric, and customers frequently ignored them and used third-party products instead. This problem was further exacerbated by Olsen's aversion to traditional advertising and his belief that well-engineered products would sell themselves. Hundreds of millions of dollars were spent on these projects, at the same time that workstations using RISC microprocessors were starting to approach VAX CPUs in performance.

Faltering in the market

As microprocessors continued to improve in the 1980s, it soon became clear that the next generation would offer performance and features equal to the best of DECs low-end minicomputer lineup. Worse, the Berkeley RISC and Stanford MIPS designs were aiming to introduce 32-bit designs that would outperform the fastest members of the VAX family, DEC's cash cow.[47]

Constrained by the huge success of their VAX/VMS products, which followed the proprietary model, the company was very late to respond to these threats. In the early 1990s, DEC found its sales faltering and its first layoffs followed. The company that created the minicomputer, a dominant networking technology, and arguably the first computers for personal use, had abandoned the "low end" market, whose dominance with the PDP-8 had built the company in a previous generation. Decisions about what to do about this threat led to infighting within the company that seriously delayed their responses.

One group suggested that every possible development in the industry be poured into the construction of a new VAX family that would leapfrog the performance of the existing machines. This would limit the market erosion in the top-end segment, where profit margins were maximized and DEC could continue to survive as a minicomputer vendor. This line of thought led, eventually, to the VAX 9000 series, which were plagued with problems when they were first introduced in October 1989, already two years late.[48] The problems took so long to work out, and the prices of the systems were so high, that DEC was never able to make the line the success they hoped.

Others within the company felt that the proper response was to introduce their own RISC designs and use those to build new machines. However, there was little official support for these efforts, and no less than four separate small projects ran in parallel at various labs around the US. Eventually these were gathered into the DEC PRISM project, which delivered a credible 32-bit design with some unique features allowing it to serve as the basis of a new VAX implementation.[49] Infighting with teams dedicated to DEC's big iron made funding difficult, and the design was not finalized until April 1988, and then cancelled shortly thereafter.[50]

Another group concluded that new workstations like those from Sun Microsystems and Silicon Graphics would take away a large part of DEC's existing customer base before the new VAX systems could address the issues, and that the company needed its own Unix workstation as soon as possible. Fed up with slow progress on both the RISC and VAX fronts, a group in Palo Alto started a skunkworks project to introduce their own systems. Selecting the MIPS processor, which was widely available, introducing the new DECstation series with the model 3100 on 11 January 1989.[51] These systems would see some success in the market, but were later displaced by similar models running the Alpha.

32-bit MIPS and 64-bit Alpha systems

Inside view of AlphaServer 2100.

Eventually, in 1992, DEC launched the DECchip 21064 processor, the first implementation of their Alpha instruction set architecture, initially named Alpha AXP (the "AXP" was a "non-acronym" and was later dropped). This was a 64-bit RISC architecture (as opposed to the 32-bit CISC architecture used in the VAX) and one of the first "pure" (not an extension of an earlier 32-bit architecture) 64-bit microprocessor architectures and implementations. The Alpha offered class-leading performance at its launch, and subsequent variants continued to do so into the 2000s. An AlphaServer SC45 supercomputer was still ranked No. 6 in the world in November 2004.[52] Alpha-based computers (the DEC AXP series, later the AlphaStation and AlphaServer series) superseded both the VAX and MIPS architecture in DEC's product lines, and could run OpenVMS, DEC OSF/1 AXP (later, Digital Unix or Tru64 UNIX) and Microsoft's then-new operating system, Windows NT.

In 1998, following the takeover by Compaq Computers, a decision was made that Microsoft would no longer support and develop Windows NT for the Alpha series computers, a decision that was seen as the beginning of the end for the Alpha series computers.

DEC tried to compete in the Unix market by adding POSIX-compatibility features to the VAX/VMS operating system (becoming "OpenVMS") and by selling its own version of Unix (Ultrix on PDP-11, VAX and MIPS architectures; OSF/1 on Alpha), and began to advertise more aggressively. DEC was simply not prepared to sell into a crowded Unix market however, and the low end PC-servers running NT (based on Intel processors) took market share from Alpha-based computers. DEC's workstation and server line never gained much popularity beyond former DEC customers.

StrongARM

In the mid-1990s, Digital Semiconductor collaborated with ARM Limited to produce the StrongARM microprocessor. This was based in part on ARM7 and in part on DEC technologies like Alpha, and was targeted at embedded systems and portable devices. It was highly compatible with the ARMv4 architecture and was very successful, competing effectively against rivals such as the SuperH and MIPS architectures in the portable digital assistant market. Microsoft subsequently dropped support for these other architectures in their Pocket PC platform. In 1997, as part of a lawsuit settlement, the StrongARM intellectual property was sold to Intel. They continued to produce StrongARM, as well as developing it into the XScale architecture. Intel subsequently sold this business to Marvell Technology Group in 2006.

Designing solutions

Beyond DECsystem-10/20, PDP, VAX and Alpha, Digital was well respected for its communication subsystem designs, such as Ethernet, DNA (Digital Network Architecture – predominantly DECnet products), DSA (Digital Storage Architecture – disks/tapes/controllers), and its "dumb terminal" subsystems including VT100 and DECserver products.[53]

Final years

In June 1992, Ken Olsen was replaced by Robert Palmer as the company's president. Digital's board of directors also granted Palmer the title of chief executive officer ("CEO"), a title that had never been used during Digital's 35-year existence. Palmer had joined DEC in 1985 to run Semiconductor Engineering and Manufacturing. His relentless campaign to be CEO, and success with the Alpha microprocessor family, made him a candidate to succeed Olsen. At the same time a more modern logo was designed[54]

New 1993 corporate logo

During the profitable years up until the early 1990s, DEC was a company that boasted that it never had a general layoff;[55] following the 1992 economic downturn, layoffs became regular events as the company continually downsized to try to stay afloat.[56] Palmer was tasked with the goal of bringing DEC back to profitability, which he attempted to do by changing the established DEC business culture, hiring new executives from outside the company, and selling off various non-core business units:[57]

- Worldwide training was spun off to form an independent/new company called Global Knowledge Network.
- Rdb, DEC's database product, was sold to Oracle.
- Rights to the PDP-11 line and several PDP-11 operating systems were sold to Mentec in 1994, though DEC continued to produce some PDP-11 hardware for a few years.[58]
- Disk and DLT technologies was sold to Quantum Corporation in 1994, immediately propelling Quantum to the No1 spot in disk manufacturing.
- Text terminal business (VT100 and its successors) was sold in August 1995 to Boundless Technologies.
- CORBA-based product, ObjectBroker, and its messaging software, MessageQ, were sold to BEA Systems, Inc in March 1997.
- In May 1997, DEC sued Intel for allegedly infringing on its Alpha patents in designing the original Pentium, Pentium Pro, and Pentium II chips.[59] As part of a settlement, much of DEC's chip design and fabrication business was sold to Intel. This included DEC's StrongARM implementation of the ARM computer architecture, which Intel marketed as the XScale processors commonly used in Pocket PCs. The core of Digital Semiconductor, the Alpha microprocessor group, remained with DEC, while the associated office buildings went to Intel as part of the Hudson, Mass. fabrication site.

- Printer business was sold in 1997 to GENICOM (now TallyGenicom), which then produced models bearing the Digital logo.
- Networking business was sold c.1997 to Cabletron Systems, and subsequently spun off as Digital Network Products Group.
- DECtalk and DECvoice voice products were spun off, and eventually arrived at Fonix.

By 1997 Digital had subsidiary companies in more than two dozen countries including Austria, Australia, Belgium, Brazil, Canada, China (People's Republic), Colombia, Cyprus, Czech Republic, Denmark, Finland, France, Germany, Ireland, Israel, Japan, Jersey States, New Zealand, Netherlands, Norway, Russia, Singapore, Spain, Sweden, Switzerland, Taiwan, and the United Kingdom.[60]

Eventually, on 26 January 1998, what remained of the company (including Digital's multivendor global services organization and customer support centers) was sold to Compaq, which was acquired by Hewlett-Packard in 2002. The remainder of Digital Semiconductor (the Alpha microprocessor group) was sold to Intel, which placed those employees back in their Hudson, Mass. office which they had vacated when the site was sold to Intel in 1997. Compaq, and later HP, continued to sell many of the former Digital products but rebranded with their own logos. For example, HP now sells what were formerly Digital's StorageWorks disk/tape products,[61] as a result of the Compaq acquisition.

The Digital logo survived for a while after the company ceased to exist, as the logo of Digital GlobalSoft, an IT services company in India (which was a 51 percent subsidiary of Compaq). Digital GlobalSoft was later renamed "HP GlobalSoft" (also known as the "HP Global Delivery India Center" or HP GDIC) and no longer uses the Digital logo.

The digital.com and DEC.com domain names are now owned by Hewlett-Packard and redirect to their US website.[62] Digital once held the Class A IP address block 16.0.0.0/8.[63]

The Digital Federal Credit Union (DCU, now DFCU), which was chartered in 1979 for employees of DEC, is now open to essentially everyone. DFCU has over 700 different sponsors, including the companies that acquired pieces of DEC.

Research

DEC's Research Laboratories (or Research Labs, as they were commonly known) conducted Digital's corporate research. Some of them were operated by Compaq and are still operated by Hewlett-Packard. The laboratories were:

- Western Research Laboratory (WRL) in Palo Alto, California, USA
- Systems Research Center (SRC) in Palo Alto, California, USA
- Network Systems Laboratory (NSL) in Palo Alto, California, USA
- Cambridge Research Laboratory (CRL) in Cambridge, Massachusetts, USA
- Paris Research Laboratory (PRL) in Paris, France
- MetroWest Technology Campus (MTC) in Maynard, Massachusetts, USA

Some of the former employees of Digital's Research Labs or Digital's R&D in general include:

- Gordon Bell — technical visionary, VP Engineering 1972-1983; Microsoft Research
- Leonard Bosack —
- Henry Burkhardt III — co-founder of Data General Corporation and Kendall Square Research
- Mike Burrows
- Luca Cardelli —
- Dave Cutler — led RSX-11M and VAX/VMS operating systems development; then led Windows NT development at MicrosoftTalk:Digital Equipment Corporation#unsourced/exaggerated synopses of notable people
- Ed deCastro — co-founder of Data General Corporation

- Jim Gettys — early developer of X Window SystemTalk:Digital Equipment Corporation#unsourced/exaggerated synopses of notable people
- Henri Gouraud —
- Jim Gray —
- Alan Kotok —
- Leslie Lamport —
- Butler Lampson —
- Louis Monier —
- Isaac Nassi —
- Radia Perlman —
- Marcus Ranum —
- Brian Reid —
- Paul Vixie —

Some of the former employees of Digital Equipment Corp who were responsible for developing Alpha and StrongARM

- Daniel W. Dobberpuhl —
- Jill Keller —
- Rich Witek —

Some of the work of the Research Labs was published in the *Digital Technical Journal*,[64] which was in published from 1985 until 1998.[65]

Accomplishments

Digital supported the ANSI standards, especially the ASCII character set, which survives in Unicode and the ISO 8859 character set family. Digital's own Multinational Character Set also had a large influence on ISO 8859-1 (Latin-1) and, by extension, Unicode .

The first versions of the C language and the Unix operating system ran on Digital's PDP series of computers (first on a PDP-7, then the PDP-11's), which were among the first commercially viable minicomputers, although for several years Digital itself did not encourage the use of Unix.

Digital also produced the popular VAX computer family, the first pure 64-bit microprocessor architecture (Alpha AXP), the first commercially successful workstation (the VT-78), and some commercially unsuccessful personal computers. The central computing system of the Soviet reusable Buran spaceship was based on two clones of MicroVAX computers.

Digital produced widely used and influential interactive operating systems, including OS-8, TOPS-10, TOPS-20, RSTS/E, RSX-11, RT-11, and OpenVMS. PDP computers, in particular the PDP-11 model, inspired a generation of programmers and software developers. Some PDP-11 systems more than 25 years old (software and hardware) are still being used to control and monitor factories, transportation systems and nuclear plants. Digital was an early champion of time-sharing systems.

Digital was to the command-line interface (CLI) what Apple was to the Graphic User Interface GUI : there was history before and innovation after, but it was Digital's operating systems that put it together in a complete and definitive form . The command-line interfaces found in Digital's systems, eventually codified as DCL, would look familiar to any user of modern microcomputer CLIs; those used in earlier systems, such as CTSS, IBM's JCL, or Univac's time-sharing systems, would look utterly alien. Many features of the CP/M and MS-DOS CLI show a recognizable family resemblance to Digital's OSes, including command names such as DIR and HELP and the "name-dot-extension" file naming conventions.

VAX and MicroVAX computers (very widespread in the 1980s) running VMS formed one of the most important proprietary networks, DECnet, which linked business and research facilities. The DECnet protocols formed one of the first peer-to-peer networking standards, with DECnet phase I being released in the mid-1970s. Email, file sharing, and distributed collaborative projects existed within the company long before their value was recognized in the market.

Digital, Intel and Xerox through their collaboration to create the DIX standard, were champions of Ethernet, but Digital is the company that made Ethernet commercially successful. Initially, Ethernet-based DECnet and LAT protocols interconnected VAXes with DECserver terminal servers. Starting with the Unibus to Ethernet adapter, multiple generations of Ethernet hardware from Digital were the de facto standard. The CI "computer interconnect" adapter was the industry's first network interface controller to use separate transmit and receive "rings".

Digital also invented clustering, an operating system technology that treated multiple machines as one logical entity. Clustering permitted sharing of pooled disk and tape storage via the HSC50/70/90 and later series of Hierarchical Storage Controllers (HSC). The HSCs delivered the first hardware RAID 0 and RAID 1 capabilities and the first serial interconnects of multiple storage technologies. This technology was the forerunner to systems like Network of Workstations which are used for massively cooperative tasks such as web-searches and drug research.

The LA36 and LA120 dot matrix printers became industry standards and may have hastened the demise of the Teletype Corporation.

The VT100 computer terminal became the industry standard, implementing a useful subset of the ANSI X3.64 standard, and even today terminal emulators such as HyperTerminal, PuTTY and Xterm still emulate a VT100 (or its more capable successor, the VT220).

The X Window System, the network transparent window system used on UNIX and Linux, and also available on other operating systems, was developed at MIT jointly between Project Athena and the Laboratory for Computer Science. Digital was the primary sponsor for this project, which was one of the first large scale free software projects, a contemporary of the GNU Project but not associated with it.

Dave Cutler, who led the development of RSX-11M, RSX-11M+, VMS and then VAXeln, left Digital in 1988 to lead the development of Windows NT which was initially intended to be an "open" operating system that would run on more powerful processors than the existing predominant x86 architecture. While DEC did see value in continuing its X Window System environment to support engineering customers, it understood that future mid-range based customers would demand a faster and more user friendly Graphical User Interface (GUI), potentially offered through the Windows environment. As Microsoft had experience, technology and patents that would give them upper hand in advancing GUI technology, DEC opted to partner with Microsoft's development of Windows NT for mid-range processors and share in the R&D process of creating faster computers using their RISC Alpha processors. Microsoft was not exclusively bound to the Alpha chip so it pursued other processor makers such as IBM with the PowerPC architecture and eventually capitalized on the emerging strength of the Intel x86 based processors. While most would say that the market determined its own course through the more cost efficient processors produced by Intel, DEC quickly came to realize that its loose partnership with Microsoft would lead to its own undoing in terms of being a major player in the mid-range processor market.

Notes-11 and its follow-on product, VAX Notes, were two of the first examples of online collaboration software, a category that has become to be known as groupware. Len Kawell, one of the original Notes-11 developers later joined Lotus Development Corporation and contributed to their Lotus Notes product.

Digital was one of the first businesses connected to the Internet, with *dec.com*, registered in 1985,[66] being one of the first of the now ubiquitous *.com* domains. DEC's *gatekeeper.dec.com* was a well-known software repository during the pre-World Wide Web days, and Digital was also the first computer vendor to open a public website, on 1 October 1993.[67] The popular AltaVista, created by Digital, was one of the first comprehensive Internet search engines. (Although Lycos was earlier, it was much more limited.)

DEC invented Digital Linear Tape (DLT), formerly known as CompacTape, which began as a compact backup medium for MicroVAX systems, and later grew to capacities of 800 gigabytes.

Work on the first hard-disk-based MP3-player, the Personal Jukebox, started at the DEC Systems Research Center. (The project was started about a month before the merger into Compaq was completed.)

DEC's Western Research Lab created the Itsy Pocket Computer. This was developed into the Compaq iPaq line of PDAs, which replaced the Compaq Aero PDA.

User organizations

Originally the users' group was called DECUS (Digital Equipment Computer User Society) during the 1960s to 1990s. When Compaq acquired Digital in 1998, the users group was renamed CUO, the Compaq Users' Organisation. When HP acquired Compaq in 2002, CUO became HP-Interex, although there are still DECUS groups in several countries. In the United States, the organization is represented by the Encompass organization.

Notes

[1] "DEC used by Digital itself:" *PDP11 Processor Handbook* (1973): page 8, "DEC, PDP, UNIBUS are registered trademarks of Digital Equipment Corporation;" page 1-4, "Digital Equipment Corporation (DEC) designs and manufactures many of the peripheral devices offered with PDP-11's. As a designer and manufacturer of peripherals, DEC can offer extremely reliable equipment... The LA30 DECwriter, a totally DEC-designed and built teleprinter, can serve as an alternative to the Teletype."

[2] "MITRE's Project Whirlwind Computer Collection Transferred to MIT" (http://www.mitre.org/news/releases/09/whirlwind_07_01_2009.html), MITRE, 1 July 2009

[3] "Semi-Automatic Ground Environment (SAGE)" (http://www.mitre.org/about/sage.html), MITRE, 25 January 2005

[4] "TX-0 Computer" (http://www.computerhistory.org/collections/accession/XD154.75), Computer History Museum

[5] Highlights from *The Computer Museum Report* Volume 8 Spring 1984 (http://ed-thelen.org/comp-hist/TheCompMusRep/TCMR-V08.html), The Computer Museum, Boston, MA, archived at ed-thelen.org, retrieved 19 February 2010

[6] "Digital Equipment Corporation" (http://www.answers.com/topic/digital-equipment-corporation), *International Directory of Company Histories*, Volume 6, St. James Press, 1992

[7] "A Proposal to American Research and Development Corporation 27 May 1957" (http://archive.computerhistory.org/resources/text/dec/pdp-1/DEC.pdp_1.1957.102664472.pdf)

[8] Richard Best, Russell Doane and John McNamara, "Digital Modules, The Basis for Computers" (http://research.microsoft.com/en-us/um/people/gbell/computer_engineering/00000125.htm), *Computer Engineering, A DEC view of hardware systems design", Digital Press, 1978*

[9] "DEC Laboratory Module – FLIP-FLOP 201" (http://www.computerhistory.org/collections/accession/102633142), Computer History Museum

[10] *Present* 1978, pg. 3

[11] *Present* 1978, pg. 10

[12] Eastern Joint Computer Conference and Exhibition (http://www.computerhistory.org/collections/accession/102634161), official program of 1959 meeting in Boston

[13] "DIGITAL Computing Timeline, 1960" (http://vt100.net/timeline/1960.html)

[14] *Computers and Automation*, April 1961, pg. 8B

[15] "Bureau of Labor Statistics Inflation Calculator, 1961–2011" (http://www.bls.gov/data/inflation_calculator.htm)

[16] "History of Computing", Lexikon Services, ISBN 0-944601-78-2

[17] *Datamation*, Volume 5 Number 6 (November/December), pg. 24

[18] "Preliminary Specifications: Programmed Data Processor Model Three (PDP-3)" (http://www.gutenberg.org/etext/29461), DEC, October 1960

[19] Posting in "Announcements from The DEC Connection" (http://www.decconnection.org/announcements.htm), *The DEC Connection*, 14 January 2007

[20] Gordon Bell, "DIGITAL Computing Timeline, 1962, PDP-4" (http://research.microsoft.com/en-us/um/people/gbell/digital/timeline/1962-1.htm)

[21] Gordon Bell, "DIGITAL Computing Timeline, 1964, PDP-7" (http://research.microsoft.com/en-us/um/people/gbell/digital/timeline/1964-3.htm)

[22] Gordon Bell, "DIGITAL Computing Timeline, 1965, PDP-7A" (http://research.microsoft.com/en-us/um/people/gbell/digital/timeline/1964-3.htm)

[23] Eric Steven Raymond, "Origins and History of Unix, 1969–1995" (http://www.faqs.org/docs/artu/ch02s01.html), 19 September 2003

[24] Gordon Bell, "DIGITAL Computing Timeline, 1965, PDP-9" (http://research.microsoft.com/en-us/um/people/gbell/digital/timeline/1966-1.htm)

[25] DEC Advertisement, *Chemical and Engineering News*, Volume 46 (1968), pg. 85
[26] Miller 1997, pg. 452
[27] Wesley Clark, "The Linc, Perhaps the First Mini-Computer" (http://www.historyofscience.com/G2I/timeline/index.php?id=1006), From Cave Paintings to the Internet
[28] "DEC FAQ: What is a PDP-8?" (http://www.faqs.org/faqs/dec-faq/pdp8-models/section-1.html)
[29] "DEC PDP-8 minicomputer, 1965" (http://www.sciencemuseum.org.uk/objects/computing_and_data_processing/1982-960.aspx), *The Science Museum*
[30] "Internet History:1965" (http://www.computerhistory.org/internet_history/), Computer History Museum
[31] *Present* 1978, pg. 7
[32] *Present* 1978, pg. 8
[33] Miller 1997, pg. 456
[34] Miller 1997, pg. 457
[35] Gordon Bell, "DIGITAL Computing Timeline, 1964, PDP-6" (http://research.microsoft.com/~gbell/Digital/timeline/1964-1.htm)
[36] "PDP-6 Timesharing Software" (http://www.bitsavers.org/pdf/dec/pdp6/PDP-6_TimsharingBroch.pdf), DEC Publication F-61B
[37] Larry McGowan, "How the PDP-11 Was Born (according to Larry McGowan) (http://hampage.hu/pdp-11/birth.html), 19 August 1998
[38] alt.folklore.computers List of Frequently Asked Questions (http://www.netwhatever.com/faq/inicio.html#queIII15)
[39] "The day Jupiter went out of orbit" (http://books.google.ca/books?id=W7skAQAAIAAJ&q=dec+Jupiter+project+vax&dq=dec+Jupiter+project+vax&client=safari&cd=4), *Electronic Business*, Volume 10 (1984), pg. 76–79
[40] DEC Microprocessors: NVAX (1991) (http://simh.trailing-edge.com/semi/nvax.html)
[41] Olsen later claimed he was referring to home automation, see "Ken Olsen" (http://www.snopes.com/quotes/kenolsen.asp)
[42] Croxton, Greg. "DEC Robin (VT-180) & documentation" (http://www.digibarn.com/collections/systems/dec-robin/). *DigiBarn Computer Museum*. . Retrieved 21 March 2011.
[43] "The Rainbow 100 Frequently Asked Questions" (http://rainbow-100.com/faq/question/1/). *Drive W*. Approximatrix, LLC. 2009. . Retrieved 15 December 2010.
[44] Stravers, Kees. "The RX50 FAQ" (http://users.bart.nl/users/pb0aia/vax/rx50.html). *Kees's VAX page*. . Retrieved 21 March 2011.
[45] "Geek Historian". "MP01482 RX50 EngrDrws Jul82" (http://www.scribd.com/doc/881906/Tech-History-Digital-Equipment-Corporation-MP01482-RX50-EngrDrws-Jul82). *Tech History – Digital Equipment Corporation*. . Retrieved 21 March 2011.
[46] Wilson, John. "PUTR.COM V2.01" (http://www.dbit.com/pub/putr/). . Retrieved 21 March 2011. This relatively-recent work is a well-developed example of programs to enhance interchange of data between DEC formatted media and standard PC systems
[47] John Hennessy, David Patterson and David Goldberg, "Computer Architecture: A Quantitative Approach" (http://books.google.com/books?id=XX69oNsazH4C&pg=PA152), Morgan Kaufmann, 2003, pg. 152
[48] John Markoff, "Market Place; Digital Finally Follows a Trend", *The New York Times*, 16 July 1990
[49] Dileep Bhandarkar et al., "High performance issue oriented architecture" (http://ieeexplore.ieee.org/xpl/freeabs_all.jsp?arnumber=63667), *Proceedings of Compcon Spring '90*, pg. 153–160
[50] Mark Smotherman, "PRISM (Parallel Reduced Instruction Set Machine)" (http://www.cs.clemson.edu/~mark/prism.html), Clemson University School of Computing, October 2009
[51] Thomas Furlong et al., "Development of the DECstation 3100" (http://www.dtjcd.vmsresource.org.uk/pdfs/dtj_v02-02_1990.pdf), *Digital Technical Journal*, Volume 2 Number 2 (Spring 1990), pg. 84–88
[52] www.top500.org Top 10 Supercomputing Sites, November 2004 (http://www.top500.org/lists/2004/11)
[53] For in-depth articles regarding Digital technologies, refer to the archived Digital Technical Journal (http://www.hpl.hp.com/hpjournal/dtj/past.htm)
[54] Ned Batchelder and Vt100.net (http://vt100.net/dec/logo).
[55] Schein, *et al*, pp. 67, 109.
[56] Schein, *et al*, p. 233.
[57] Schein, *et al*, pp. 128, 144, 234.
[58] http://replay.waybackmachine.org/20060813131029/http://www.mentec-inc.com/
[59] "DEC, Cyrix sue Intel", by Gale Bradley and Jim Detar, *Electronic News* **43**, #2168 (19 May 1997), ISSN 1061-6624.
[60] SEC Web site (http://www.secinfo.com/dsvRx.83Pe.7.htm) retrieved 22 January 2008
[61] HP StorageWorks – Data and Network Storage Products and Solutions (http://h18006.www1.hp.com/storage/)
[62] Digital.com (http://www.digital.com/), DEC.com (http://www.Dec.com/)
[63] List of assigned /8 IPv4 address blocks
[64] Digital Technical Journal – Online Issues (http://www.hpl.hp.com/hpjournal/dtj/past.htm)
[65] At least some of the research reports are available online at ftp.digital.com (ftp://ftp.digital.com/pub/DEC/), in the subdirectories WRL, SRC, NSL, CRL, PRL (see Research section). Verified July 2006
[66] dec.com (http://research.microsoft.com/Users/gbell/Digital/timeline/1985-6.htm)
[67] DECTEI-L Archives – February 1994 (#2) (http://listserv.acsu.buffalo.edu/cgi-bin/wa?A2=ind9402&L=dectei-l&T=0&P=200)

References

- (*Present*), "Digital Equipment Corporation: Nineteen Fifty-Seven to the Present" (http://research.microsoft.com/en-us/um/people/gbell/digital/DEC 1957 to Present 1978.pdf), DEC Press, 1978
- David Donald Miller, "OpenVMS Operating System Concepts" (http://books.google.ca/books?id=s5lDmf3ANhEC), Elsevier, 1997
- Alan R. Earls, *Digital Equipment Corporation*; Arcadia Publishing, 2004, ISBN 0-7385-3587-7.
- Edgar H. Schein, Peter S. DeLisi, Paul J. Kampas, and Michael M. Sonduck, *DEC Is Dead, Long Live DEC – The Lasting Legacy of Digital Equipment Corporation*; San Francisco: Barrett-Koehler, 2003, ISBN 1-57675-225-9.
- Jamie P. Pearson, *Digital At Work – Snapshots of the First 35 Years* (http://research.microsoft.com/en-us/um/people/gbell/digital/Digital at work 1992.pdf); Digital Press, 1992, ISBN 1-55558-092-0
- Glenn Rifkin, and George Harrar, *The Ultimate Entrepreneur – The Story of Ken Olsen and Digital Equipment Corporation*; Contemporary Books, 1988, ISBN 0-8092-4559-0.
- C. Gordon Bell, J. Craig Mudge, and John E. McNamara, *Computer Engineering – A DEC View of Hardware Systems Design*; Digital Press, 1978, ISBN 0-932376-00-2.

External links

- GBell's CyberMuseum for Digital Equipment Corp (DEC) (http://research.microsoft.com/users/gbell/Digital/DECMuseum.htm)
- Rise and Fall of Digital (Equipment Corporation) (http://technikum29.de/en/devices/dec-history.shtm), a company chronicle at a German computer museum
- Ken Olsen (http://www.economicadventure.org/decision/olsen.pdf), New England Economic Adventure

DEC_Alpha

Designer	Digital Equipment Corporation
Bits	64-bit
Introduced	1992
Design	RISC
Type	Register-Register
Encoding	Fixed
Endianness	Bi
Extensions	Byte/Word Extension (BWX), Square-root and Floating-point Convert Extension (FIX), Count Extension (CIX), Motion Video Instructions (MVI)
Open	Yes[1]
Registers	
General purpose	32
Floating point	32

Alpha, originally known as **Alpha AXP**, is a 64-bit reduced instruction set computer (RISC) instruction set architecture (ISA) developed by Digital Equipment Corporation (DEC), designed to replace the 32-bit VAX complex instruction set computer (CISC) ISA and its implementations. Alpha was implemented in microprocessors originally developed and fabricated by DEC. These microprocessors were most prominently used in a variety of DEC workstations and servers, which eventually formed the basis for almost all of their mid-to-upper-scale lineup. Several third-party vendors also produced Alpha systems, including PC form factor motherboards.

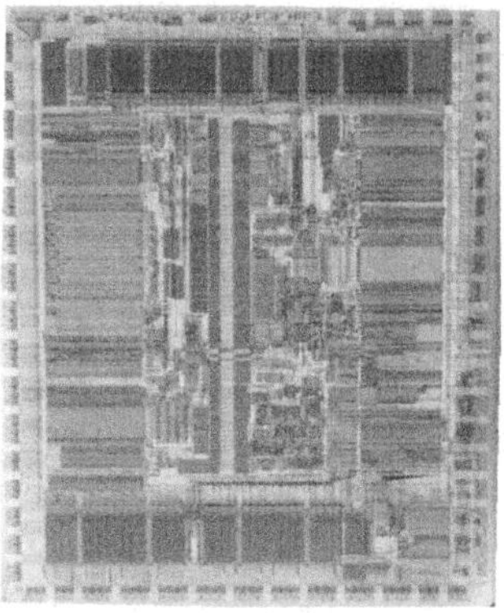

DEC Alpha AXP 21064 Microprocessor die photo

Operating systems that supported Alpha included OpenVMS (previously known as OpenVMS AXP), Tru64 UNIX (previously known as DEC OSF/1 AXP and Digital UNIX), Windows NT (until 4.0 SP6 and Windows 2000 RC1),[2] GNU/Linux (Debian GNU/Linux, Gentoo Linux and Red Hat Linux), BSD UNIX (NetBSD, OpenBSD and FreeBSD up to 6.x), as well as the L4Ka::Pistachio kernel.

The Alpha architecture was sold, along with most parts of DEC, to Compaq in 1998. Compaq, already an Intel customer, decided to phase out Alpha in favor of the forthcoming Hewlett-Packard/Intel Itanium architecture, and sold all Alpha intellectual property to Intel in 2001, effectively killing the product. Hewlett-Packard purchased Compaq later that same year, continuing development of the existing product line until 2004, and promising to continue selling Alpha-based systems, largely to the existing customer base, until October 2006 (later extended to April 2007).[3]

Package for DEC Alpha AXP 21064 Microprocessor

History

Alpha was born out of an earlier RISC project named PRISM, itself the final product of several earlier projects. PRISM was canceled after a proposal by the Palo Alto design team to build the Unix-only workstations (DECstation 3100) on a MIPS R2000 processor, allowing the DECstation to come to market sooner. Among the differences between PRISM and other RISC processors, however, was that PRISM supported a user-programmable microcode known as *Epicode*. PRISM had been designed with the intent of releasing a new operating system along with it, known as **Mica**, which would allow it to run "native" programs at full speed while also supporting Digital's existing VMS programs from the VAX after minor conversion. DEC management doubted the need to produce a new computer architecture to replace their existing VAX and DECstation lines, and eventually ended the PRISM project in 1988.

Alpha AXP 21064 bare die mounted on a business card with some statistics

By the time of cancellation, however, second-generation RISC chips (such as the newer SPARC architecture), were offering much better price/performance ratios than the VAX lineup. It was clear a third generation would completely outperform the VAX in all ways, not just on cost. Another study was started to see if a new RISC architecture could be defined that could directly support the VMS operating system. The new design used most of the basic PRISM concepts, but was re-tuned to allow VMS and VMS programs to run at reasonable speed with no conversion at all. The decision was also made to upgrade the design to a full 64-bit implementation from PRISM's 32-bit, a conversion all of the major RISC vendors were undertaking. Eventually that new architecture became Alpha. The primary Alpha instruction set architects were Richard L. Sites and Richard T. Witek. The PRISM's Epicode was developed into the Alpha's PALcode, providing an abstracted interface to platform- and processor implementation-specific features.

Compaq Alpha 21264C.

The main contribution of Alpha to the microprocessor industry, and the main reason for its performance, was not so much the architecture but rather its implementation. At that time (as it is now), the microchip industry was dominated by automated design and layout tools. The chip designers at Digital continued pursuing sophisticated manual circuit design in order to deal with the overly complex VAX architecture. The Alpha chips showed that manual circuit design applied to a simpler, cleaner architecture allowed for much higher operating frequencies than those that were possible with the more automated design systems. These chips caused a renaissance of custom circuit design within the microprocessor design community.

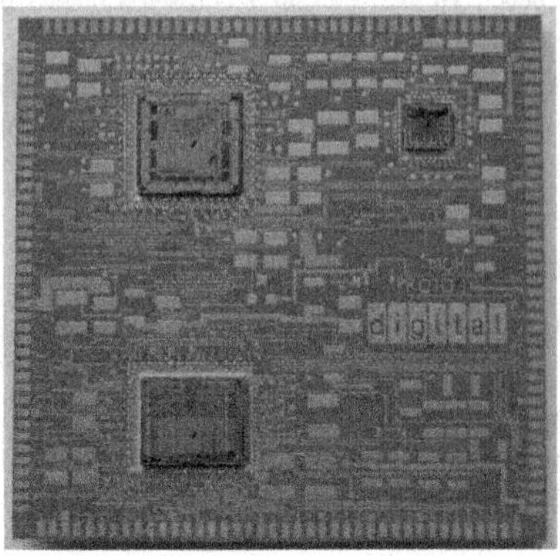

An early multi chip module prototype of the Alpha subdivided

Originally, the Alpha processors were designated the **DECchip 21x64** series, with "DECchip" replaced in the mid-1990s with "Alpha". The first two digits, "21" signifies the 21st century, and the last two digits, "64" signifies 64 bits. The Alpha was designed as 64-bit from the start and there is no 32-bit version. The middle digit corresponded to the generation of the Alpha architecture. Internally, Alpha processors were also identified by **EV** numbers, EV officially standing for "Extended VAX" but having an alternative humorous meaning of "Electric Vlasic", giving homage to the Electric Pickle experiment at Western Research Lab.[4]

The first few generations of the Alpha chips were some of the most innovative of their time. The first version, the **Alpha 21064** or **EV4**, was the first CMOS microprocessor whose operating frequency rivalled higher-powered ECL minicomputers and mainframes. The second, **21164** or **EV5**, was the first microprocessor to place a large secondary cache on chip. The third, **21264** or **EV6**, was the first microprocessor to combine both high operating frequency and the more complicated out-of-order execution microarchitecture. The **21364** or **EV7** was the first high performance processor to have an on-chip memory controller. The unproduced **21464** or **EV8** would have been the first to include simultaneous multithreading, but this version was canceled after the sale of DEC to Compaq. The **Tarantula** research project, which most likely would have been called **EV9**, would have been the first Alpha processor to feature a vector unit.[5]

A persistent report attributed to DEC insiders suggests the choice of the **AXP** tag for the processor was made by DEC's legal department, which was still smarting from the VAX trademark fiasco. After a lengthy search the tag "AXP" was found to be entirely unencumbered. Within the computer industry, a joke got started that the acronym **AXP** meant "Almost eXactly PRISM".

Design principles

The Alpha architecture was intended to be a high-performance design. Digital intended the architecture to support a one-thousandfold increase in performance over twenty-five years. To ensure this, any architectural feature that impeded multiple instruction issue, clock rate or multiprocessing was removed. As a result, the Alpha does not have:

- Branch delay slots
- Suppressed instructions
- Byte load or store instructions (later added with the Byte Word Extensions (BWX))

Condition codes

The Alpha does not have condition codes for integer instructions to remove a potential bottleneck at the condition status register. Instructions resulting in an overflow, such as adding two numbers whose result does not fit in 64 bits, write the 32 or 64 least significant bits to the destination register. The carry is generated by performing an unsigned compare on the result with either operand to see if the result is smaller than either operand. If the test was true, the value one is written to the least significant bit of the destination register to indicate the condition.

Registers

The architecture defined a set of 32 integer registers and a set of 32 floating-point registers in addition to a program counter, two lock registers and a floating-point control register (FPCR). It also defined registers that were optional, implemented only if the implementation required them. Lastly, registers for PALcode were defined.

The integer registers were denoted as R0 to R31 and floating-point registers were denoted as F0 to F31. The R31 and F31 registers were hardwired to zero and writes to those registers by instructions are ignored. Digital considered using a combined register file, but a split register file was determined to be better as it enabled two-chip implementations to have a register file located on each chip and integer-only implementations to omit the floating-point register file containing the floating point registers. A split register file was also determined to be more suitable for multiple instruction issue due to the reduced number of read and write ports. The number of registers per register file was also considered, with 32 and 64 being contenders. Digital concluded that 32 registers was more suitable as it required less die space, which improved clock frequencies. This number of registers was deemed not to be a major issue in respect to performance and future growth, as thirty-two registers could support at least eight-way instruction issue.

The program counter is a 64-bit register which contains a longword-aligned virtual byte address, that is, the low two bits of the program counter are always zero. The PC is incremented by four to the address of the next instruction when an instruction is decoded. A lock flag and locked physical address register are used by the load-locked and store-conditional instructions for multiprocessor support. The floating-point control register (FPCR) is a 64-bit register defined by the architecture intended for use by Alpha implementations with IEEE 754-compliant floating-point hardware.

Data types

In the Alpha architecture, a byte was defined as an 8-bit datum, a word as a 16-bit datum, a longword as a 32-bit datum, a quadword as a 64-bit datum and an octaword as a 128-bit datum.

The Alpha architecture originally defined six data types:

- Quadword (64-bit) integer
- Longword (32-bit) integer
- IEEE T-floating-point (double precision, 64-bit)
- IEEE S-floating-point (single precision, 32-bit)

To maintain a level of compatibility with VAX, the 32-bit architecture the Alpha succeeded, two VAX data types were included:

- VAX G-floating point (double precision, 64-bit)
- VAX F-floating point (single precision, 32-bit)

The Alpha had some provision for future expansion of the instruction set to include 128-bit data types.

Memory

The Alpha has a 64-bit linear virtual address space with no memory segmentation. Implementations can implement a smaller virtual address space with a minimum size of 43 bits. Although the unused bits were not implemented in hardware such as TLBs, the architecture required implementations to check if they are zero to ensure software compatibility with implementations that implemented a larger or the full virtual address space.

Instruction formats

<table>
<tr><td>31</td><td>30</td><td>29</td><td>28</td><td>27</td><td>26</td><td>25</td><td>24</td><td>23</td><td>22</td><td>21</td><td>20</td><td>19</td><td>18</td><td>17</td><td>16</td><td>15</td><td>14</td><td>13</td><td>12</td><td>11</td><td>10</td><td>9</td><td>8</td><td>7</td><td>6</td><td>5</td><td>4</td><td>3</td><td>2</td><td>1</td><td>0</td><td>Type</td></tr>
<tr><td colspan="6">Opcode</td><td colspan="5">Ra</td><td colspan="5">Rb</td><td colspan="3">Unused</td><td>0</td><td colspan="7">Function</td><td colspan="5">Rc</td><td>Integer operate</td></tr>
<tr><td colspan="6">Opcode</td><td colspan="5">Ra</td><td colspan="8">Literal</td><td>1</td><td colspan="7">Function</td><td colspan="5">Rc</td><td>Integer operate, literal</td></tr>
<tr><td colspan="6">Opcode</td><td colspan="5">Ra</td><td colspan="5">Rb</td><td colspan="11">Function</td><td colspan="5">Rc</td><td>Floating-point operate</td></tr>
<tr><td colspan="6">Opcode</td><td colspan="5">Ra</td><td colspan="5">Rb</td><td colspan="16">Displacement</td><td>Memory format</td></tr>
<tr><td colspan="6">Opcode</td><td colspan="5">Ra</td><td colspan="21">Displacement</td><td>Branch format</td></tr>
<tr><td colspan="6">Opcode</td><td colspan="26">Function</td><td>CALL_PAL format</td></tr>
</table>

The Alpha ISA has a fixed instruction length of 32 bits. It has six instruction formats.

The integer operate format is used by integer instructions. It contains a 6-bit opcode field, followed by the Ra field, which specifies the register containing the first operand and the Rb field, specifies the register containing the second operand. Next is a 3-bit field which is unused and reserved. A 1-bit field contains a "0", which distinguished this format from the integer literal format. A 7-bit function field follows, which is used in conjunction with the opcode to specify an operation. The last field is the Rc field, which specifies the register which the result of a computation should be written to. The register fields are all 5 bits long, required to address 32 unique locations, the 32 integer registers.

The integer literal format is used by integer instructions which use a literal as one of the operands. The format is the same as the integer operate format except for the replacement of the 5-bit Rb field and the 3 bits of unused space with an 8-bit literal field which is zero-extended to a 64-bit operand.

The floating-point operate format is used by floating-point instructions. It is similar to the integer operate format, but has an 11-bit function field made possible by using the literal and unused bits which are reserved in integer operate format.

The memory format is used mostly by load and store instructions. It has a 6-bit opcode field, a 5-bit Ra field, a 5-bit Rb field and a 16-bit displacement field.

Branch instructions have a 6-bit opcode field, a 5-bit Ra field and a 21-bit displacement field. The Ra field specifies a register to be tested by a conditional branch instruction, and if the condition is met, the program counter is updated by adding the contents of the displacement field with the program counter. The displacement field contains a signed integer and if the value of the integer is positive, if the branch is taken then the program counter is incremented. If the value of the integer is negative, then program counter is decremented if the branch is taken. The range of a branch is 1,048,576. The Alpha Architecture was designed with a large range as part of the architecture's forward-looking goal.

The CALL_PAL format is used by the CALL_PAL instruction, which is used to call PALcode subroutines. The format retains the opcode field but replaces the others with a 26-bit function field, which contains an integer specifying a PAL subroutine.

Instruction set

Control instructions

The control instructions consist of conditional and unconditional branches, and jumps. The conditional and unconditional branch instructions use the branch instruction format, while the jump instructions use the memory instruction format.

Conditional branches test the least significant bit of a register is set or clear, or compare a register as a signed quadword to zero, and branch if the specified condition is true. These conditions available for comparing a register to zero are equality, inequality, less than, less than or equal to, greater than or equal to, and greater than. The new address is computed by longword aligning and sign extending the 21-bit displacement and adding it to the address of the instruction following the conditional branch.

Unconditional branches update the program counter with a new address computed in the same way as conditional branches. They also save the address of the instruction following the unconditional branch to a register. There are two such instructions, and they differ only in the hints provided for the branch prediction hardware.

There are four jump instructions. These all perform the same operation, saving the address of the instruction following the jump, and providing the program counter with a new address from a register. They differ in the hints provided to the branch prediction hardware. The unused displacement field is used for this purpose.

Integer arithmetic

The integer arithmetic instructions perform addition, multiplication, and subtraction on longwords and quadwords; and comparison on quadwords. There is no instruction(s) for division as the architects considered the implementation of division in hardware to be adverse to simplicity. In addition to the standard add and subtract instructions, there are *scaled* versions. These versions shift the second operand to the left by two or three bits before adding or subtracting. The *Multiply Longword* and *Multiply Quadword* instructions write the least significant 32 or 64 bits of a 64- or 128-bit result to the destination register, respectively. Since it is useful to obtain the most significant half, the *Unsigned Multiply Quadword High* (UMULH) instruction is provided. UMULH is used for implementing multi-precision arithmetic and division algorithms. The concept of a separate instruction for multiplication that returns the most significant half of a result was taken from PRISM.

The instructions that operate on longwords ignore the most significant half of the register and the 32-bit result is sign-extended before it is written to the destination register. By default, the add, multiply, and subtract instructions, with the exception of UMULH and scaled versions of add and subtract, do no trap on overflow. When such functionality is required, versions of these instructions that perform overflow detection and trap on overflow are provided.

The compare instructions compare two registers or a register and a literal and write '1' to the destination register if the specified condition is true or '0' if not. The conditions are equality, inequality, less than or equal to, and less than. With the exception of the instructions that specify the former two conditions, there are versions that perform signed and unsigned compares.

The integer arithmetic instructions use the integer operate instruction formats.

Logical and shift

The logical instructions consist of those for performing bitwise logical operations and conditional moves on the integer registers. The bitwise logical instructions perform AND, NAND, NOR, OR, XNOR, and XOR between two registers or a register and literal. The conditional move instructions test a register as a signed quadword to zero and move if the specified condition is true. The specified conditions are equality, inequality, less than or equal to, less than, greater than or equal to, and greater than. The shift instructions perform arithmetic right shift, and logical left and right shifts. The shift amount is given by a register or literal. Logical and shift instructions use the integer operate instruction formats.

Extensions

Byte-Word Extensions (BWX)

Later, the Alpha included byte-word extensions, a set of instructions to manipulate 8-bit and 16-bit data types. These instructions were first introduced in the 21164A (EV56) microprocessor and are present in all subsequent implementations. These instructions performed operations that previously required multiple instructions to implement, which improved code density and the performance of certain applications. BWX also made the emulation of x86 machine code and the writing of device drivers easier.[6]

Mnemonic	Instruction
LDBU	Load Zero-Extended Byte from Memory to Register
LDWU	Load Zero-Extended Word from Memory to Register
SEXTB	Sign Extend Byte
SEXTW	Sign Extend Word
STB	Store Byte from Register to Memory
STW	Store Word from Register to Memory

Motion Video Instructions (MVI)

Motion Video Instructions (MVI) was an instruction set extension to the Alpha ISA that added instructions for single instruction, multiple data (SIMD) operations.[7] Alpha implementations that implement MVI, in chronological order, are the Alpha 21164PC (PCA56 and PCA57), Alpha 21264 (EV6) and Alpha 21364 (EV7). Unlike other SIMD instruction sets of the same period such as MIPS' MDMX or Sun Microsystems' Visual Instruction Set, MVI was a simple instruction set composed of a few instructions that operate on integer data types stored in existing integer registers.

MVI's simplicity was due to two reasons. Firstly, Digital had determined that the Alpha 21164 was already capable of performing DVD decoding through software, therefore not requiring hardware provisions for the purpose, but was inefficient in MPEG-2 encoding. The second reason was the requirement to retain the fast cycle times of implementations. Adding many instructions would have complicated and enlarged the instruction decode logic, reducing an implementation's clock frequency.

MVI consisted of 13 instructions:

Mnemonic	Instruction
MAXSB8	Vector Signed Byte Maximum
MAXSW4	Vector Signed Word Maximum
MAXUB8	Vector Unsigned Byte Maximum
MAXUW4	Vector Unsigned Word Maximum
MINSB8	Vector Signed Byte Minimum
MINSW4	Vector Signed Word Minimum
MINUB8	Vector Unsigned Byte Minimum
MINUW4	Vector Unsigned Word Minimum
PERR	Pixel Error
PKLB	Pack Longwords to Bytes
PKWB	Pack Words to Bytes
UNPKBL	Unpack Bytes to Longwords
UNPKBW	Unpack Bytes to Words

Floating-point Extensions (FIX)

Floating-point extensions (FIX) was an extension the Alpha Architecture. It introduced nine instructions for floating-point square-root and for transferring data to and from the integer registers and floating-point registers. The Alpha 21264 (EV6) was the first microprocessor to implement these instructions.

Mnemonic	Instruction
FTOIS	Floating-point to Integer Register Move, S_floating
FTOIT	Floating-point to Integer Register Move, T_floating
ITOFF	Integer to Floating-point Register Move, F_floating
ITOFS	Integer to Floating-point Register Move, S_floating
ITOFT	Integer to Floating-point Register Move, T_floating
SQRTF	Square root F_floating
SQRTG	Square root G_floating
SQRTS	Square root S_floating
SQRTT	Square root T_floating

Count Extensions (CIX)

Count Extensions (CIX) was an extension to the architecture which introduced three instructions for counting bits. These instructions were categorized as integer arithmetic instructions. They were first implemented on the Alpha 21264A (EV67).

Mnemonic	Instruction
CTLZ	Count Leading Zero
CTPOP	Count Population
CTTZ	Count Trailing Zero

Implementations

At the time of its announcement, Alpha was heralded as an architecture for the next 25 years. While this was not to be, Alpha has nevertheless had a reasonably long life. The first version, the **Alpha 21064** (otherwise known as the **EV4**) was introduced in November 1992 running at up to 192 MHz; a slight shrink of the die (the **EV4S**, shrunk from 0.75 µm to 0.675 µm) ran at 200 MHz a few months later. The 64-bit processor was a superpipelined and superscalar design, like other RISC designs, but nevertheless outperformed them all and DEC touted it as the world's fastest processor. Careful attention to circuit design, a hallmark of the Hudson design team, like a huge centralized clock circuitry, allowed them to run the CPU at higher speeds, even though the microarchitecture was fairly similar to other RISC chips. In comparison, the less expensive Intel Pentium ran at 66 MHz when it was launched the following spring.

The **Alpha 21164** or **EV5** became available in 1995 at processor frequencies of up to 333 MHz. In July 1996 the line was speed bumped to 500 MHz, in March 1998 to 666 MHz. Also in 1998 the **Alpha 21264** (**EV6**) was released at 450 MHz, eventually reaching (in 2001 with the **21264C/EV68CB**) 1.25 GHz. In 2003, the **Alpha 21364** or **EV7** *Marvel* was launched, essentially an EV68 core with four 1.6 GB/s[8] inter-processor communication links for improved multiprocessor system performance, running at 1 or 1.15 GHz.

In 1996, the production of Alpha chips was licensed to Samsung Electronics Company. Following the purchase of Digital by Compaq the majority of the Alpha products were placed with API NetWorks, Inc. (previously Alpha Processor Inc.), a private company funded by Samsung and Compaq. In October 2001, Microway became the exclusive sales and service provider of API NetWorks' Alpha-based product line.

On June 25, 2001, Compaq announced that Alpha would be phased out by 2004 in favor of Intel's Itanium, canceled the planned **EV8** chip, and sold all Alpha intellectual property to Intel.[9] HP, new owner of Compaq later the same year, announced that development of the Alpha series would continue for a few more years, including the release of a 1.3 GHz EV7 variant called the **EV7z**. This would be the final iteration of Alpha, the 0.13 µm **EV79** also being canceled.

Alpha was also implemented in the *Piranha*, a research prototype developed by Compaq's Corporate Research and Nonstop Hardware Development groups at the Western Research Laboratory and Systems Research Center. *Piranha* was a multicore design for transaction processing workloads that contained eight simple cores. It was described at the 27th Annual International Symposium on Computer Architecture in June 2000.[10]

Model history

Model	Model number	Year	Frequency [MHz]	Process [μm]	Transistors [millions]	Die size [mm²]	IO Pins	Power [W]	Voltage	Dcache [KB][11]	Icache [KB]	Scache	Bcache	ISA
EV4	21064	1992	100–200	0.75	1.68	234	290	30	3.3	8	8	–	128 KB–16 MB	
EV4S	21064	1993	100–200	0.675	1.68	186	290	27	3.3	8	8	–	128 KB–16 MB	
EV45	21064A	1994	200–300	0.5	2.85	164		33	3.3	16	16	–	256 KB–16 MB	
LCA4	21066	1993	100–166	0.675	1.75	209		21	3.3	8	8	–		
LCA4	21068	1994	66	0.675	1.75	209		9	3.3	8	8	–		
LCA45	21066A	1994	100–266	0.5	1.8	161		23	3.3	8	8	–		
LCA45	21068A	1994	100	0.5	1.8	161			3.3	8	8	–		
EV5	21164	1995	266–500	0.5	9.3	299	296	56	3.3/2.5	8	8	96 KB	Up to 64 MB	R
EV56	21164A	1996	366–666[12]	0.35	9.66[12]	209		31–55[12]	3.3/2.5[12]	8	8	96 KB	Up to 64 MB	R,B
PCA56	21164PC	1997	400–533	0.35	3.5	141	264	26–35	3.3/2.5	8	16	–	512 KB–4 MB	R,B,M
PCA57	21164PC		600–666	0.28	5.7	101	283	18–23	2.5/2.0	16	32[12]	–	512 KB–4 MB	R,B,M
EV6	21264	1998	450–600	0.35	15.2	314	389	73	2.0	64	64	–	2–8 MB	R,B,M,F
EV67	21264A	1999	600–750	0.25	15.2	210	389		2.0	64	64	–	2–8 MB	R,B,M,F,C
EV68AL	21264B	2001	800–833	0.18	15.2	125			1.7	64	64	–	2–8 MB	R,B,M,F,C,T
EV68CB	21264C	2001	1000–1250	0.18	15.2	125		65–75	1.65	64	64	–	2–8 MB	R,B,M,F,C,T
EV68CX	21264D								1.65	64	64	–	2–8 MB	R,B,M,F,C,T
EV7	21364	2003	1000–1150	0.18	130	397		125	1.5	64	64	1.75 MB	–	R,B,M,F,C,T
EV7z	21364	2004	1300	0.18	130	397		125	1.5	64	64	1.75 MB	–	R,B,M,F,C,T
Cancelled														
EV78/EV79	21364A	Slated for 2004	1700	0.13	152	300		120	1.2	64	64	1.75 MB	–	R,B,M,F,C,T
EV8	21464	Slated for 2003	1200–2000	0.125	250	420	1800	??	1.2	64	64	3 MB	–	R,B,M,F,C,T
Model	**Model number**	**Year**	**Frequency [MHz]**	**Process [μm]**	**Transistors [millions]**	**Die size [mm²]**	**IO Pins**	**Power [W]**	**Voltage**	**Dcache [KB]**	**Icache [KB]**	**Scache**	**Bcache**	**ISA**

ISA extensions

- **R** – Hardware support for rounding to infinity and negative infinity.[13]
- **B** – BWX, the "Byte/Word Extension", adding instructions to allow 8- and 16-bit operations from memory and I/O
- **M** – MVI, "multimedia" instructions

- **F** – FIX, instructions to move data between integer and floating point registers and for square root
- **C** – CIX, instructions for counting and finding bits
- **T** – Support for prefetch with modify intent to improve the performance of the first attempt to acquire a lock

Performance

To illustrate the comparative performance of Alpha-based systems, some SPEC performance numbers (SPECint95, SPECfp95) are listed below. Note that the SPEC results claim to report the measured performance of a whole computer system (CPU, bus, memory, compiler optimizer), not just the CPU. Also note that the benchmark and scale changed from 1992 to 1995. However, the figures give a rough impression of the performance of the Alpha architecture (64-bit), compared with the contemporary HP (64-bit) and Intel-based offerings (32-bit). Perhaps the most obvious trend is that while Intel could always get reasonably close to Alpha in integer performance, in floating point performance the difference was considerable. On the other side, HP (PA-RISC) is also reasonably close to Alpha, but these CPUs are running at significantly lower clock rates (MHz).

System	**CPU**	**MHz**	**integer**	**floating point**
AlphaServer 8400 5/350	21164 (EV5)	350	10.1	14.2
Intel Alder System (200 MHz, 256KB L2)	Pentium Pro	200	8.9	6.75
HP 9000 C160	PA 8000	160	10.4	16.3

I+SPEC Benchmark 1995 Performance comparison (using *SPECint95* and *SPECfp95* Result [14])

System	**CPU**	**MHz**	**integer**	**floating point**
AlphaServer ES40 6/833	21264 (EV6)	833	50.0	100.0
Intel VC820 motherboard	Pentium III	1000	46.8	31.9
HP 9000 C3600	PA-8600	552	42.1	64.0

I+2000 Performance comparison (using *SPECint95* and *SPECfp95* Result)

Alpha-based systems

The first generation of DEC Alpha-based systems comprised the DEC 3000 AXP series workstations and low-end servers, DEC 4000 AXP series mid-range servers, and DEC 7000 AXP and 10000 AXP series high-end servers. The DEC 3000 AXP systems used the same TURBOchannel bus as the previous MIPS-based DECstation models, whereas the 4000 was based on FutureBus+ and the 7000/10000 shared an architecture with corresponding VAX models.

DEC also produced a PC-like Alpha workstation with an EISA bus, the DECpc AXP 150 (codename "Jensen", also known as the DEC 2000 AXP). This was the first Alpha system to support Windows NT. DEC later produced Alpha versions of their Celebris XL and Digital Personal Workstation PC lines, with 21164 processors.

Digital also produced single board computers based on the VMEbus for embedded and industrial use. The first generation included the 21068-based AXPvme 64 and AXPvme 64LC, and the 21066-based AXPvme 160. These were introduced on March 1, 1994. Later models such as the AXPvme 100, AXPvme 166 and AXPvme 230 were based on the 21066A processor, while the Alpha VME 4/224 and Alpha VME 4/288 were based on the 21064A processor. The last models, the Alpha VME 5/352 and Alpha VME 5/480, were based on the 21164 processor.

The 21066 chip was used in the DEC Multia VX40/41/42 compact workstation and the ALPHAbook 1 laptop from Tadpole Technology.

In 1994, DEC launched a new range of AlphaStation and AlphaServer systems. These used 21064 or 21164 processors and introduced the PCI bus, VGA-compatible frame buffers and PS/2-style keyboards and mice. The

AlphaServer 8000 series superseded the DEC 7000/10000 AXP and also employed XMI and FutureBus+ buses.

The AlphaStation XP1000 was the first workstation based on the 21264 processor. Later AlphaServer/Station models based on the 21264 were categorised into *DS* (departmental server), *ES* (enterprise server) or *GS* (global server) families.

The final 21364 chip was used in the AlphaServer ES47, ES80 and GS1280 models and the AlphaStation ES47.

A number of OEM motherboards were produced by DEC, such as the 21066 and 21068-based AXPpci 33 "NoName", which was part of a major push into the OEM market by the company,[15] the 21164-based AlphaPC 164 and AlphaPC 164LX, the 21164PC-based AlphaPC 164SX and AlphaPC 164RX and the 21264-based AlphaPC 264DP. Several third-parties such as Samsung and API also produced OEM motherboards such as the API UP1000 and UP2000.

To assist third parties in developing hardware and software for the platform, DEC produced Evaluation Boards, such as the EB64+ and EB164 for the Alpha 21064A and 21164 microprocessors respectively.

The 21164 and 21264 processors were used by NetApp in various Network Attached Storage systems, while the 21064 and 21164 processors were used by Cray in their T3D and T3E massively parallel supercomputers.

Supercomputers

The fastest supercomputers based on Alpha processors:

- ASCI Q at Los Alamos National Laboratory. Machine: HP AlphaServer SC45/GS Cluster. CPU: 4096 Alpha (21264 EV-68, 1.25 GHz). Rmax: 7.727 Teraflops.[16]

References

[1] Bolotoff, Paul V. (14 April 2005). "Alpha: The History in Facts and Comments" (http://alasir.com/articles/alpha_history/dec_collapse.shtml). Alasir. .

[2] Aaron Sakovich (2001). "Windows 2000?" (http://www.alphant.com/articles/windows2000.html). The AlphaNT Source. . Retrieved 2007-01-01.

[3] "Transforming your AlphaServer environment" (http://h18002.www1.hp.com/alphaserver/evolution.html). HP. . Retrieved 2007-01-11.

[4] Bill Hamburgen, Jeff Mogul, Brian Reid, Alan Eustace, Richard Swan, Mary Jo Doherty, Joel Bartlett (1989) (PDF). *WRL Technical Note TN-13: Characterization of Organic Illumination Systems* (http://www.hpl.hp.com/techreports/Compaq-DEC/WRL-TN-13.html). Digital Equipment Corporation. . Retrieved 2007-10-04.

[5] Espasa, Roger; Federico Ardanaz, Julio Gago, Roger Gramunt, Isaac Hernandez, Toni Juan, Joel Emer, Stephen Felix, Geoff Lowney, Matthew Mattina, Andre Seznec (2002). "Tarantula: A Vector Extension to the Alpha Architecture" (http://ieeexplore.ieee.org/search/wrapper.jsp?arnumber=1003586). In Danielle C. Martin (PDF). *Proceedings: 29th Annual International Symposium on Computer Architecture (ISCA '02).* 29th Annual International Symposium on Computer Architecture (ISCA '02) (http://systems.cs.colorado.edu/ISCA2002), Joe Daigle/Studio Productions. Los Alamitos, Calif: IEEE Computer Society. pp. Page(s): 281–292. doi:10.1109/ISCA.2002.1003586. ISBN 0-7695-1605-X. . Retrieved 2007-10-04.

[6] Gronowski, *et al.*; Bowhill, W.J.; Donchin, D.R.; Blake-Campos, R.P.; Carlson, D.A.; Equi, E.R.; Loughlin, B.J.; Mehta, S. et al. (1996). "A 433-MHz 64-b quad-issue RISC microprocessor". *IEEE Journal of Solid-State Circuits* **31** (11): 1687–1696. doi:10.1109/JSSC.1996.542313.

[7] Gwennap, Linley (18 November 1996). "Digital, MIPS Add Multimedia Extensions". *Microprocessor Report.*

[8] In the context of data transfer, 1 GB is used to mean 1 billion bytes

[9] Popovich, Ken (2001-06-28). "Alpha proved costly for Compaq" (http://news.zdnet.co.uk/itmanagement/0,1000000308,2090197,00.htm). *www.zdnet.co.uk*. ZDNet. . Retrieved 2009-05-01.

[10] Luiz André Barroso, Kourosh Gharachorloo, Robert McNamara, Andreas Nowatzyk, Shaz Qadeer, Barton Sano, Scott Smith, Robert Stets, and Ben Verghese (2000). "Piranha: A Scalable Architecture Based on Single-Chip Multiprocessing". *Proceedings of the 27th Annual International Symposium on Computer Architecture.*

[11] In the context of cache memory, 1 KB = 1024 bytes; 1 MB = 1024 KB

[12] Paul V. Bolotoff (21st of April 2007). "Alpha: The History in Facts and Comments" (http://www.alasir.com/articles/alpha_history/). . Retrieved Nov 22 2008.

[13] David Mosberger. "Overview of Alpha Family" (http://www.mostang.com/~davidm/papers/expo97/paper/doc003.html). . Retrieved Dec 9 2009.

[14] http://www.spec.org/cpu95/results/

[15] Reinhardt Krause. "DEC launching Alpha board push". Electronic News, April 4, 1994.

[16] Los Alamos National Laboratories (2002). "The ASCI Q System: 30 TeraOPS Capability at Los Alamos National Laboratory" (http://www.sandia.gov/supercomp/sc2002/flyers/ASCI_Q_rev.pdf). . Retrieved 2010-06-06.

External links

- The Alpha Architecture Handbook, Version 4 (http://www.compaq.com/cpq-alphaserver/technology/literature/alphaahb.pdf)
- The Alpha Architecture Handbook, Version 3 (http://www.cs.cmu.edu/afs/cs/academic/class/15213-f98/doc/alpha-ref.pdf)
- Digital Technical Journal, Volume 4, Number 4, Special Issue 1992 Alpha AXP Architecture and Systems (http://www.hpl.hp.com/hpjournal/dtj/vol4num4/toc.htm) This issue contains several articles from Alpha's Architects
- Archived technical documentation library (http://h18002.www1.hp.com/alphaserver/technology/chip-docs.html) This link features the hardware reference manuals and datasheets for Alpha microprocessors, chipsets and OEM motherboards. Includes the Alpha Architecture Handbook and various programming manuals.
- "DEC Alpha DECchip 21064 - Images of the first DEC Alpha Microprocessor (1992)." http://www.chipsetc.com/dec---digital-equipment-corporation.html]

Instruction_set

An **instruction set**, or **instruction set architecture** (ISA), is the part of the computer architecture related to programming, including the native data types, instructions, registers, addressing modes, memory architecture, interrupt and exception handling, and external I/O. An ISA includes a specification of the set of opcodes (machine language), and the native commands implemented by a particular processor.

Instruction set architecture is distinguished from the microarchitecture, which is the set of processor design techniques used to implement the instruction set. Computers with different microarchitectures can share a common instruction set. For example, the Intel Pentium and the AMD Athlon implement nearly identical versions of the x86 instruction set, but have radically different internal designs.

Some virtual machines that support bytecode for Smalltalk, the Java virtual machine, and Microsoft's Common Language Runtime virtual machine as their ISA implement it by translating the bytecode for commonly used code paths into native machine code, and executing less-frequently-used code paths by interpretation; Transmeta implemented the x86 instruction set atop VLIW processors in the same fashion.

Classification of instruction sets

A complex instruction set computer (CISC) has many specialized instructions, which may only be rarely used in practical programs. A reduced instruction set computer (RISC) simplifies the processor by only implementing instructions that are frequently used in programs; unusual operations are implemented as subroutines, where the extra processor execution time is offset by their rare use. Theoretically important types are the minimal instruction set computer and the one instruction set computer but these are not implemented in commercial processors. Another variation is the very long instruction word (VLIW) where the processor receives many instructions encoded and retrieved in one instruction word.

Machine language

Machine language is built up from discrete *statements* or *instructions*. On the processing architecture, a given instruction may specify:

- Particular registers for arithmetic, addressing, or control functions
- Particular memory locations or offsets
- Particular addressing modes used to interpret the operands

More complex operations are built up by combining these simple instructions, which (in a von Neumann architecture) are executed sequentially, or as otherwise directed by control flow instructions.

Instruction types

Some operations available in most instruction sets include:

- Data handling and Memory operations
  - **set** a register (a temporary "scratchpad" location in the CPU itself) to a fixed constant value
  - **move** data from a memory location to a register, or vice versa. This is done to obtain the data to perform a computation on it later, or to store the result of a computation.
  - **read** and **write** data from hardware devices
- Arithmetic and Logic
  - **add**, **subtract**, **multiply**, or **divide** the values of two registers, placing the result in a register, possibly setting one or more condition codes in a status register
  - perform bitwise operations, taking the **conjunction** and **disjunction** of corresponding bits in a pair of registers, or the **negation** of each bit in a register
  - **compare** two values in registers (for example, to see if one is less, or if they are equal)
- Control flow
  - **branch** to another location in the program and execute instructions there
  - **conditionally branch** to another location if a certain condition holds
  - **indirectly branch** to another location, while saving the location of the next instruction as a point to return to (a *call*)

Complex instructions

Some computers include "complex" instructions in their instruction set. A single "complex" instruction does something that may take many instructions on other computers. Such instructions are typified by instructions that take multiple steps, control multiple functional units, or otherwise appear on a larger scale than the bulk of simple instructions implemented by the given processor. Some examples of "complex" instructions include:

- saving many registers on the stack at once
- moving large blocks of memory
- complex and/or floating-point arithmetic (sine, cosine, square root, etc.)
- performing an atomic test-and-set instruction
- instructions that combine ALU with an operand from memory rather than a register

A complex instruction type that has become particularly popular recently is the SIMD or Single-Instruction Stream Multiple-Data Stream operation or vector instruction, an operation that performs the same arithmetic operation on multiple pieces of data at the same time. SIMD have the ability of manipulating large vectors and matrices in minimal time. SIMD instructions allow easy parallelization of algorithms commonly involved in sound, image, and video processing. Various SIMD implementations have been brought to market under trade names such as MMX, 3DNow! and AltiVec.

Specialised processor types like GPUs for example also provide complex instruction sets. Nonetheless many of these specialised processor complex instruction sets do not have a publicly available native instruction set and native assembly language for proprietary hardware related reasons and are usually only accessible to software developers through standardized higher level languages and APIs. The OpenGL virtual instruction set and virtual assembly language ARB (GPU assembly language) and CUDA are examples of such hardware abstraction layers on top of the specialised processor native instruction set.

Parts of an instruction

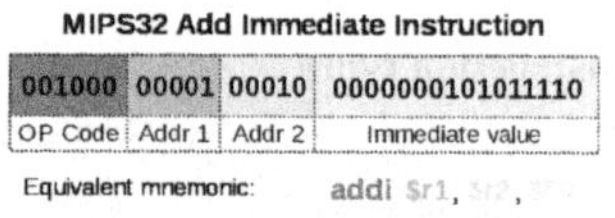

One instruction may have several fields, which identify the logical operation to be done, and may also include source and destination addresses and constant values. This is the MIPS "Add Immediate" instruction which allows selection of source and destination registers and inclusion of a small constant.

On traditional architectures, an instruction includes an opcode specifying the operation to be performed, such as "add contents of memory to register", and zero or more operand specifiers, which may specify registers, memory locations, or literal data. The operand specifiers may have addressing modes determining their meaning or may be in fixed fields.

In very long instruction word (VLIW) architectures, which include many microcode architectures, multiple simultaneous opcodes and operands are specified in a single instruction.

Some exotic instruction sets do not have an opcode field (such as Transport Triggered Architectures (TTA) or the Forth virtual machine), only operand(s). Other unusual "0-operand" instruction sets lack any operand specifier fields, such as some stack machines including NOSC [1].

Instruction length

The size or length of an instruction varies widely, from as little as four bits in some microcontrollers to many hundreds of bits in some VLIW systems. Processors used in personal computers, mainframes, and supercomputers have instruction sizes between 8 and 64 bits. The longest possible instruction on x86 is 18 bytes (144 bits) [2] . Within an instruction set, different instructions may have different lengths. In some architectures, notably most reduced instruction set computers (RISC), instructions are a fixed length, typically corresponding with that architecture's word size. In other architectures, instructions have variable length, typically integral multiples of a byte or a halfword.

Representation

The instructions constituting a program are rarely specified using their internal, numeric form; they may be specified by programmers using an assembly language or, more commonly, may be generated by compilers.

Design

The design of instruction sets is a complex issue. There were two stages in history for the microprocessor. The first was the CISC (Complex Instruction Set Computer) which had many different instructions. In the 1970s, however, places like IBM did research and found that many instructions in the set could be eliminated. The result was the RISC (Reduced Instruction Set Computer), an architecture which uses a smaller set of instructions. A simpler instruction set may offer the potential for higher speeds, reduced processor size, and reduced power consumption. However, a more complex set may optimize common operations, improve memory/cache efficiency, or simplify programming.

Some instruction set designers reserve one or more opcodes for some kind of system call or software interrupt For example, MOS Technology 6502 uses 00_H, Zilog Z80 uses the eight codes C7,CF,D7,DF,E7,EF,F7,FF_H [3] while

Motorola 68000 use codes in the range A000..$AFFF_H$.

Fast virtual machines are much easier to implement if an instruction set meets the Popek and Goldberg virtualization requirements.

The NOP slide used in Immunity Aware Programming is much easier to implement if the "unprogrammed" state of the memory is interpreted as a NOP.

On systems with multiple processors, non-blocking synchronization algorithms are much easier to implement if the instruction set includes support for something such as "fetch-and-add", "load-link/store-conditional" (LL/SC), or "atomic compare and swap".

Instruction set implementation

Any given instruction set can be implemented in a variety of ways. All ways of implementing an instruction set give the same programming model, and they all are able to run the same binary executables. The various ways of implementing an instruction set give different tradeoffs between cost, performance, power consumption, size, etc.

When designing the microarchitecture of a processor, engineers use blocks of "hard-wired" electronic circuitry (often designed separately) such as adders, multiplexers, counters, registers, ALUs etc. Some kind of register transfer language is then often used to describe the decoding and sequencing of each instruction of an ISA using this physical microarchitecture. There are two basic ways to build a control unit to implement this description (although many designs use middle ways or compromises):

1. Early computer designs and some of the simpler RISC computers "hard-wired" the complete instruction set decoding and sequencing (just like the rest of the microarchitecture).
2. Other designs employ microcode routines and/or tables to do this—typically as on chip ROMs and/or PLAs (although separate RAMs have been used historically).

There are also some new CPU designs which compile the instruction set to a writable RAM or flash inside the CPU (such as the Rekursiv processor and the Imsys Cjip),[4] or an FPGA (reconfigurable computing). The Western Digital MCP-1600 is an older example, using a dedicated, separate ROM for microcode.

An ISA can also be emulated in software by an interpreter. Naturally, due to the interpretation overhead, this is slower than directly running programs on the emulated hardware, unless the hardware running the emulator is an order of magnitude faster. Today, it is common practice for vendors of new ISAs or microarchitectures to make software emulators available to software developers before the hardware implementation is ready.

Often the details of the implementation have a strong influence on the particular instructions selected for the instruction set. For example, many implementations of the instruction pipeline only allow a single memory load or memory store per instruction, leading to a load-store architecture (RISC). For another example, some early ways of implementing the instruction pipeline led to a delay slot.

The demands of high-speed digital signal processing have pushed in the opposite direction—forcing instructions to be implemented in a particular way. For example, in order to perform digital filters fast enough, the MAC instruction in a typical digital signal processor (DSP) must be implemented using a kind of Harvard architecture that can fetch an instruction and two data words simultaneously, and it requires a single-cycle multiply–accumulate multiplier.

Code density

In early computers, program memory was expensive, so minimizing the size of a program to make sure it would fit in the limited memory was often central. Thus the combined size of all the instructions needed to perform a particular task, the *code density*, was an important characteristic of any instruction set. Computers with high code density also often had (and have still) complex instructions for procedure entry, parameterized returns, loops etc. (therefore retroactively named *Complex Instruction Set Computers*, CISC). However, more typical, or frequent, "CISC" instructions merely combine a basic ALU operation, such as "add", with the access of one or more operands in memory (using addressing modes such as direct, indirect, indexed etc.). Certain architectures may allow two or three operands (including the result) directly in memory or may be able to perform functions such as automatic pointer increment etc. Software-implemented instruction sets may have even more complex and powerful instructions.

Reduced instruction-set computers, RISC, were first widely implemented during a period of rapidly growing memory subsystems and sacrifice code density in order to simplify implementation circuitry and thereby try to increase performance via higher clock frequencies and more registers. RISC instructions typically perform only a single operation, such as an "add" of registers or a "load" from a memory location into a register; they also normally use a fixed instruction width, whereas a typical CISC instruction set has many instructions shorter than this fixed length. Fixed-width instructions are less complicated to handle than variable-width instructions for several reasons (not having to check whether an instruction straddles a cache line or virtual memory page boundary[5] for instance), and are therefore somewhat easier to optimize for speed. However, as RISC computers normally require more and often longer instructions to implement a given task, they inherently make less optimal use of bus bandwidth and cache memories.

Minimal instruction set computers (MISC) are a form of stack machine, where there are few separate instructions (16-64), so that multiple instructions can be fit into a single machine word. These type of cores often take little silicon to implement, so they can be easily realized in an FPGA or in a multi-core form. Code density is similar to RISC; the increased instruction density is offset by requiring more of the primitive instructions to do a task.

There has been research into executable compression as a mechanism for improving code density. The mathematics of Kolmogorov complexity describes the challenges and limits of this.

Number of operands

Instruction sets may be categorized by the maximum number of operands *explicitly* specified in instructions.

(In the examples that follow, *a*, *b*, and *c* are (direct or calculated) addresses referring to memory cells, while *reg1* and so on refer to machine registers.)

- 0-operand (*zero-address machines*), so called stack machines: All arithmetic operations take place using the top one or two positions on the stack; 1-operand push and pop instructions are used to access memory: **push** a, **push** b, **add**, **pop** c.
- 1-operand (*one-address machines*), so called accumulator machines, include early computers and many small microcontrollers: most instructions specify a single right operand (that is, constant, a register, or a memory location), with the implicit accumulator as the left operand (and the destination if there is one): **load** *a*, **add** *b*, **store** *c*. A related class is practical stack machines which often allow a single explicit operand in arithmetic instructions: **push** a, **add** b, **pop** c.
- 2-operand — many CISC and RISC machines fall under this category:
  - CISC — often **load** *a,reg1*; **add** *reg1,b*; **store** *reg1,c* on machines that are limited to one memory operand per instruction; this may be load and store at the same location
  - CISC — **move** *a->c*; **add** *c+=b*.
  - RISC — Requiring explicit memory loads, the instructions would be: **load** *a,reg1*; **load** *b,reg2*; **add** *reg1,reg2*; **store** *reg2,c*
- 3-operand, allowing better reuse of data:.[5]
  - CISC — It becomes either a single instruction: **add** *a,b,c*, or more typically: **move** *a,reg1*; **add** *reg1,b,c* as most machines are limited to two memory operands.
  - RISC — arithmetic instructions use registers only, so explicit 2-operand load/store instructions are needed: **load** *a,reg1*; **load** *b,reg2*; **add** *reg1+reg2->reg3*; **store** *reg3,c*; unlike 2-operand or 1-operand, this leaves all three values a, b, and c in registers available for further reuse[5].

- more operands—some CISC machines permit a variety of addressing modes that allow more than 3 operands (registers or memory accesses), such as the VAX "POLY" polynomial evaluation instruction.

Due to the large number of bits needed to encode the three registers of a 3-operand instruction, RISC processors using 16-bit instructions are invariably 2-operand machines, such as the Atmel AVR, the TI MSP430, and some versions of the ARM Thumb. RISC processors using 32-bit instructions are usually 3-operand machines, such as processors implementing the Power Architecture, the SPARC architecture, the MIPS architecture, the ARM architecture, and the AVR32 architecture.

Each instruction specifies some number of operands (registers, memory locations, or immediate values) *explicitly*. Some instructions give one or both operands implicitly, such as by being stored on top of the stack or in an implicit register. When some of the operands are given implicitly, the number of specified operands in an instruction is smaller than the arity of the operation. When a "destination operand" explicitly specifies the destination, the number of operand specifiers in an instruction is larger than the arity of the operation. Some instruction sets have different numbers of operands for different instructions.

See also

- Comparison of CPU architectures
- Computer architecture
- CPU design
- Emulator
- Instruction set simulator
- Register transfer language (RTL)
- List of instruction sets

Categories of ISA

- EPIC: Explicitly Parallel Instruction Computing
- Vector processor
- SIMD: Single Instruction Multiple Data
- Flynn's Taxonomy
- Orthogonal instruction set

References

[1] http://strangegizmo.com/forth/NOSC/
[2] John L. Hennessy and David Patterson (2006). *Computer Architecture: A Quantitative Approach* (http://www.elsevierdirect.com/product.jsp?isbn=9780123704900) (Fourth Edition ed.). Morgan Kaufmann. ISBN 978-0-12-370490-0. .
[3] Ganssle, Jack. "Proactive Debugging" (http://embedded.com/showArticle.jhtml?articleID=9900044). Published February 26, 2001.
[4] http://cpushack.net/CPU/cpu7.html
[5] The evolution of RISC technology at IBM by John Cocke (http://domino.watson.ibm.com/tchjr/journalindex.nsf/0/22d06c5aa961e78085256bfa0067fa93?OpenDocument) – IBM Journal of R&D, Volume 44, Numbers 1/2, p.48 (2000)

External links

- Mark Smotherman's Historical Computer Designs Page (http://www.cs.clemson.edu/~mark/hist.html)
- Microprocessor Instruction Set Cards (http://vmoc.museophile.org/cards/)
- A Set of Standard Microprocessor Programming Cards (http://archive.comlab.ox.ac.uk/cards/cards.html) by Jonathan Bowen
- Randy Hyde's discussion on ISA (http://webster.cs.ucr.edu/AoA/Windows/HTML/ISA.html)

Alpha_21064

The **Alpha 21064** is a microprocessor developed and fabricated by Digital Equipment Corporation that implemented the Alpha (introduced as the Alpha AXP) instruction set architecture (ISA). It was introduced as the **DECchip 21064** before it was renamed in 1994. The 21064 is also known by its code name, **EV4**. It was announced in February 1992 with volume availability in September 1992. The 21064 was the first commercial implementation of the Alpha ISA, and the first microprocessor from Digital to be available commercially. It was succeeded by a derivative, the Alpha 21064A in October 1993.

The 21064 microprocessor

History

The first Alpha processor was a test chip codenamed **EV3**. This test chip was fabricated using Digital's 1.0-micrometre (μm) CMOS-3 process. The test chip lacked a floating point unit and only had 1 KB caches. The test chip was used to confirm the operation of the aggressive circuit design techniques. The test chip (along with simulators and emulators) was also used to bring up firmware and the various operating systems that the company supported. The production chip, codenamed **EV4**, was fabricated using Digital's 0.75 μm CMOS-4 process. Dirk Meyer and Edward McLellan were the micro-architects. Ed designed the issue logic while Dirk designed the other major blocks. Jim Montanaro lead the circuit implementation. The EV3 was used in the Alpha Development Unit (ADU), a computer used by Digital to develop software for the Alpha platform before the availability of EV4 parts.

The 21064 microprocessor mounted on a business card

The 21064 was unveiled at the 39th International Solid-State Circuits Conference (ISSCC) in mid-February 1992. It was announced on 25 February 1992, with a 150 MHz sample introduced on the same day. It was priced at $3,375 in quantities of 100, $1,650 in quantities between 100 and 1,000, and $1,560 for quantities over 1,000. Volume shipments begun in September 1992.

In early February 1993, the price of the 150 MHz version was reduced to $1,096 from $1,559 in quantities greater than 1,000.

On 25 February 1993, a 200 MHz was introduced, with sample kits available, priced at $3,495. In volume, it was priced at $1,231 per unit in quantities greater than 10,000. Volume orders were accepted in June 1993, with shipments in August 1993. The price of the 150 MHz version was reduced in response. The sample kit was reduced to $1,690 from $3,375, effective in April 1993; and in volume, it was reduced to $853 from $1,355 per unit in quantities greater than 10,000, effective in July 1993.

With the introduction of the Alpha 21066 and the Alpha 21068 on 10 September 1993, Digital adjusted the positioning of the existing 21064s and introduced a 166 MHz version priced at $499 per unit in quantities of 5,000. The price of the 150 MHz version was reduced to $455 per unit in quantities of 5,000.

On 6 June 1994, the price of the 200 MHz version was reduced by 31% to $544 to position it against the 60 MHz Pentium; and the 166 MHz version by 19% to $404 per unit in quantities of 5,000, effective on 3 July 1994.

The Alpha 21064 was fabricated at Digital's Hudson, Massachusetts and South Queensferry, Scotland facilities.

Users

The 21064 was mostly used in high-end computers such as workstations and servers. Users included:

- Aspen Systems in its Alpine workstations
- Carrera Computers in its Hercules 150, Hercules 200, and Pantera II workstations
- Cray Research, used the 150 MHz 21064 in its Cray T3D supercomputers
- Digital, in its DECpc AXP 150 entry-level workstations, DEC 2000 AXP entry-level servers, DEC 3000 AXP workstations and entry-level servers, DEC 4000 AXP mid-range servers and DEC 7000/10000 AXP high-end servers
- Encore Computer, in its Infinity R/T high-end real-time computer

Performance

The 21064 was the highest performing microprocessor from when it was introduced until 1993, after International Business Machines (IBM) introduced the multi-chip POWER2. It subsequently became the highest performing single-chip microprocessor, a position it held until the 275 MHz 21064A was introduced in October 1993.[1]

Description

The Alpha 21064 is a superpipelined dual-issue superscalar microprocessor that executes instructions in-order. It is capable of issuing up to two instructions every clock cycle to four functional units: an integer unit, a floating-point unit (FPU), an address unit, and a branch unit. The integer pipeline is seven stages long, and the floating-point pipeline ten stages. The first four stages of both pipelines are identical and are implemented by the I-Box.

I-box

The I-box is the control unit; it fetches, issues and decodes instructions; and controls the pipeline.[2] During stage one, two instructions are fetched from the I-cache. Branch prediction is performed by logic in the I-box during stage two. Either static prediction or dynamic prediction is used. Static prediction examined the sign bit of the displacement field of a branch instruction, predicted the branch as taken if the sign bit indicated a backwards branch (if sign bit contained 1). Dynamic prediction examined an entry in the 2,048-entry by 1-bit branch history table. If an entry contained 1, the branch was predicted as taken.[3] If dynamic prediction was utilized, the branch prediction is approximately 80% accurate for most programs.[4] The branch misprediction penalty is four cycles.[5]

These instructions are decoded during stage three. The I-box then checks if the resources required by the two instructions are available during stage four. If so, the instructions are issued, providing they can be paired. Which instructions could be paired was determined by the number of read and write ports in the integer register file.[6] The 21064 could issue: an integer operate with a floating-point operate, any load/store instruction with any operate instruction, an integer operate with an integer branch, or a floating-point operate with a floating-point branch. Two combinations were not permitted: an integer operate and a floating-point store, and a floating-point operate and an integer store. If one of the two instructions cannot be issued together, the first four stages are stalled until the remaining instruction is issued. The first four stages are also stalled in the event that no instruction can be issued due to resource unavailability, dependencies, or similar conditions.

The I-box contains two translation lookaside buffers (TLBs) for translating virtual addresses to physical addresses. These TLBs are referred to as *instruction translation buffers* (ITBs). The ITBs cache recently used page table entries for the instruction stream. An eight-entry ITB is used for 8 KB pages and a four-entry ITB for 4 MB pages. Both ITBs are fully associative and use a not-last used replacement algorithm.[7]

Execution

Execution begins during stage five for all instructions. The register files are read during stage four. The pipelines beginning at stage five cannot be stalled.

Integer unit

The integer unit is responsible for executing integer instructions. It consists of the integer register file (IRF) and the E-box. The IRF contains thirty-two 64-bit registers and has four read ports and two write ports that are equally divided between the integer unit and the branch unit.[8] The E-box contains an adder, a logic unit, barrel shifter and multiplier. Except for multiply, shift and byte manipulation instructions, most integer instructions are completed by the end of stage five and thus have a latency of one cycle. The barrel shifter is pipelined, but shift and byte manipulation instructions are not completed by the end of stage six, and thus have a latency of two cycles. The multiplier was not pipelined in order to save die area,[4] thus multiply instructions have a variable latency of 19 to 23 cycles depending on the operands. In stage seven, integer instructions write their results to the IRF.

Address unit

The address unit, also known as the "A-box", executed load and store instructions. To enable the address unit and integer unit to operate in parallel, the address unit has its own displacement adder, which it uses to calculate virtual addresses, instead of using the adder in the integer unit.[9] A 32-entry fully associative translation lookaside buffer (TLB) is used to translate virtual addresses into physical addresses.[9] This TLB is referred to as the *data translation buffer* (DTB). The 21064 implemented a 43-bit virtual address and a 34-bit physical address, and is therefore is capable of addressing 8 TB of virtual memory and 16 GB of physical memory.

Store instructions result in data buffered in a 4-entry by 32-byte write buffer. The write buffer improved performance by reducing the number of writes on the system bus by merging data from adjacent stores and by temporarily delaying stores, enabling loads to be serviced quicker as the system bus is not utilized as often.[9]

Floating-point unit

The floating-point unit consists of the floating-point register file (FRF) and the F-box.[6] The FRF contains thirty-two 64-bit registers and has three read ports and two write ports. The F-box contained a floating-point pipeline and a non-pipelined divide unit which retired one bit per cycle.

The floating-point register file is read and the data formatted into fraction, exponent, and sign in stage four. If executing add instructions, the adder calculates the exponent difference, and a predictive leading one or zero detector using input operands for normalizing the result is initiated. If executing multiply instructions, a 3 X multiplicand is generated.

In stages five and six, alignment or a normalization shift and sticky-bit calculations are performed for adds and subtracts. Multiply instructions are multiplied in a pipelined, two-way interleaved array which uses a radix-8 Booth algorithm.[4] [10] In stage eight, final addition is performed in parallel with rounding. Floating-point instructions write their results to the FRF in stage ten.[10]

Instructions executed in the pipeline have a six-cycle latency.[10] Single-precision (32-bit) and double-precision (64-bit) divides, which are executed in the non-pipelined divide unit, have a latency of 31 and 61 cycles, respectively.[11]

Caches

The 21064 has two on-die primary caches: an 8 KB data cache (known as the D-cache) using a write-through write policy and an 8 KB instruction cache (known as the I-cache). Both caches are direct-mapped for single-cycle access and have 32-byte line size. The caches are built with six-transistor static random access memory (SRAM) cells that have an area of 98 μm^2. The caches are 1,024 cells wide by 66 cells tall, with the top two rows used for redundancy.

An optional external secondary cache, known as the B-cache, with capacities of 128 KB to 16 MB was supported. The cache operated at one-third to one-sixteenth of the internal clock frequency, or 12.5 to 66.67 MHz at 200 MHz.[12] The B-cache is direct-mapped and has a 128-byte line size by default that could be configured to use larger quantities. The B-cache is accessed via the system bus.

External interface

The external interface is a 128-bit data bus that operated at half to one-eighth the internal clock rate, or 25 to 100 MHz at 200 MHz. The width of the bus was configurable, systems using the 21064 could have a 64-bit external interface. The external interface also consisted of a 34-bit address bus.

Fabrication

The 21064 contained 1.68 million transistors.[13] The original EV4 was fabricated by Digital in its CMOS-4 process, which has a 0.75 μm feature size and three levels of aluminium interconnect.[13] The EV4 measures 13.9 mm by 16.8 mm, for an area of 233.52 mm^2. The later EV4S was fabricated in CMOS-4S, a 10% optical shrink of CMOS-4 with a 0.675 μm feature size. This version measured 12.4 mm by 15.0 mm, for an area 186 mm^2.[14]

The 21064 used a 3.3-volt (V) power supply.[13] The EV4 dissipated a maximum of 30 W at 200 MHz. The EV4S dissipates a maximum of 21.0 W at 150 MHz, 22.5 W at 166 MHz, and 27.0 W at 200 MHz.[15]

Package

The 21064 is packaged in a 431-pin alumina-ceramic pin grid array (PGA) measuring 61.72 mm by 61.72 mm.[16] Of the 431 pins, 291 were for signals and 140 were for power and ground.[13] [17] The heatsink is directly attached to the package, secured by nuts attached to two studs protruding from the tungsten heat spreader.

A packaged 21064 microprocessor

Derivatives

Alpha 21064A

The **Alpha 21064A**, introduced as the **DECchip 21064A**, code-named **EV45**, is a further development of the Alpha 21064 introduced in October 1993. It operated at clock frequencies of 200, 225, 233, 275 and 300 MHz. The 225 MHz model was replaced by the 233 MHz model on 6 July 1994, which at introduction, was priced at US$788 in quantities of 5,000, 10% less than the 225 MHz model it replaced. On the same day, prices for the 275 MHz was also reduced by 25% to US$1,083 in quantities of 5,000. The 300 MHz model was announced and sampled on 2 October 1995 and was shipped in December 1995. There was also one model, the 21064A-275-PC, that was restricted to running the Windows NT or operating systems that use the Windows NT memory management model.

The 21064A succeeded the original 21064 as the high-end Alpha microprocessor. It subsequently saw the most use in high-end systems. Users included:

- Digital in some models of its DEC 3000 AXP, DEC 4000 AXP and DEC 7000/10000 AXP systems
- Aspen Systems in its Alpine workstation
- BTG, who used a 275 MHz model in its Action AXP275 RISC PC
- Carrera Computers in its Cobra AXP 275 workstation
- NekoTech, who used a 275 MHz model overclocked by 5% to 289 MHz in their Mach 2-289-T workstation
- Network Appliance (now NetApp), who used a 275 MHz model in its storage systems

The 21064A had a number of microarchitectural improvements over the 21064. The primary caches were improved in two ways: the capacity of the I-cache and D-cache was doubled from 8 KB to 16 KB and parity protection was added to the cache tag and cache data arrays. Floating-point divides have a lower latency due to an improved divider that retires two bits per cycle on average. Branch prediction was improved by a larger 4,096-entry by 2-bit BHT.

The 21064A contains 2.8 million transistors and is 14.5 by 10.5 mm large, for an area of 152.25 mm^2. It was fabricated by Digital in their fifth-generation CMOS process, CMOS-5, a 0.5 μm process with four levels of aluminium interconnect.[18]

Alpha 21066

The **Alpha 21066**, introduced as the **DECchip 21066**, code-named **LCA4** (*Low Cost Alpha*), is a low-cost variant of Alpha 21064. Samples were introduced on 10 September 1993, with volume shipments in early 1994. At the time of introduction, the 166 MHz Alpha 21066 was priced at US$385 in quantities of 5,000. A 100 MHz model, intended for embedded systems, also existed. Sampling begun in late 1994, with volume shipments in the third quarter of 1995. The *Microprocessor Report* recognized the Alpha 21066 as the first microprocessor with an integrated PCI controller.

The Alpha 21066 was intended for use in low-cost applications, specifically personal computers running Windows NT. Digital used various models of the Alpha 21066 in their Multia clients, AXPpci 33 original equipment manufacturer (OEM) motherboards and AXPvme single board computers. Outside of Digital, users included Aspen Systems in its Alpine workstation, Carrera Computers in its Pantera I workstation, NekoTech used a 166 MHz model in its Mach 1-166 personal computer, and Parsys in its TransAlpha TA9000 Series supercomputers.

Due to the process shrink, it was able to include features that were desirable in cost-sensitive embedded systems. These features include an on-die B-cache and memory controller with ECC support, a functionally limited graphics accelerator supporting up to 8 MB of VRAM for implementing a framebuffer, a PCI controller and a phase locked loop (PLL) clock generator for multiplying a 33 MHz external clock signal to the desired internal clock frequency.

The memory controller supported 64 KB to 2 MB of B-cache and 2 to 512 MB of memory. The ECC implementation was capable of detecting 1-, 2- and 4-bit errors and correcting 1-bit errors. To reduce cost, the Alpha 21066 has a 64-bit system bus, which reduced the number of pins and thus the size of the package. The reduced width of the system bus also reduced bandwidth and thus performance by 20%, which was deemed acceptable.

The 21066 contained 1.75 million transistors and measured 17.0 by 12.3 mm, for an area of 209.1 mm^2. It was fabricated in CMOS-4S, a 0.675 μm process with three levels of interconnect. The 21066 was packaged in a 287-pin CPGA measuring 57.404 by 57.404 mm.

Alpha 21066A

The **Alpha 21066A**, code-named **LCA45**, is a low-cost variant of the Alpha 21064A. It was announced on 14 November 1994, with samples of 100 and 233 MHz models introduced on the same day. Both models were shipped in March 1995. When announced, the 100 and 233 MHz models were priced at $175 and $360, respectively, in quantities of 5,000. A 266 MHz model was later made available.

DEC Alpha 21066A.

The 21066A was second sourced by Mitsubishi Electric as the **M36066A**. It was the first Alpha microprocessor to be fabricated by the company. 100 and 233 MHz parts were announced in November 1994. At the time of the announcement, engineering samples were set for December 1994, commercial samples in July 1995 and volume quantities in September 1995. The 233 MHz part was priced at $490 in quantities of 1,000.[19]

Although it was based on the 21064A, the 21066A did not have the 16 KB instruction and data caches. A feature specific to the 21066A was power management – the microprocessor's internal clock frequency could be adjusted by software.

Digital used various models of 21066A in their products which had previously used the 21066. Outside of Digital, Tadpole Technology used a 233 MHz model in their ALPHAbook 1 notebook.

The 21066A contained 1.8 million transistors on a die measuring 14.8 by 10.9 mm, for an area of 161.32 mm^2. It was fabricated in Digital's fifth-generation CMOS process, CMOS-5, a 0.5 μm process with three levels of interconnect. Mitsubishi Electric fabricated the M36066A in its own 0.5 μm three-level-metal process.

Alpha 21068

The **Alpha 21068**, introduced as the **DECchip 21068**, is a version of the 21066 positioned for embedded systems. It was identical to the 21066 but was offered at a lower clock rate to reduce power dissipation and cost. Samples were introduced on 10 September 1993 with volume shipments in early 1994. It operated at 66 MHz and had a 9 W maximum power dissipation. At the time of introduction, the 21068 was priced at US$221 each in quantities of 5,000. On 6 June 1994, Digital announced that it was cutting the price by 16% to US$186, effective on 3 July 1994.

The Alpha 21068 was used by Digital in their AXPpci 33 motherboard and the AXPvme 64 and 64LC single-board computers.

Alpha 21068A

The **Alpha 21068A**, introduced as the **DECchip 21068A**, is a variant of the Alpha 21066A for embedded systems. It operated at a clock frequency of 100 MHz.

Chipsets

Initially, there was no standard chipset for the 21064 and 21064A. Digital's computers used custom application-specific integrated circuits (ASICs) to interface the microprocessor to the system. As this raised development cost for third-parties who wished to develop Alpha-based products, Digital developed a standard chipset, the DECchip 21070 (*Apecs*), for original equipment manufacturers (OEMs).

There were two models of the 21070, the **DECchip 21071** and the **DECchip 21072**. The 21071 was intended for workstations whereas the 21072 was intended for high-end workstations or low-end uniprocessor servers. The two models differed in memory subsystem features: the 21071 has a 64-bit memory bus and supports 8 MB to 2 GB of parity-protected memory whereas the 21072 has a 128-bit memory bus and supports 16 MB to 4 GB of ECC-protected memory.

The chipset consisted of three chip designs, the COMANCHE B-cache and memory controller, the DECADE data slice and the EPIC PCI controller. The DECADE chips implemented the data paths in 32-bit slices and therefore the 21071 has two such chips while the 21072 has four. The EPIC chip has a 32-bit path to the DECADE chips.

The 21070 was introduced on 10 January 1994,[20] with samples available. Volume shipments began in mid-1994. In quantities of 5,000, the 21071 was priced at $90 and the 21072 at $120.

21070 users included Carrera Computers for its Pantera workstations and Digital in some models of its AlphaStations and uniprocessor AlphaServers.

Notes

[1] Ryan 1994
[2] Digital Equipment Corporation 1996, p. 2-3–2-4
[3] Digital Equipment Corporation 1996, p. 2-5
[4] McLellan 1993, p. 42
[5] Dobberpuhl 1992, p. 37
[6] Dobberpuhl 1992, p. 36
[7] Digital Equipment Corporation 1996, p. 2-6
[8] Dobberpuhl 1992, pp. 35–36
[9] McLellan 1993, p. 43
[10] Dobberpuhl 1992, p. 38
[11] Gwennap 1994
[12] McLellan 1993, p. 44
[13] Dobberpuhl 1992, p. 35
[14] Bhandarkar 1995, pp. 2–4
[15] Digital Equipment Corporation 1996, p. 8-3
[16] Digital Equipment Corporation 1996, p. 8-2
[17] Bhandarkar 1995, p. 2
[18] Bhandarkar 1995, p. 3
[19] Krause 1994
[20] Digital Equipment Corporation 1994

References

- *Alpha 21064 and 21064A Microprocessors Hardware Reference Manual*, June 1996. Order number: EC-Q92UC-TE. Digital Equipment Corporation.
- Apiki, Steve; Grehan, Rick (March 1995). "Fastest NT Workstations" (http://web.archive.org/web/20070928031257/http://www.byte.com/art/9503/sec11/art1.htm). *Byte*.
- Bhandarkar, Dileep. "Alpha Implementations" (http://tab.computer.org/tcca/NEWS/DEC95/dec95_dileep.ps), *IEEE Computer Society Technical Committee on Computer Architecture Newsletter*, December 1995.
- Computergram (25 February 1992). "DEC Reveals More On Alpha, Challenges Hewlett-Packard's Precision Architecture RISC" (http://www.cbronline.com/news/dec_reveals_more_on_alpha_challenges_hewlett_packards_precision_architecture_risc). *Computer Business Review*.
- Computergram (26 February 1992). "DEC Describes Its Alpha RISC, Kubota Discloses Its Plans" (http://www.cbronline.com/news/dec_describes_its_alpha_risc_kubota_discloses_its_plans). *Computer Business Review*.
- Computergram (7 June 1994). "DEC slashes Alpha AXP Chip Prices by up to 31%" (http://www.cbronline.com/news/dec_slashes_alpha_axp_chip_prices_by_up_to_31). *Computer Business Review*.
- Computergram (13 September 1993). "DEC adds Alphas for Personal Computers, Control" (http://www.cbronline.com/news/dec_adds_alphas_for_personal_computers_control). *Computer Business Review*.

- Computergram (11 January 1994). "Microprocessor Report's Annual Chip Awards Declare Motorola 88110 the Part least likely to..." (http://www.cbronline.com/news/microprocessor_reports_annual_chip_awards_declare_motorola_88110_the_part_least_likely_to_1). *Computer Business Review*.
- Computergram (11 November 1994). "Mitsubishi Electric Is Ready To Sample Its First Alpha At Last" (http://www.cbronline.com/news/mitsubishi_electric_is_ready_to_sample_its_first_alpha_at_last). *Computer Business Review*.
- Computergram (25 November 1994). "Mitsubishi's First Alpha Provides The Same Functionality As DEC's 21066A". *Computer Business Review*.
- Digital Equipment Corporation (10 January 1994). "Digital Introduces PCI-Based System Logic Chipsets For Alpha AXP 21064 Microprocessors And Announces The Industry's First PCI To PCI Bridge Chip". Press release.
- Dobberpuhl, Daniel W., Witek, Richard T. et al. "A 200-MHz 64-bit Dual-issue CMOS Microprocessor", *Digital Technical Journal*, Volume 4, Number 4, Special Issue 1992, pp. 35–50.
- Gwennap, Linley (12 September 1994). "Digital Leads the Pack with 21164", *Microprocessor Report*, Volume 8, Number 12.
- Krause, Reinhardt (13 September 1993). "DEC unveils two Alphas in PCI, embedded drive". *Electronic News*.
- Krause, Reinhardt (18 October 1993). "DEC readies 225/275MHz Alphas". *Electronic News*.
- Krause, Reinhardt (21 November 1994). "Alpha partners roll 233MHz 21066A". *Electronic News*.
- McKinney, Dina L. et al. "Digital's DECchip 21066: The First Cost-focused Alpha AXP Chip". *Digital Technical Journal*, Volume 6, Number 1, Winter 1994, pp. 66–77.
- McLellan, Edward (June 1993). "The Alpha AXP Architecture and 21064 Processor". *IEEE Micro*. pp. 36–47.
- Ryan, Bob; Thompson, Tom (January 1994). "RISC Grows Up" (http://web.archive.org/web/20050218003618/http://www.byte.com/art/9401/sec7/art5.htm). *Byte*.

Further reading

- "DEC Enters Microprocessor Business with Alpha". (4 March 1992). *Microprocessor Report*, Volume 6, Number 3.
- "DEC's Alpha Architecture Premiers". (4 March 1992). *Microprocessor Report*, Volume 6, Number 3.
- "Digital Plans Broad Alpha Processor Family" (18 November 1992). *Microprocessor Report*, Volume 6, Number 3.
- "Digital Reveals PCI Chip Sets For Alpha". (12 July 1993). *Microprocessor Report*, Volume 7, Number 9.
- "Alpha Hits Low End with Digital's 21066". (13 September 1993). *Microprocessor Report*, Volume 7, Number 12.
- Bhandarkar, Dileep P. (1995). *Alpha Architecture and Implementations*. Digital Press.
- Fox, Thomas F. (1994). "The design of high-performance microprocessors at Digital". *Proceedings of the 31st Annual ACM-IEEE Design Automation Conference*. pp. 586–591.
- Gronowski, Paul E. et al. (May 1998). "High-performance microprocessor design". *IEEE Journal of Solid-State Circuits* **33** (5): pp. 676–686.

Alpha_21264

The **Alpha 21264** was a Digital Equipment Corporation RISC microprocessor introduced in October, 1996. The 21264 implemented the Alpha instruction set architecture (ISA).

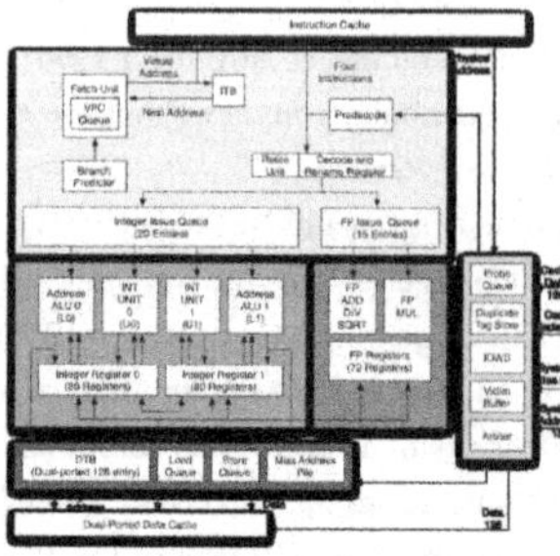

Alpha 21264 microarchitecture.

Description

The Alpha 21264 was a four-issue superscalar microprocessor with out-of-order execution and speculative execution. It has a peak execution rate of six instructions per cycle and can sustain four instructions per cycle. It has a seven-stage instruction pipeline.

Out of order execution

At any given stage, the microprocessor could have up to 80 instructions in various stages of execution, surpassing every other contemporary microprocessor.

Decoded instructions are queued in instruction queues and are issued when their operands are available. The integer queue contained 20 entries and the floating-point queue 15. Each queue could issue as many instructions as there were pipelines.

Ebox

The Ebox executed integer, load and store instructions. It has two integer units, two load store units and two integer register files. Each integer register file contained 80 entries, of which 31 are architectural registers, 41 are rename registers and 8 are PALshadow registers. There was no entry for register R31 because in the Alpha architecture, R31 is hardwired to zero and can only be read from.

Each register file served an integer unit and a load store unit, and the register file and its two units are referred to as a "cluster". The two clusters were designated U0 and U1. This scheme was used as it reduced the number of write and read ports required to serve operands and receive results, thus reducing the physical size of the register file, enabling the microprocessor to operate at higher clock frequencies. Writes to any of the register files thus have to be synchronized, which required a clock cycle to complete, negatively impacting performance by one percent. The reduction of performance resulting from the synchronization was compensated in two ways. Firstly, the higher clock frequency achievable offset the loss. Secondly, the logic responsible for instruction issue avoided creating situations where the register file had to be synchronized by issuing instructions that were not dependent on data held in other register file where possible.

The clusters are near identical except for two differences: U1 has a seven-cycle pipelined multiplier while U0 has a three-cycle pipeline for executing Motion Video Instructions (MVI), an extension to the Alpha Architecture defining single instruction multiple data (SIMD) instructions for multimedia.

The load store units are simple arithmetic logic units used to calculate virtual addresses for memory access. They are also capable of executing simple arithmetic and logic instructions. The Alpha 21264 instruction issue logic utilized this capability, issuing instructions to these units when they were available for use (not performing address arithmetic).

The Ebox therefore has four 64-bit adders, four logic units, two barrel shifters, byte-manipulation logic, two sets of conditional branch logic equally divided between U1 and U0.

Fbox

The Fbox is responsible for executing floating-point instructions. It consists of two floating-point pipelines and a floating-point register file. The pipelines are not identical, one executes the majority of instructions and the other only multiply instructions. The adder pipeline has two non-pipelined units connected to it, a divide unit and a square root unit. Adds, multiplies and most other instructions have a 4-cycle latency, a double-precision divide has 16-cycle latency and a double-precision square root has a 33-cycle latency. The floating point register file contains 72 entries, of which 32 are architectural registers and 40 are rename registers.

Cache

The Alpha 21264 has two levels of cache, a primary cache and secondary cache. The three-level cache of the Alpha 21164 was not used due to problems with bandwidth.

Primary caches

The primary cache is split into separate caches for instructions and data, the I-cache and D-cache respectively. Both caches have a capacity of 64 KB. The D-cache is dual-ported by transferring data on both the rising and falling edges of the clock signal. This method of dual-porting enabled any combination of reads or writes to the cache every processor cycle. It also avoided duplication the cache so there are two, as in the Alpha 21164. Duplicating the cache restricted the capacity of the cache, as it required more transistors to provide the same amount of capacity, and in turn increased the area required and power consumed.

B-cache

The secondary cache, termed the B-cache, is an external cache with a capacity of 1 to 16 MB. It is controlled by the microprocessor and is implemented by synchronous static random access memory (SSRAM) chips that operate at two thirds, half, one-third or one-fourth the internal clock frequency, or 133 to 333 MHz at 500 MHz. The B-cache was accessed with a dedicated 128-bit bus that operates at the same clock frequency as the SSRAM or at twice the clock frequency if double data rate SSRAM is used. The B-cache is direct-mapped.[1]

Branch prediction

Branch prediction is performed by a tournament branch prediction algorithm. The algorithm was developed by Scott McFarling at Digital's Western Research Laboratory (WRL) and was described in a 1993 paper. This predictor was used as the Alpha 21264 has a minimum branch misprediction penalty of seven cycles. Due to the instruction cache's two cycle latency and the instruction queues, the average branch misprediction penalty is 11 cycles. The algorithm maintains two history tables, Local and Global, and the table used to predict the outcome of a branch is determined by a Choice predictor.

The local predictor is a two-level table which records the history of individual branches. It consists of a 1,024-entry by 10-bit branch history table. A two-level table was used as the prediction accuracy is similar to that of a larger single-level table while requiring fewer bits of storage. It has a 1,024-entry branch history table. Each entry is a 3-bit saturating counter. The value of the counter determines whether the current branch is taken or not taken.

The choice predictor records the history of the local and global predictors to determine which predictor is the best for a particular branch. It has a 4,096-entry branch history table. Each entry is a 2-bit saturating counter. The value of the counter determines if the local or global predictor is used.

External interface

The external interface consisted of a bidirectional 64-bit double data rate (DDR) data bus and two 15-bit unidirectional time-multiplexed address and control buses, one for signals originating from the Alpha 21264 and one for signals originating from the system. Digital licensed the bus to Advanced Micro Devices (AMD), and it was subsequently used in their Athlon microprocessors, where it was known as the EV6 bus.

Fabrication

The Alpha 21264 contained 15.2 million transistors. The logic consisted of approximately six million transistors, with the rest contained in the caches and branch history tables. The die measured 16.7 mm by 18.8 mm (313.96 mm²).[2] It was fabricated in a 0.35 µm complementary metal–oxide–semiconductor (CMOS) process with six levels of interconnect.

Packaging

The Alpha 21264 was packaged in a 587-pin ceramic interstitial pin grid array (IPGA).

Alpha Processor, Inc. later sold the Alpha 21264 in a Slot B package containing the microprocessor mounted on a printed circuit board with the B-cache and voltage regulators. The design was intended to use the success of slot-based microprocessors from Intel and AMD. Slot B was originally developed to be used by AMD's Athlon as well, so that API could obtain materials for the Slot B at commodity prices in order to reduce the cost of the Alpha 21264 to gain a wider market share. This never materialized as AMD chose to use Slot A for their slot-based Athlons.

Derivatives

Alpha 21264A

The **Alpha 21264A**, code-named **EV67** was a shrink of the Alpha 21264 introduced in late 1999. There were six versions: 600, 667, 700, 733, 750, 833 MHz. The EV67 was the first Alpha microprocessor to implement the count extension (CIX), which extended the instruction set with instructions for performing population count. It was fabricated by Samsung Electronics in a 0.25 µm CMOS process that had 0.25 µm transistors but 0.35 µm metal layers. The die had an area of 210 mm². The EV68 used a 2.0 V power supply. It dissipated a maximum of 73 W at 600 MHz, 80 W at 667 MHz, 85 W at 700 MHz, 88 W at 733 MHz and 90 W at 750 MHz.

Alpha 21264B

The **Alpha 21264B** is a further development for increased clock frequencies. There were two models, one fabricated by IBM, code-named **EV68C**, and one by Samsung, code-named **EV68A**.

The EV68A was fabricated in a 0.18 µm CMOS process with aluminium interconnects. It had a die size of 125 mm², a third smaller than the Alpha 21264A, and used a 1.7 V power supply. It was available in volume in 2001 at clock frequencies of 750, 833, 875 and 940 MHz. The EV68A dissipated a maximum of 60 W at 750 MHz, 67 W at 833 MHz, 70 W at 875 MHz and 75 W at 940 MHz.[3]

The EV68C was fabricated in a 0.18 µm CMOS process with copper interconnects. It was sampled in early 2000 and achieved a maximum clock frequency of 1.25 GHz.

In September 1998, Samsung announced they would fabricate a variant of the Alpha 21264B in a 0.18 µm fully depleted silicon-on-insulator (SOI) process with copper interconnects that was capable of achieving a clock frequency of 1.5 GHz. This version never materialized.

Alpha 21264C

The **Alpha 21264C**, code-named **EV68CB** was a derivative of the Alpha 21264. It was available at clock frequencies of 1.0, 1.25 and 1.33 GHz. The EV68CB contained 15.5 million transistors and measured 120 mm². It was fabricated by IBM in a 0.18 µm CMOS process with seven levels of copper interconnect and low-K dielectric. It was packaged in a 675-pad flip-chip ceramic land grid array (CLGA) measuring 49.53 by 49.53 mm. The EV68A used a 1.7 V power supply, dissipating a maximum of 64 W at 1.0 GHz, 75 W at 1.25 GHz and 80 W at 1.33 GHz.[4]

Alpha 21264D

The **Alpha 21264D**, code-named **EV68CD** is a faster derivative fabricated by IBM.

Alpha 21264E

The **Alpha 21264E**, code-named **EV68E**, was a cancelled derivative developed by Samsung first announced on 10 October 2000 at Microprocessor Forum 2000 slated for introduction at around mid-2001. Improvements were a higher operating frequency of 1.25 GHz and the addition of an on-die 1.85 MB secondary cache. It was to be fabricated in a 0.18 micrometre CMOS process with copper interconnects.

Chipsets

Digital and Advanced Micro Devices (AMD) both developed chipsets for the Alpha 21264.

21272

The Digital **21272**, also known as the **Tsunami** and **Typhoon** was the first chipset for the Alpha 21264. The 21272 chipset supported two-, three- or four-way multiprocessing and one or two 64-bit 33 MHz PCI buses. It had 128- to 512-bit memory bus which operated at 83 MHz, yielding a maximum bandwidth of 5,312 MB/s. The chipset supported 100 MHz registered ECC SDRAM.

The chipset consisted of three devices, a C-chip, a D-chip and a P-chip. The number of devices which made up the chipset varied as it was determined by the configuration of the chipset. The C-chip is the control chip containing the memory controller. One C-chip was required for every microprocessor.

The P-chip is the PCI controller, implementing a 33 MHz PCI bus. The 21272 could have one or two P-chips.

The 21272 was used extensively by Digital, Compaq and Hewlett Packard in their entry-level to mid-range AlphaServers and in all models of the AlphaStation. It was also used in third-party products from Alpha Processor, Inc. (later known as API NetWorks) such as their UP2000+ motherboard.

Irongate

AMD developed two Alpha 21264-compatible chipsets, the **Irongate**, also known as the **AMD-751**, and its successor, **Irongate-2**, also known as the **AMD-761**. These chipsets were developed for their Athlon microprocessors but due to AMD licensing the EV6 bus used in the Alpha from Digital, the Athlon and Alpha 21264 were compatible in terms of bus protocol. The Irongate was used by Samsung in their UP1000 and UP1100 motherboards. The Irongate-2 was used by Samsung in their UP1500 motherboard.

Notes

[1] The Alpha 21264 Microprocessor Architecture, p. 5.
[2] Gronowski, "High Performance Microprocessor Design", p. 676.
[3] Compaq, "21264/EV68A Microprocessor Hardware Reference Manual".
[4] Compaq, "21264/EV68CB and 21264/EV68DC Hardware Reference Manual".

References

- Compaq Computer Corporation (July 1999). *Alpha 21264 Microprocessor Hardware Reference Manual.*
- Compaq Computer Corporation (June 2001). *21264/EV68CB and 21264/EV68DC Hardware Reference Manual.*
- Compaq Computer Corporation (March 2002). *21264/EV67 Microprocessor Hardware Reference Manual.*
- Compaq Computer Corporation (March 2002). *21264/EV68A Microprocessor Hardware Reference Manual.*
- Gronowski, Paul E. et al. (1998). "High Performance Microprocessor Design". *IEEE Journal of Solid-State Circuits*, Volume 33, Number 5, pp. 676–686.
- Gwennap, Linley (28 October 1996). "Digital 21264 Sets New Standard". *Microprocessor Report*, Volume 10, Number 14. MicroDesign Resources.
- Kessler, R. E.; McLellan, E. J. and Webb, D. A. (1998) "The Alpha 21264 Microprocessor Architecture". *Proceedings of the International Conference on Computer Design: VLSI in Computers and Processors*. pp. 90–95.
- Kessler, R. E. (1999). "The Alpha 21264 Microprocessor". *IEEE Micro*, March–April 1999. pp. 24–36.
- Leibholz, Daniel and Razdan, Rahul (1997). "The Alpha 21264: A 500 MHz Out-of-Order Execution Microprocessor". *Proceedings of Compcon '97*. pp. 28–36.
- Matson, M. et al. "Circuit Implementation of a 600MHz Superscalar RISC Microprocessor". *Proceedings of the International Conference on Computer Design: VLSI in Computers and Processors*. pp. 104–110.
- AlphaVM-free (http://emuvm.com/) freeware Alpha emulator supporting 21264 processors line

Further reading

- Benschneider, B.J. et al. (2000). "A 1 GHz Alpha microprocessor" (http://ieeexplore.ieee.org/xpls/abs_all.jsp?arnumber=839702). *ISSCC Digest of Technical Papers*, pp. 86–87.
- Clouser, J. et al. (July 1999). "A 600-MHz superscalar floating-point processor" (http://ieeexplore.ieee.org/xpls/abs_all.jsp?arnumber=772419). *IEEE Journal of Solid-State Circuits* **34** (7): pp. 1026–1029.
- Fischer, T.; Leibholz, D. (1998). "Design trade offs in stall-control circuits for 600 MHz instruction queues" (http://ieeexplore.ieee.org/xpls/abs_all.jsp?arnumber=672448). *ISSCC Digest of Technical Papers*, pp. 232–234, 444.
- Gieseke, B.A. et al. (1997). "A 600 MHz superscalar RISC microprocessor with out-of-order execution". *ISSCC Digest of Technical Papers*, pp. 176–177, 451.
- Gronowski, Paul E. et al. (May 1998). "High-performance microprocessor design". *IEEE Journal of Solid-State Circuits* **33** (5): pp. 676–686.
- Hokinson, R. et al. (2001). "Design and migration challenges for an Alpha microprocessor in a 0.18 μm copper process" (http://ieeexplore.ieee.org/xpls/abs_all.jsp?arnumber=912656). *ISSCC Digest of Technical Papers*, pp. 320–321, 460.

Windows_NT

Microsoft WindowsNT	
Company / developer	Microsoft
Programmed in	C, C++ and Assembly language[1]
Working state	Current
Source model	Closed source / Shared source
Initial release	27 July 1993 (as Windows NT 3.1)
Latest stable release	[[Windows 7 [2]], Windows Server 2008 R2 NT 6.1 (Build 7601: Service Pack 1)] (February 22, 2011) [2] [±]
Latest unstable release	[[Windows 8 [3]] NT 6.2 (Build 8400)] (May 31, 2012) [3] [±]
Update method	Windows Update
Supported platforms	IA-32, x86-64, Alpha, MIPS, PowerPC, ARM, Itanium
Kernel type	Hybrid
Default user interface	Graphical (Windows Explorer)
License	MS-EULA
Official website	www.microsoft.com/windows/ [4]

Windows NT is a family of operating systems produced by Microsoft, the first version of which was released in July 1993. It was a powerful high-level-language-based, processor-independent, multiprocessing, multiuser operating system with features comparable to Unix. It was intended to complement consumer versions of Windows that were based on MS-DOS. NT was the first fully 32-bit version of Windows, whereas its consumer-oriented counterparts, Windows 3.1x and Windows 9x, were 16-bit/32-bit hybrids. Windows 2000, Windows XP, Windows Server 2003, Windows Vista, Windows Home Server, Windows Server 2008, and Windows 7 are effectively Windows NT, although they are not branded using that name.

It is popularly believed that Dave Cutler[5] intended the initialism 'WNT' as a pun on VMS, incrementing each letter by one. However, the project was named NT OS/2 before receiving the Windows brand.[6] One of the original OS/2 3.0 developers, Mark Lucovsky, states that the name was taken from the original target processor—the Intel i860, code-named N10 ('N-Ten').[7] Various Microsoft publications, including a 1998 question-and-answer session with Bill Gates, reveal that the letters were expanded to 'New Technology' for marketing purposes but no longer carry any specific meaning.[8] The letters were dropped from the name of Windows 2000, though Microsoft described the product as 'Built on NT technology.'

Major features

A main design goal of NT was hardware and software portability. Various versions of NT family operating systems have been released for a variety of processor architectures, initially Intel IA-32, MIPS R3000/R4000, and Alpha, with PowerPC, Itanium, AMD64 and ARM supported in later releases. The idea was to have a common code base with a custom Hardware Abstraction Layer (HAL) for each platform. However, support for MIPS, Alpha, and PowerPC was later dropped after NT 4.0. Broad software compatibility was achieved with support for several API "personalities", including Win32, POSIX,[9] and OS/2[10] APIs - the latter two were phased out starting with Windows XP.[11] Partial MS-DOS compatibility was achieved via an integrated DOS Virtual Machine - although this feature is being phased out in the x86-64 architecture.[12] NT supported per-object (file, function, and role) access control lists allowing a rich set of security permissions to be applied to systems and services. NT supported Windows network protocols, inheriting the previous OS/2 LAN Manager networking, as well as TCP/IP networking (for which Microsoft would implement a TCP/IP stack derived at first from STREAMS, then later rewritten in-house.[13])

Windows NT 3.1 was the first version of Windows to utilize 32-bit "flat" virtual memory addressing on 32-bit processors. Its companion product, Windows 3.1, used segmented addressing and switches from 16-bit to 32-bit addressing in pages.

Windows NT 3.1 featured a core kernel providing a system API, running in supervisor mode, and a set of user-space environments with their own APIs which included the new Win32 environment, an OS/2 1.3 text-mode environment and a POSIX environment. The full preemptive multitasking kernel could interrupt running tasks to schedule other tasks, without relying on user programs to voluntarily give up control of the CPU, as in Windows 3.1 Windows applications (although MS-DOS applications were preemptively multitasked in Windows starting with Windows 1.0).

Notably, in Windows NT 3.x, several I/O driver subsystems, such as video and printing, were user-mode subsystems. In Windows NT 4, the video, server, and printer spooler subsystems were integrated into the kernel. Windows NT's first GUI was strongly influenced by (and programmatically compatible with) that from Windows 3.1; Windows NT 4's interface was redesigned to match that of the brand new Windows 95, moving from the Program Manager to the Start Menu/Taskbar design.

NTFS, a journaled, secure file system, was created for NT. Windows NT also allows for other installable file systems, and with versions 3.1 and 3.51, NT could also be installed on DOS's FAT or OS/2's HPFS file systems. Later versions could be installed on a FAT32 partition, in select cases, including Vista versions.[14] Windows Vista and Windows 7 require a FAT32 partition to boot on an EFI based system.[15]

Development

Microsoft decided to create a portable operating system, compatible with OS/2 and POSIX and supporting multiprocessing, in October 1988.[16] When development started in November 1989, Windows NT was to be known as OS/2 3.0,[17] the third version of the operating system developed jointly by Microsoft and IBM. To ensure portability, initial development was targeted at the Intel i860XR RISC processor, switching to the MIPS R3000 in late 1989, and then the Intel i386 in 1990.[18] Microsoft also continued parallel development of the DOS-based and less resource-demanding Windows environment, resulting in the release of Windows 3.0 in May 1990. Windows 3 was eventually so successful that Microsoft decided to change the primary application programming interface for the still unreleased NT OS/2 (as it was then known) from an extended OS/2 API to an extended Windows API. This decision caused tension between Microsoft and IBM and the collaboration ultimately fell apart. IBM continued OS/2 development alone while Microsoft continued work on the newly renamed Windows NT. Though neither operating system would immediately be as popular as Microsoft's MS-DOS or Windows products, Windows NT would eventually be far more successful than OS/2.

Microsoft hired a group of developers from Digital Equipment Corporation led by Dave Cutler to build Windows NT, and many elements of the design reflect earlier DEC experience with Cutler's VMS [19] and RSX-11. The operating system was designed to run on multiple instruction set architectures and multiple hardware platforms within each architecture. The platform dependencies are largely hidden from the rest of the system by a kernel mode module called the HAL (Hardware Abstraction Layer).

Windows NT's kernel mode code further distinguishes between the "kernel", whose primary purpose is to implement processor and architecture dependent functions, and the "executive". This was designed as a modified microkernel, as the Windows NT kernel was influenced by the Mach microkernel developed at Carnegie Mellon University[20] , but does not meet all of the criteria of a pure microkernel. Both the kernel and the executive are linked together into the single loaded module ntoskrnl.exe; from outside this module there is little distinction between the kernel and the executive. Routines from each are directly accessible, as for example from kernel-mode device drivers.

API sets in the Windows NT family are implemented as subsystems atop the publicly undocumented "native" API; this allowed the late adoption of the Windows API (into the Win32 subsystem). Windows NT was one of the earliest operating systems to use Unicode internally.

Driver models

Windows NT introduced its own driver model, the Windows NT driver model, and is incompatible with older driver frameworks. With Windows 2000, the Windows NT driver model was enhanced to become the Windows Driver Model, which was first introduced with Windows 98, but was based on the NT driver model.[21] Windows Vista added native support for the Windows Driver Foundation, which is also available for Windows XP, Windows Server 2003 and to an extent, Windows 2000.

Releases

Windows NT releases

Version	Marketing name	Editions	Release date	RTM build
NT 3.1	Windows NT 3.1	Workstation (named just *Windows NT*), Advanced Server	27 July 1993	528
NT 3.5	Windows NT 3.5	Workstation, Server	21 September 1994	807
NT 3.51	Windows NT 3.51	Workstation, Server	30 May 1995	1057
NT 4.0	Windows NT 4.0	Workstation, Server, Server Enterprise Edition, Terminal Server, Embedded	29 July 1996	1381
NT 5.0	Windows 2000	Professional, Server, Advanced Server, Datacenter Server, Advanced/Datacenter Server Limited Edition	17 February 2000	2195
NT 5.1	Windows XP	Home, Professional, 64-bit Edition, Media Center (original, 2003, 2004 & 2005), Tablet PC (original and 2005), Starter, Embedded, Home N, Professional N	25 October 2001	2600
NT 5.1	Windows Fundamentals for Legacy PCs	N/A	8 July 2006	2600
NT 5.2	Windows XP	64-bit Edition Version 2003[22]	28 March 2003	3790
NT 5.2	Windows Server 2003	Standard, Enterprise, Datacenter, Web, Storage, Small Business Server, Compute Cluster	24 April 2003	3790
NT 5.2	Windows XP	Professional x64 Edition	25 April 2005	3790

NT 5.2	Windows Server 2003 R2	Standard, Enterprise, Datacenter, Web, Storage, Small Business Server, Compute Cluster	6 December 2005	3790
NT 5.2	Windows Home Server	N/A	16 July 2007	3790
NT 6.0	Windows Vista	Starter, Home Basic, Home Premium, Business, Enterprise, Ultimate, Home Basic N, Business N	Business: 30 November 2006 Consumer: 30 January 2007	6000 6001(SP1) 6002(SP2)
NT 6.0	Windows Server 2008	Foundation, Standard, Enterprise, Datacenter, Web Server, HPC Server, Itanium-Based Systems[23]	27 February 2008	6001 6002(SP2)
NT 6.1[24]	Windows 7	Starter, Home Basic, Home Premium, Professional, Enterprise, Ultimate[25]	22 October 2009[26]	7600 7601(SP1)
NT 6.1[24]	Windows Server 2008 R2	Foundation, Standard, Enterprise, Datacenter, Web Server, HPC Server, Itanium-Based Systems	22 October 2009[27]	7600 7601(SP1)
NT 6.2[28]	Windows 8	Windows 8 (x86), Windows 8 Pro (x86), Windows 8 Enterprise (x86), Windows RT (ARM)[29]	TBA	TBA
TBA	Windows Server 2012	TBA	TBA	TBA

Windows NT 3.1 to 3.51 incorporated the Program Manager and File Manager from the Windows 3.x series. Windows NT 4.0 onwards replaced those programs with Windows Explorer (including a taskbar and Start menu), which originally appeared in Windows 95.

The first release was given version number 3.1 to match the contemporary 16-bit Windows; magazines of that era claimed the number was also used to make that version seem more reliable than a '.0' release. There were also some issues related to Novell IPX protocol licensing, which was apparently limited to 3.1 versions of Windows software.

The NT version number is not now generally used for marketing purposes, but is still used internally, and said to reflect the degree of changes to the core of the operating system;[30] however, for application compatibility reasons, Microsoft have kept the major version number as 6 in releases following Vista.[31] The build number is an internal identifier used by Microsoft's developers and beta testers.

Supported platforms

NT was written in C and C++,[32] and is reasonably portable, although (as of 2009) only three architectures are currently supported. That said, it proved far more difficult to port applications such as Microsoft Office which were sensitive to issues such as data structure alignment on RISC processors. Unlike Windows CE which routinely runs on a variety of processors, the lack of success of RISC-based systems in the desktop market has resulted in nearly all NT deployments being on x86 architecture processors.

32-bit platforms

In order to prevent Intel x86-specific code from slipping into the operating system by developers used to developing on x86 chips, Windows NT 3.1 was initially developed using non-x86 development systems and then ported to the x86 architecture. This work was initially based on the Intel i860-based *Dazzle* system and, later, the MIPS R4000-based *Jazz* platform. Both systems were designed internally at Microsoft.[33]

Windows NT 3.1 was released for Intel x86 PC compatible, DEC Alpha, and ARC-compliant MIPS platforms. Windows NT 3.51 added support for the PowerPC processor in 1995, specifically PReP-compliant systems such as the IBM Power Series desktops/laptops and Motorola PowerStack series; but despite meetings between Michael Spindler and Bill Gates, not on the Power Macintosh as the PReP compliant Power Macintosh project failed to ship.

Intergraph Corporation ported Windows NT to its Clipper architecture and later announced intention to port Windows NT 3.51 to Sun Microsystems' SPARC architecture,[34] but neither version was sold to the public as a retail product.

Only two of the Windows NT 4.0 variants (IA-32 and Alpha) have a full set of service packs available. All of the other ports done by third parties (Motorola, Intergraph, etc.) have few, if any, publicly available updates.

Windows NT 4.0 was the last major release to support Alpha, MIPS, or PowerPC, though development of Windows 2000 for Alpha continued until August 1999, when Compaq stopped support for Windows NT on that architecture; and then three days later Microsoft also canceled their AlphaNT program, even though the Alpha NT 5 (Windows 2000) release had reached RC2 (build 2128).

Microsoft announced on 5 January 2011 that the next major version of the Windows NT family will include support for the ARM architecture. Microsoft demonstrated a preliminary version of Windows (version 6.2.7867) running on an ARM-based computer at the 2011 Consumer Electronics Show.[35]

According to Microsoft, it is a common misconception that the Xbox and Xbox 360 use a modified Windows 2000 kernel.[36] They claim that the Xbox operating system was built from scratch but implements a subset of Windows APIs. The idea that it does, indeed, run a modified copy of the Windows kernel still persists in the community.

64-bit platforms

Released versions of NT for Alpha were 32-bit only. The 64-bit port of Windows was originally intended to run on Itanium as well as on Alpha. Alpha hardware was accordingly used internally at Microsoft during early development of 64-bit Windows.[37] [38] This continued for some time after Microsoft publicly announced that it was cancelling plans to ship 64-bit Windows for Alpha, because Itanium hardware was not yet available for development.[39]

As of June 2010, Microsoft has released seven editions for Itanium and seventeen editions for the x64 processor architecture:

Itanium editions	x64 editions
• Windows 2000 Advanced Server Limited Edition[40]	• Windows XP Professional x64 Edition[41]
• Windows 2000 Datacenter Server[40]	• Windows Server 2003 Standard x64 Edition[41]
• Windows XP 64-Bit Edition[42]	• Windows Server 2003 Enterprise x64 Edition[41]
• Windows Server 2003 Enterprise[40]	• Windows Server 2003 Datacenter x64 Edition[41]
• Windows Server 2003 Datacenter[40]	• Windows Vista Home Basic x64 Edition
• Windows Server 2008 for Itanium-Based Systems[43]	• Windows Vista Home Premium x64 Edition
• Windows Server 2008 R2 for Itanium-Based Systems[44]	• Windows Vista Enterprise x64 Edition
	• Windows Vista Ultimate x64 Edition
	• Windows Server 2008 Web Server x64 Edition
	• Windows Server 2008 Standard x64 Edition
	• Windows Server 2008 Enterprise x64 Edition
	• Windows Server 2008 Datacenter x64 Edition
	• Windows 7 Home Basic x64 Edition
	• Windows 7 Home Premium x64 Edition
	• Windows 7 Professional x64 Edition
	• Windows 7 Enterprise x64 Edition
	• Windows 7 Ultimate x64 Edition

Hardware requirements

The minimum hardware specification required to run each release of the professional workstation version of Windows NT has been fairly slow-moving until the 6.0 Vista release, which requires a minimum of 15 GB of free disk space, a 10-fold increase in free disk space alone over the previous version.

Windows NT desktop (x86) minimum hardware requirements

NT version	CPU	RAM	Free disk space
NT 3.1 NT 3.1 Advanced Server	386, 25 MHz	12 MB 16 MB	90 MB
NT 3.5 Workstation NT 3.5 Server	386, 25 MHz	12 MB 16 MB	90 MB[45]
NT 3.51 Workstation NT 3.51 Server	386, 25 MHz	12 MB 16 MB	90 MB[45]
NT 4.0 Workstation NT 4.0 Server	486, 25 MHz	12 MB 16 MB	124 MB[46]
2000 Professional 2000 Server	Pentium, 133 MHz	32 MB 128 MB	650 MB[47]
XP	Pentium, 233 MHz	64 MB*	1.5 GB[48]
Server 2003	Pentium, 133 MHz	128 MB	1.5 GB[47]
Vista	Pentium III, 800 MHz	512 MB	15 GB[49]
7	Pentium III, 1 GHz	1GB	16 GB[50]

*Windows XP can be run with 64 MB of RAM. Some features require 128 MB RAM.[51]

See also

- Architecture of Windows NT
- Criticism of Microsoft Windows
- F6 disk
- Microsoft Windows
- NT Domain
- NTFS
- ReactOS (an open source project with the goal of providing binary- and device driver-level compatibility with Windows NT)
- Windows NT Startup Process
- Windows Preinstallation Environment
- Windows Server System
- Windows Embedded

References

[1] Lextrait, Vincent (January 2010). "The Programming Languages Beacon, v10.0" (http://www.lextrait.com/Vincent/implementations.html). . Retrieved 4 January 2010.

[2] http://en.wikipedia.org/wiki/Template%3Alatest_stable_software_release%2Fwindows_nt

[3] http://en.wikipedia.org/wiki/Template%3Alatest_preview_software_release%2Fwindows_nt

[4] http://www.microsoft.com/windows/

[5] Zachary, G. Pascal (1994). *Show Stopper!: The Breakneck Race to Create Windows NT and the Next Generation at Microsoft*. Free Press. ISBN 978-0-02-935671-5.

[6] "Microsoft Windows NT OS/2 Design Workbook" (http://americanhistory.si.edu/collections/object.cfm?key=35&objkey=124). . Retrieved 2008-11-15.

[7] "Paul Thurrott's History of Windows Server 2003: The Road To Gold" (http://www.winsupersite.com/article/windows-server/windows-server-2003-the-road-to-gold-part-one-the-early-years-127432). .

[8] Gates, Bill (1998-06-05). "Q&A: Protecting children from information on the Internet" (http://www.microsoft.com/billgates/columns/1998q&a/QA5-6.asp). . Retrieved 2005-06-26.

[9] "Paul Thurrott's SuperSite for Windows" (http://www.winsupersite.com/showcase/winvista_ff_x64.asp). Winsupersite.com. . Retrieved 2010-11-24.

[10] "Chapter 28 - OS/2 Compatibility" (http://www.microsoft.com/resources/documentation/windowsnt/4/workstation/reskit/en-us/os2comp.mspx?mfr=true). Microsoft. . Retrieved 2010-11-24.

[11] "POSIX and OS/2 are not supported in Windows XP or in Windows Server 2003" (http://support.microsoft.com/kb/308259). Support.microsoft.com. 2007-11-05. . Retrieved 2010-11-24.

[12] "x64 editions deployment" (http://download.microsoft.com/download/8/1/e/81eabaf4-1907-4967-87a9-be242b1402e9/x64_Editions_Deployment.doc). . Retrieved 2010-11-24.

[13] Barr, Adam Microsoft, TCP/IP, Open Source, and Licensing (http://www.kuro5hin.org/story/2001/6/19/05641/7357), Kuro5hin, June 19, 2001. Retrieved October 3, 2010.

[14] "File Systems" (http://technet.microsoft.com/en-us/library/cc766145(WS.10).aspx). Technet.microsoft.com. . Retrieved 2010-11-24.

[15] "UEFI Support and Requirements for Windows Operating Systems" (http://www.microsoft.com/whdc/system/platform/firmware/uefireg.mspx). Microsoft.com. 2009-05-13. . Retrieved 2010-11-24.

[16] Dave Cutler's preface to Mark Russinovich, David A. Solomon. *Microsoft Windows Internals, (Fourth Edition)*, Microsoft Press. ISBN 0-7356-1917-4

[17] Andrew Pollack (1991-07-27). "Microsoft Widens Its Split With I.B.M. Over Software - New York Times" (http://query.nytimes.com/gst/fullpage.html?res=9D0CE0D81339F934A15754C0A967958260). *New York Times*. . Retrieved 2008-09-02.

[18] Paul Thurrott (2003-01-24). "Windows Server 2003: The Road To Gold" (http://www.winsupersite.com/reviews/winserver2k3_gold1.asp). . Retrieved 2010-01-05.

[19] Mark Russinovich (01 December 1998). "Windows NT and VMS: The Rest of the Story" (http://www.windowsitpro.com/article/windows-2000/windows-nt-and-vms-the-rest-of-the-story). . Retrieved 5 May, 2012.

[20] "Supporting Windows NT and 2000 Workstation and Server" (http://technet.microsoft.com/en-us/library/cc768132.aspx). Prentice Hall. 1999-12-01. ISBN 978-0-13-083068-5. . Retrieved 2011-08-29.

[21] "NT Drivers - FAQ - WDM" (http://www.cmkrnl.com/faq02.html). .

[22] "Microsoft Releases Windows XP 64-Bit Edition Version 2003 to Manufacturing" (http://www.microsoft.com/presspass/press/2003/mar03/03-28WinXP64BitPR.mspx). March 2003. . Retrieved 2008-01-14.

[23] "Windows Server 2008: Overview of Editions" (http://www.microsoft.com/windowsserver2008/en/us/editions-overview.aspx). *www.microsoft.com*. . Retrieved 2009-05-18.

[24] "Operating System Versioning" (http://msdn.microsoft.com/en-gb/library/dd371754(VS.85).aspx). *Microsoft Developer Network*. Microsoft. 2009-05-20. . Retrieved 2009-07-06.

[25] LeBlanc, Brandon (2009-02-04). "A closer look at the Windows 7 SKUs" (http://windowsteamblog.com/blogs/windows7/archive/2009/02/04/a-closer-look-at-the-windows-7-skus.aspx). *Blogging Windows*. Microsoft. . Retrieved 2009-02-05.

[26] Rothman, Wilson (2009-06-02). "Windows 7 To Be Released October 22" (http://gizmodo.com/5275938/windows-7-to-be-released-october-22). *Gizmodo*. . Retrieved 2009-06-06.

[27] "Windows Server 2008: Product Roadmap" (http://www.microsoft.com/windowsserver2008/en/us/roadmap.aspx). *www.microsoft.com*. . Retrieved 2009-05-18.

[28] http://msdn.microsoft.com/en-us/windows/apps/br229516/

[29] LeBlanc, Brandon (2012-04-16). "Announcing the Windows 8 Editions" (http://windowsteamblog.com/windows/b/bloggingwindows/archive/2012/04/16/announcing-the-windows-8-editions.aspx). *Blogging Windows*. Microsoft. . Retrieved 2012-04-17.

[30] Russinovich, Mark; Solomon, David (2001-12), *Windows XP: Kernel Improvements Create a More Robust, Powerful, and Scalable OS* (http://web.archive.org/web/20030424123732/http://msdn.microsoft.com/msdnmag/issues/01/12/XPKernel/), archived from the original (http://msdn.microsoft.com/msdnmag/issues/01/12/XPKernel/) on 2003-04-23, , retrieved 2006-12-19

[31] "Why 7?" (http://windowsteamblog.com/windows/archive/b/windowsvista/archive/2008/10/14/why-7.aspx). *Windows Team Blog*. 2008-10-14. . Retrieved 2012-03-30.

[32] "Windows NT System Overview" (http://www.microsoft.com/technet/archive/winntas/training/ntarchitectoview/ntarc_2.mspx). Microsoft.com. . Retrieved 2010-11-24.
[33] Lucovsky, Mark (2000-08-09). "Windows: A Software Engineering Odyssey" (http://www.usenix.org/events/usenix-win2000/invitedtalks/lucovsky_html/). . Retrieved 2006-11-02.
[34] "Intergraph Announces Port of Windows NT to SPARC Architecture" (http://ftp.lanet.lv/ftp/sun-info/sunflash/1993/Jul/55.11-Sun-Intergraph:-SPARC-and-Windows-NT). The Florida SunFlash. 1993-07-07. .
[35] Microsoft demonstrates early build of Windows 8 (http://www.winrumors.com/microsoft-demonstrates-early-build-of-windows-8/)
[36] Shaheen Gandhi. "Xbox Team: The Xbox Operating System" (http://blogs.msdn.com/xboxteam/archive/2006/02/17/534421.aspx). . Retrieved 2008-05-29.
[37] Paul Thurott (December 1999). "The Road to Gold: The development of Windows 2000 Reviewed" (http://www.winsupersite.com/reviews/win2k_gold.asp). . Retrieved 2008-01-05.
[38] Raymond Chen (August 2008). "Windows Confidential" (http://technet.microsoft.com/en-us/magazine/2008.08.windowsconfidential.aspx). .
[39] Paul Thurott (June 2000). "Windows 2000 Reportedly Returning to Alpha Platform" (http://www.windowsitpro.com/Article/ArticleID/19345/19345.html). . Retrieved 2008-01-05.
[40] Fontana, John (30 August 2001). "Microsoft Ships 64-Bit Windows for Itanium" (http://www.pcworld.com/article/60024/microsoft_ships_64bit_windows_for_itanium.html). *PC World*. PCWorld Communications, Inc. . Retrieved 14 October 2011.
[41] "A description of the x64-based versions of Windows Server 2003 and of Windows XP Professional x64 Edition" (http://support.microsoft.com/kb/888733). *Microsoft Support Center*. Microsoft Corporation. . Retrieved 14 October 2011.
[42] "Microsoft Windows XP 64-Bit Edition" (http://technet.microsoft.com/en-us/library/bb457053.aspx). *Microsoft TechNet*. Microsoft Corporation. 15 August 2001. . Retrieved 14 October 2011.
[43] "Windows Server 2008 for Itanium-Based Systems Feature Support" (http://technet.microsoft.com/en-us/library/cc772344(WS.10).aspx). *Microsoft TechNet*. Microsoft Corporation. . Retrieved 14 October 2011.
[44] "Windows Server 2008 R2 for Itanium-Based Systems" (http://www.microsoft.com/en-us/server-cloud/windows-server/2008-r2-itanium.aspx). *Windows Server Editions*. Microsoft Corporation. . Retrieved 14 October 2011.
[45] "Windows NT 3.5x Setup Troubleshooting Guide (MSKB 139733)" (http://support.microsoft.com/kb/139733). Support.microsoft.com. 2006-11-01. . Retrieved 2010-11-24.
[46] "INFO:Windows NT 4.0 Setup Troubleshooting Guide" (http://support.microsoft.com/kb/126690). Support.microsoft.com. 2006-10-31. . Retrieved 2010-11-24.
[47] "System requirements for Microsoft Windows 2000 operating systems" (http://support.microsoft.com/kb/304297). Support.microsoft.com. 2007-11-13. . Retrieved 2010-11-24.
[48] "System requirements for Microsoft Windows XP operating systems" (http://support.microsoft.com/kb/314865). Support.microsoft.com. 2007-09-14. . Retrieved 2010-11-24.
[49] "System requirements for Microsoft Windows Vista" (http://support.microsoft.com/kb/919183). Support.microsoft.com. 2007-11-13. . Retrieved 2010-11-24.
[50] "Windows 7 system requirements" (http://windows.microsoft.com/en-us/windows7/products/system-requirements). *Microsoft*. . Retrieved 2009-08-30.
[51] "Windows XP Professional System Requirements" (http://www.microsoft.com/windowsxp/sysreqs/pro.mspx). . Retrieved 7 March 2010.

External links

- Official Page (http://www.microsoft.com/windows)
- *Windows NT and VMS: The Rest of the Story*, discussion of ancestry of NT by Mark Russinovich (http://web.archive.org/web/20020503172231/http://www.win2000mag.com/Articles/Print.cfm?ArticleID=4494)
- *A Brief History of the Windows NT Operating System* a Microsoft PressPass Fact Sheet (http://web.archive.org/web/20040610122846/http://www.microsoft.com/presspass/features/1998/winntfs.asp)

Operating_system

An **operating system** (**OS**) is a set of software that manages computer hardware resources and provides common services for computer programs. The operating system is a vital component of the system software in a computer system. Application programs require an operating system to function.

Time-sharing operating systems schedule tasks for efficient use of the system and may also include accounting for cost allocation of processor time, mass storage, printing, and other resources.

For hardware functions such as input and output and memory allocation, the operating system acts as an intermediary between programs and the computer hardware,[1] [2] although the application code is usually executed directly by the hardware and will frequently make a system call to an OS function or be interrupted by it. Operating systems can be found on almost any device that contains a computer—from cellular phones and video game consoles to supercomputers and web servers.

Examples of popular modern operating systems include Android, BSD, iOS, GNU/Linux, Mac OS X, Microsoft Windows,[3] Windows Phone, and IBM z/OS. All these, except Windows and z/OS, share roots in UNIX.

Types

Real-time

A real-time operating system is a multitasking operating system that aims at executing real-time applications. Real-time operating systems often use specialized scheduling algorithms so that they can achieve a deterministic nature of behavior. The main objective of real-time operating systems is their quick and predictable response to events. They have an event-driven or time-sharing design and often aspects of both. An event-driven system switches between tasks based on their priorities or external events while time-sharing operating systems switch tasks based on clock interrupts.

Multi-user

A multi-user operating system allows multiple users to access a computer system concurrently. Time-sharing system can be classified as multi-user systems as they enable a multiple user access to a computer through the sharing of time. Single-user operating systems, as opposed to a multi-user operating system, are usable by a single user at a time. Being able to use multiple accounts on a Windows operating system does not make it a multi-user system. Rather, only the network administrator is the real user. But for a UNIX-like operating system, it is possible for two users to login at a time and this capability of the OS makes it a multi-user operating system.

Multi-tasking vs. Single-tasking

When only a single program is allowed to run at a time, the system is grouped under a single-tasking system. However, when the operating system allows the execution of multiple tasks at one time, it is classified as a multi-tasking operating system. Multi-tasking can be of two types: pre-emptive or co-operative. In pre-emptive multitasking, the operating system slices the CPU time and dedicates one slot to each of the programs. Unix-like operating systems such as Solaris and Linux support pre-emptive multitasking, as does AmigaOS. Cooperative multitasking is achieved by relying on each process to give time to the other processes in a defined manner. 16-bit versions of Microsoft Windows used cooperative multi-tasking. 32-bit versions, both Windows NT and Win9x, used pre-emptive multi-tasking. Mac OS prior to OS X used to support cooperative multitasking.

Distributed

Further information: Distributed system

A distributed operating system manages a group of independent computers and makes them appear to be a single computer. The development of networked computers that could be linked and communicate with each other gave rise to distributed computing. Distributed computations are carried out on more than one machine. When computers in a group work in cooperation, they make a distributed system.

Embedded

Embedded operating systems are designed to be used in embedded computer systems. They are designed to operate on small machines like PDAs with less autonomy. They are able to operate with a limited number of resources. They are very compact and extremely efficient by design. Windows CE and Minix 3 are some examples of embedded operating systems.

Summary

Early computers were built to perform a series of single tasks, like a calculator. Operating systems did not exist in their modern and more complex forms until the early 1960s.[4] Basic operating system features were developed in the 1950s, such as resident monitor functions that could automatically run different programs in succession to speed up processing. Hardware features were added that enabled use of runtime libraries, interrupts, and parallel processing. When personal computers by companies such as Apple Inc., Atari, IBM and Amiga became popular in the 1980s, vendors included operating systems in them that had previously become widely used on mainframe and mini computers.

History

In the 1940s, the earliest electronic digital systems had no operating systems. Electronic systems of this time were so primitive compared to those of today that instructions were often entered into the system one bit at a time on rows of mechanical switches or by jumper wires on plug boards. These were special-purpose systems that, for example, generated ballistics tables for the military or controlled the printing of payroll checks from data on punched paper cards. After programmable general purpose computers were invented, machine languages (consisting of strings of the binary digits 0 and 1 on punched paper tape) were introduced that sped up the programming process (Stern, 1981).

In the early 1950s, a computer could execute only one program at a time. Each user had sole use of the computer for a limited period of time and would arrive at a scheduled time with program and data on punched paper cards and/or punched tape. The program would be loaded into the machine, and the machine would be set to work until the program completed or crashed. Programs could generally be debugged via a front panel using toggle switches and panel lights. It is said that Alan Turing was a master of this on the early Manchester Mark 1 machine, and he was already deriving the primitive conception of an operating system from the principles of the Universal Turing machine.[4]

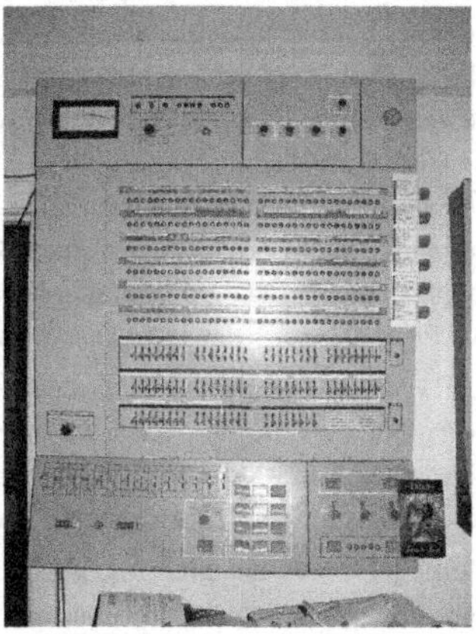

OS/360 was used on most IBM mainframe computers beginning in 1966, including the computers that helped NASA put a man on the moon.

Later machines came with libraries of programs, which would be linked to a user's program to assist in operations such as input and output and generating computer code from human-readable symbolic code. This was the genesis of the modern-day computer system. However, machines still ran a single job at a time. At Cambridge University in England the job queue was at one time a washing line from which tapes were hung with different colored clothes-pegs to indicate job-priority.

Mainframes

Through the 1950s, many major features were pioneered in the field of operating systems, including batch processing, input/output interrupt, buffering, multitasking, spooling, runtime libraries, link-loading, and programs for sorting records in files. These features were included or not included in application software at the option of application programmers, rather than in a separate operating system used by all applications. In 1959 the SHARE Operating System was released as an integrated utility for the IBM 704, and later in the 709 and 7090 mainframes, although it was quickly supplanted by IBSYS/IBJOB on the 709, 7090 and 7094.

During the 1960s, IBM's OS/360 introduced the concept of a single OS spanning an entire product line, which was crucial for the success of the System/360 machines. IBM's current mainframe operating systems are distant descendants of this original system and applications written for OS/360 can still be run on modern machines.

OS/360 also pioneered the concept that the operating system keeps track of all of the system resources that are used, including program and data space allocation in main memory and file space in secondary storage, and file locking during update. When the process is terminated for any reason, all of these resources are re-claimed by the operating system.

The alternative CP-67 system for the S/360-67 started a whole line of IBM operating systems focused on the concept of virtual machines. Other operating systems used on IBM S/360 series mainframes included systems developed by IBM: COS/360 (Compatibility Operating System), DOS/360 (Disk Operating System), TSS/360 (Time Sharing System), TOS/360 (Tape Operating System), BOS/360 (Basic Operating System), and ACP (Airline Control Program), as well as a few non-IBM systems: MTS (Michigan Terminal System), MUSIC (Multi-User System for Interactive Computing), and ORVYL (Stanford Timesharing System).

Control Data Corporation developed the SCOPE operating system in the 1960s, for batch processing. In cooperation with the University of Minnesota, the Kronos and later the NOS operating systems were developed during the 1970s, which supported simultaneous batch and timesharing use. Like many commercial timesharing systems, its interface was an extension of the Dartmouth BASIC operating systems, one of the pioneering efforts in timesharing and programming languages. In the late 1970s, Control Data and the University of Illinois developed the PLATO operating system, which used plasma panel displays and long-distance time sharing networks. Plato was remarkably innovative for its time, featuring real-time chat, and multi-user graphical games. Burroughs Corporation introduced the B5000 in 1961 with the MCP, (Master Control Program) operating system. The B5000 was a stack machine designed to exclusively support high-level languages with no machine language or assembler, and indeed the MCP was the first OS to be written exclusively in a high-level language – ESPOL, a dialect of ALGOL. MCP also introduced many other ground-breaking innovations, such as being the first commercial implementation of virtual memory. During development of the AS400, IBM made an approach to Burroughs to licence MCP to run on the AS400 hardware. This proposal was declined by Burroughs management to protect its existing hardware production. MCP is still in use today in the Unisys ClearPath/MCP line of computers.

UNIVAC, the first commercial computer manufacturer, produced a series of EXEC operating systems. Like all early main-frame systems, this was a batch-oriented system that managed magnetic drums, disks, card readers and line printers. In the 1970s, UNIVAC produced the Real-Time Basic (RTB) system to support large-scale time sharing, also patterned after the Dartmouth BC system.

General Electric and MIT developed General Electric Comprehensive Operating Supervisor (GECOS), which introduced the concept of ringed security privilege levels. After acquisition by Honeywell it was renamed to General Comprehensive Operating System (GCOS).

Digital Equipment Corporation developed many operating systems for its various computer lines, including TOPS-10 and TOPS-20 time sharing systems for the 36-bit PDP-10 class systems. Prior to the widespread use of UNIX, TOPS-10 was a particularly popular system in universities, and in the early ARPANET community.

In the late 1960s through the late 1970s, several hardware capabilities evolved that allowed similar or ported software to run on more than one system. Early systems had utilized microprogramming to implement features on their systems in order to permit different underlying computer architectures to appear to be the same as others in a series. In fact most 360s after the 360/40 (except the 360/165 and 360/168) were microprogrammed implementations. But soon other means of achieving application compatibility were proven to be more significant.

The enormous investment in software for these systems made since 1960s caused most of the original computer manufacturers to continue to develop compatible operating systems along with the hardware. The notable supported mainframe operating systems include:

- Burroughs MCP – B5000, 1961 to Unisys Clearpath/MCP, present.
- IBM OS/360 – IBM System/360, 1966 to IBM z/OS, present.
- IBM CP-67 – IBM System/360, 1967 to IBM z/VM, present.
- UNIVAC EXEC 8 – UNIVAC 1108, 1967, to OS 2200 Unisys Clearpath Dorado, present.

Microcomputers

The first microcomputers did not have the capacity or need for the elaborate operating systems that had been developed for mainframes and minis; minimalistic operating systems were developed, often loaded from ROM and known as *monitors*. One notable early disk operating system was CP/M, which was supported on many early microcomputers and was closely imitated by Microsoft's MS-DOS, which became wildly popular as the operating system chosen for the IBM PC (IBM's version of it was called IBM DOS or PC DOS). In the '80s, Apple Computer Inc. (now Apple Inc.) abandoned its popular Apple II series of microcomputers to introduce the Apple Macintosh computer with an innovative Graphical User Interface (GUI) to the Mac OS.

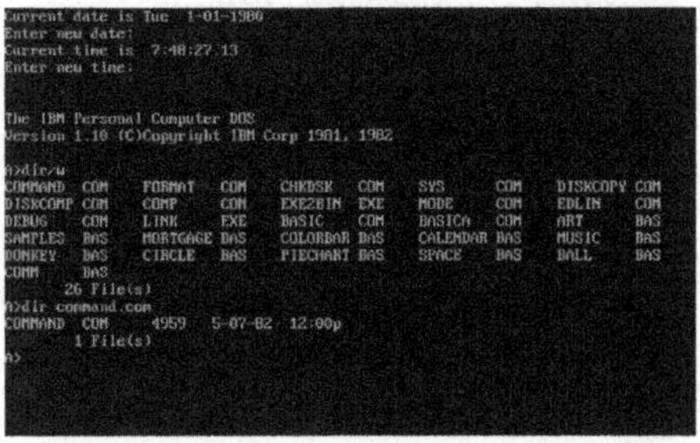

PC-DOS was an early personal computer OS that featured a command line interface.

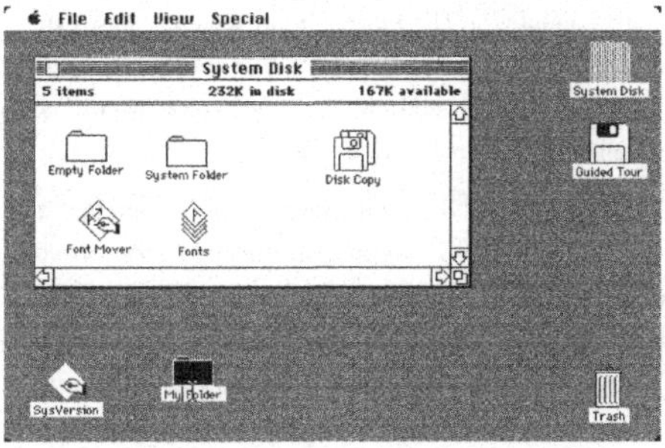

Mac OS by Apple Computer became the first widespread OS to feature a graphical user interface. Many of its features such as windows and icons would later become commonplace in GUIs.

The introduction of the Intel 80386 CPU chip with 32-bit architecture and paging capabilities, provided personal computers with the ability to run multitasking operating systems like those of earlier minicomputers and mainframes. Microsoft responded to this progress by hiring Dave Cutler, who had developed the VMS operating system for Digital Equipment Corporation. He would lead the development of the Windows NT operating system, which continues to serve as the basis for Microsoft's operating systems line. Steve Jobs, a co-founder of Apple Inc., started NeXT Computer Inc., which developed the Unix-like NEXTSTEP operating system. NEXTSTEP would later be acquired by Apple Inc. and used, along with code from FreeBSD as the core of Mac OS X.

The GNU Project was started by activist and programmer Richard Stallman with the goal of a complete free software replacement to the proprietary UNIX operating system. While the project was highly successful in duplicating the functionality of various parts of UNIX, development of the GNU Hurd kernel proved to be unproductive. In 1991, Finnish computer science student Linus Torvalds, with cooperation from volunteers collaborating over the Internet, released the first version of the Linux kernel. It was soon merged with the GNU user space components and system software to form a complete operating system. Since then, the combination of the two major components has usually been referred to as simply "Linux" by the software industry, a naming convention that Stallman and the Free Software Foundation remain opposed to, preferring the name GNU/Linux. The Berkeley Software Distribution, known as BSD, is the UNIX derivative distributed by the University of California, Berkeley, starting in the 1970s. Freely distributed and ported to many minicomputers, it eventually also gained a following for use on PCs, mainly as FreeBSD, NetBSD and OpenBSD.

Examples of operating systems

UNIX and UNIX-like operating systems

Ken Thompson wrote B, mainly based on BCPL, which he used to write Unix, based on his experience in the MULTICS project. B was replaced by C, and Unix developed into a large, complex family of inter-related operating systems which have been influential in every modern operating system (see History).

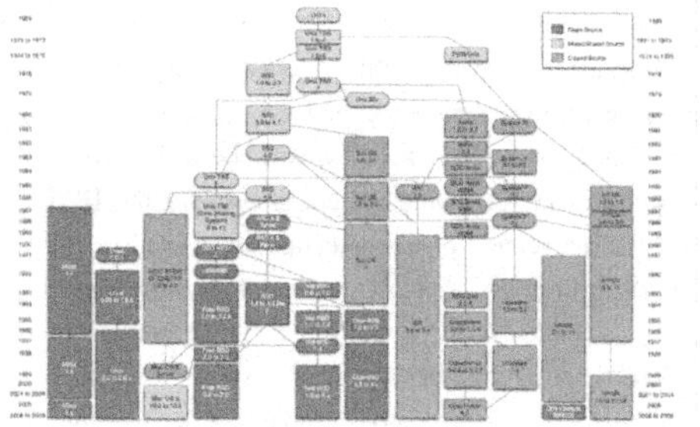

Evolution of Unix systems

The *UNIX-like* family is a diverse group of operating systems, with several major sub-categories including System V, BSD, and GNU/Linux. The name "UNIX" is a trademark of The Open Group which licenses it for use with any operating system that has been shown to conform to their definitions. "UNIX-like" is commonly used to refer to the large set of operating systems which resemble the original UNIX.

Unix-like systems run on a wide variety of computer architectures. They are used heavily for servers in business, as well as workstations in academic and engineering environments. Free UNIX variants, such as GNU/Linux and BSD, are popular in these areas.

Four operating systems are certified by the The Open Group (holder of the Unix trademark) as Unix. HP's HP-UX and IBM's AIX are both descendants of the original System V Unix and are designed to run only on their respective vendor's hardware. In contrast, Sun Microsystems's Solaris Operating System can run on multiple types of hardware, including x86 and Sparc servers, and PCs. Apple's Mac OS X, a replacement for Apple's earlier (non-Unix) Mac OS, is a hybrid kernel-based BSD variant derived from NeXTSTEP, Mach, and FreeBSD.

Unix interoperability was sought by establishing the POSIX standard. The POSIX standard can be applied to any operating system, although it was originally created for various Unix variants.

BSD and its descendants

A subgroup of the Unix family is the Berkeley Software Distribution family, which includes FreeBSD, NetBSD, and OpenBSD, PC-BSD. These operating systems are most commonly found on webservers, although they can also function as a personal computer OS. The Internet owes much of its existence to BSD, as many of the protocols now commonly used by computers to connect, send and receive data over a network were widely implemented and refined in BSD. The world wide web was also first demonstrated on a number of computers running an OS based on BSD called NextStep.

The first server for the World Wide Web ran on NeXTSTEP, based on BSD.

BSD has its roots in Unix. In 1974, University of California, Berkeley installed its first Unix system.

Over time, students and staff in the computer science department there began adding new programs to make things easier, such as text editors. When Berkely received new VAX computers in 1978 with Unix installed, the school's undergraduates modified Unix even more in order to take advantage of the computer's hardware possibilities. The Defense Advanced Research Projects Agency of the US Department of Defense took interest, and decided to fund the project. Many schools, corporations, and government organizations took notice and started to use Berkeley's version of Unix instead of the official one distributed by AT&T.

Steve Jobs, upon leaving Apple Inc. in 1985, formed NeXT Inc., a company that manufactured high-end computers running on a variation of BSD called NeXTSTEP. One of these computers was used by Tim Berners-Lee as the first webserver to create the World Wide Web.

Developers like Keith Bostic encouraged the project to replace any non-free code that originated with Bell Labs. Once this was done, however, AT&T sued. Eventually, after two years of legal disputes, the BSD project came out ahead and spawned a number of free derivatives, such as FreeBSD and NetBSD.

Mac OS X

Mac OS X is a line of open core graphical operating systems developed, marketed, and sold by Apple Inc., the latest of which is pre-loaded on all currently shipping Macintosh computers. Mac OS X is the successor to the original Mac OS, which had been Apple's primary operating system since 1984. Unlike its predecessor, Mac OS X is a UNIX operating system built on technology that had been developed at NeXT through the second half of the 1980s and up until Apple purchased the company in early 1997.

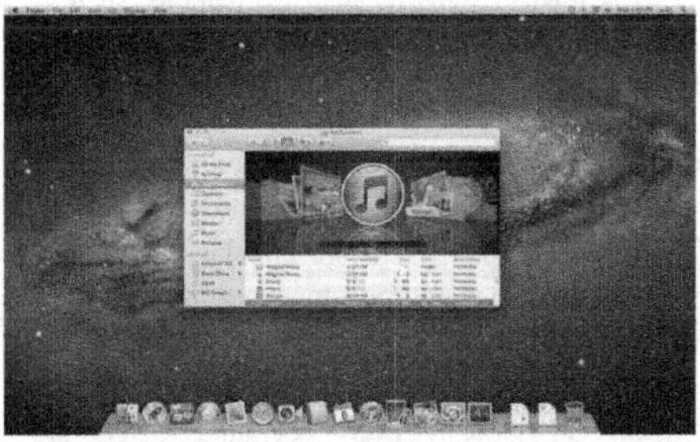

The standard user interface of Mac OS X

The operating system was first released in 1999 as Mac OS X Server 1.0, with a desktop-oriented version (Mac OS X v10.0 "Cheetah") following in March 2001. Since then, six more distinct "client" and "server" editions of Mac OS X have been released, the most recent being OS X 10.8 "Mountain Lion", which was first made available on February 16, 2012 for developers, and to be released to the public late summer 2012. Releases of Mac OS X are named after big cats.

The server edition, Mac OS X Server, is architecturally identical to its desktop counterpart but usually runs on Apple's line of Macintosh server hardware. Mac OS X Server includes work group management and administration software tools that provide simplified access to key network services, including a mail transfer agent, a Samba server, an LDAP server, a domain name server, and others. In Mac OS X v10.7 Lion, all server aspects of Mac OS X Server have been integrated into the client version.[5]

Linux and GNU

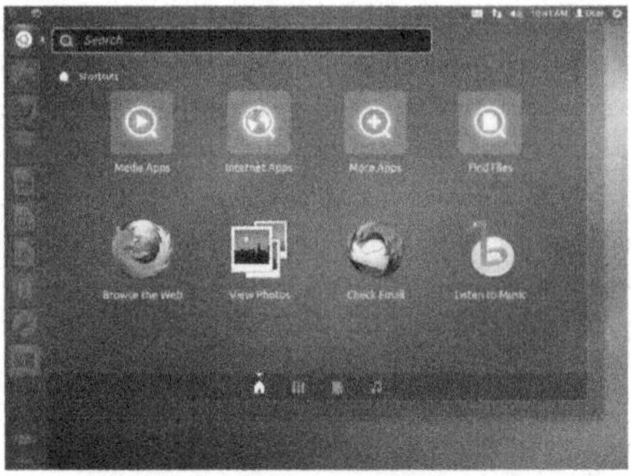

Ubuntu, desktop Linux distribution

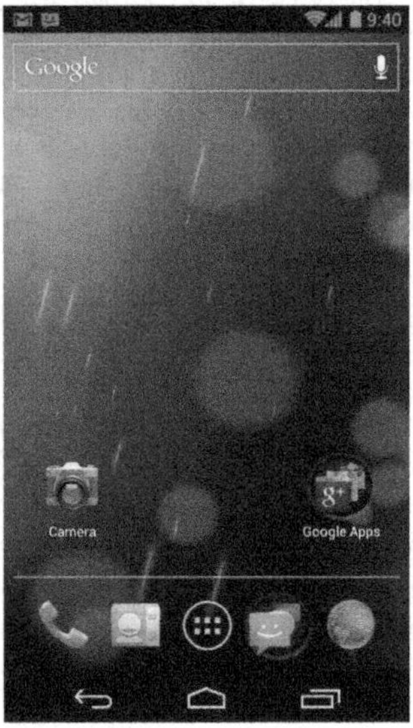

Android, a popular mobile operating system using the Linux kernel

Linux (or GNU/Linux) is a Unix-like operating system that was developed without any actual Unix code, unlike BSD and its variants. Linux can be used on a wide range of devices from supercomputers to wristwatches. The Linux kernel is released under an open source license, so anyone can read and modify its code. It has been modified to run on a large variety of electronics. Although estimates suggest that Linux is used on 1.82% of all personal computers,[6] [7] it has been widely adopted for use in servers[8] and embedded systems[9] (such as cell phones). Linux has superseded Unix in most places, and is used on the 10 most powerful supercomputers in the world.[10] The Linux kernel is used in some popular distributions, such as Red Hat, Debian, Ubuntu, Linux Mint and Google's Android.

The GNU project is a mass collaboration of programmers who seek to create a completely free and open operating system that was similar to Unix but with completely original code. It was started in 1983 by Richard Stallman, and is responsible for many of the parts of most Linux variants. Thousands of pieces of software for virtually every operating system are licensed under the GNU General Public License. Meanwhile, the Linux kernel began as a side project of Linus Torvalds, a university student from Finland. In 1991, Torvalds began work on it, and posted information about his project on a newsgroup for computer students and programmers. He received a wave of support and volunteers who ended up creating a full-fledged kernel. Programmers from GNU took notice, and members of both projects worked to integrate the finished GNU parts with the Linux kernel in order to create a full-fledged operating system.

Google Chrome OS

Chrome is an operating system based on the Linux kernel and designed by Google. Since Chrome OS targets computer users who spend most of their time on the Internet, it is mainly a web browser with no ability to run applications. It relies on Internet applications (or Web apps) used in the web browser to accomplish tasks such as word processing and media viewing, as well as online storage for storing most files.

Microsoft Windows

Bootable Windows To Go USB flash drive

Microsoft Windows is a family of proprietary operating systems designed by Microsoft Corporation and primarily targeted to Intel architecture based computers, with an estimated 88.9 percent total usage share on Web connected computers.[7] [11] [12] [13] The newest version is Windows 7 for workstations and Windows Server 2008 R2 for servers. Windows 7 recently overtook Windows XP as most used OS.[14] [15] [16]

Microsoft Windows 7 Desktop

Microsoft Windows originated in 1985 as an application running on top of MS-DOS, which was the standard operating system shipped on most Intel architecture personal computers at the time. In 1995, Windows 95 was released which only used MS-DOS as a bootstrap. For backwards compatibility, Win9x could run real-mode MS-DOS[17] [18] and 16 bits Windows 3.x[19] drivers. Windows Me, released in 2000, was the last version in the Win9x family. Later versions have all been based on the Windows NT kernel. Current versions of Windows run on IA-32 and x86-64 microprocessors, although Windows 8 will support ARM architecture. In the past, Windows NT supported non-Intel architectures.

Server editions of Windows are widely used. In recent years, Microsoft has expended significant capital in an effort to promote the use of Windows as a server operating environment. However, Windows' usage on servers is not as widespread as on personal computers, as Windows competes against Linux and BSD for server market share.[20] [21]

Other

There have been many operating systems that were significant in their day but are no longer so, such as AmigaOS; OS/2 from IBM and Microsoft; Mac OS, the non-Unix precursor to Apple's Mac OS X; BeOS; XTS-300; RISC OS; MorphOS and FreeMint. Some are still used in niche markets and continue to be developed as minority platforms for enthusiast communities and specialist applications. OpenVMS formerly from DEC, is still under active development by Hewlett-Packard. Yet other operating systems are used almost exclusively in academia, for operating systems education or to do research on operating system concepts. A typical example of a system that fulfills both roles is MINIX, while for example Singularity is used purely for research.

Other operating systems have failed to win significant market share, but have introduced innovations that have influenced mainstream operating systems, not least Bell Labs' Plan 9.

Components

The components of an operating system all exist in order to make the different parts of a computer work together. All software—from financial databases to film editors—needs to go through the operating system in order to use any of the hardware, whether it be as simple as a mouse or keyboard or complex as an Internet connection.

Kernel

With the aid of the firmware and device drivers, the kernel provides the most basic level of control over all of the computer's hardware devices. It manages memory access for programs in the RAM, it determines which programs get access to which hardware resources, it sets up or resets the CPU's operating states for optimal operation at all times, and it organizes the data for long-term non-volatile storage with file systems on such media as disks, tapes, flash memory, etc.

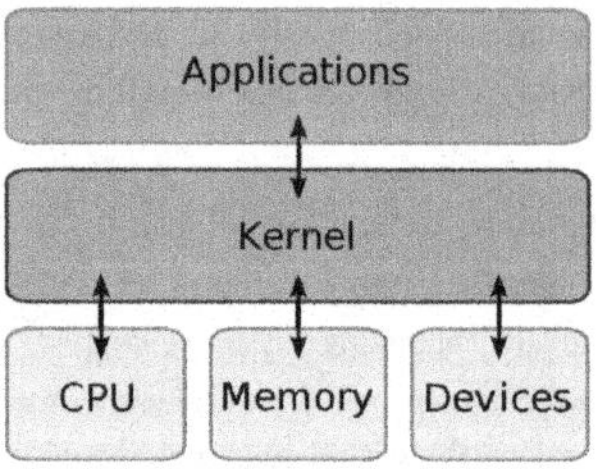

A kernel connects the application software to the hardware of a computer.

Program execution

The operating system provides an interface between an application program and the computer hardware, so that an application program can interact with the hardware only by obeying rules and procedures programmed into the operating system. The operating system is also a set of services which simplify development and execution of application programs. Executing an application program involves the creation of a process by the operating system kernel which assigns memory space and other resources, establishes a priority for the process in multi-tasking systems, loads program binary code into memory, and initiates execution of the application program which then interacts with the user and with hardware devices.

Interrupts

Interrupts are central to operating systems, as they provide an efficient way for the operating system to interact with and react to its environment. The alternative — having the operating system "watch" the various sources of input for events (polling) that require action — can be found in older systems with very small stacks (50 or 60 bytes) but are unusual in modern systems with large stacks. Interrupt-based programming is directly supported by most modern CPUs. Interrupts provide a computer with a way of automatically saving local register contexts, and running specific code in response to events. Even very basic computers support hardware interrupts, and allow the programmer to specify code which may be run when that event takes place.

When an interrupt is received, the computer's hardware automatically suspends whatever program is currently running, saves its status, and runs computer code previously associated with the interrupt; this is analogous to placing a bookmark in a book in response to a phone call. In modern operating systems, interrupts are handled by the operating system's kernel. Interrupts may come from either the computer's hardware or from the running program.

When a hardware device triggers an interrupt, the operating system's kernel decides how to deal with this event, generally by running some processing code. The amount of code being run depends on the priority of the interrupt (for example: a person usually responds to a smoke detector alarm before answering the phone). The processing of hardware interrupts is a task that is usually delegated to software called device driver, which may be either part of the operating system's kernel, part of another program, or both. Device drivers may then relay information to a running program by various means.

A program may also trigger an interrupt to the operating system. If a program wishes to access hardware for example, it may interrupt the operating system's kernel, which causes control to be passed back to the kernel. The kernel will then process the request. If a program wishes additional resources (or wishes to shed resources) such as memory, it will trigger an interrupt to get the kernel's attention.

Modes

Modern CPUs support multiple modes of operation. CPUs with this capability use at least two modes: protected mode and supervisor mode. The supervisor mode is used by the operating system's kernel for low level tasks that need unrestricted access to hardware, such as controlling how memory is written and erased, and communication with devices like graphics cards. Protected mode, in contrast, is used for almost everything else. Applications operate within protected mode, and can only use hardware by communicating with the kernel, which controls everything in supervisor mode. CPUs might have other modes similar to protected mode as well, such as the virtual modes in order to emulate older processor types, such as 16-bit processors on a 32-bit one, or 32-bit processors on a 64-bit one.

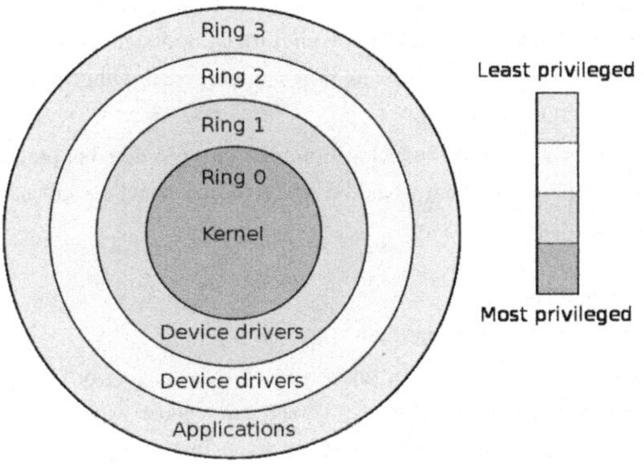

Privilege rings for the x86 available in protected mode. Operating systems determine which processes run in each mode.

When a computer first starts up, it is automatically running in supervisor mode. The first few programs to run on the computer, being the BIOS or EFI, bootloader, and the operating system have unlimited access to hardware - and this is required because, by definition, initializing a protected environment can only be done outside of one. However, when the operating system passes control to another program, it can place the CPU into protected mode.

In protected mode, programs may have access to a more limited set of the CPU's instructions. A user program may leave protected mode only by triggering an interrupt, causing control to be passed back to the kernel. In this way the operating system can maintain exclusive control over things like access to hardware and memory.

The term "protected mode resource" generally refers to one or more CPU registers, which contain information that the running program isn't allowed to alter. Attempts to alter these resources generally causes a switch to supervisor mode, where the operating system can deal with the illegal operation the program was attempting (for example, by killing the program).

Memory management

Among other things, a multiprogramming operating system kernel must be responsible for managing all system memory which is currently in use by programs. This ensures that a program does not interfere with memory already in use by another program. Since programs time share, each program must have independent access to memory.

Cooperative memory management, used by many early operating systems, assumes that all programs make voluntary use of the kernel's memory manager, and do not exceed their allocated memory. This system of memory management is almost never seen any more, since programs often contain bugs which can cause them to exceed their allocated memory. If a program fails, it may cause memory used by one or more other programs to be affected or overwritten. Malicious programs or viruses may purposefully alter another program's memory, or may affect the operation of the operating system itself. With cooperative memory management, it takes only one misbehaved program to crash the system.

Memory protection enables the kernel to limit a process' access to the computer's memory. Various methods of memory protection exist, including memory segmentation and paging. All methods require some level of hardware support (such as the 80286 MMU), which doesn't exist in all computers.

In both segmentation and paging, certain protected mode registers specify to the CPU what memory address it should allow a running program to access. Attempts to access other addresses will trigger an interrupt which will cause the CPU to re-enter supervisor mode, placing the kernel in charge. This is called a segmentation violation or Seg-V for short, and since it is both difficult to assign a meaningful result to such an operation, and because it is usually a sign of a misbehaving program, the kernel will generally resort to terminating the offending program, and will report the error.

Windows 3.1-Me had some level of memory protection, but programs could easily circumvent the need to use it. A general protection fault would be produced, indicating a segmentation violation had occurred; however, the system would often crash anyway.

Virtual memory

Further information: Page fault

The use of virtual memory addressing (such as paging or segmentation) means that the kernel can choose what memory each program may use at any given time, allowing the operating system to use the same memory locations for multiple tasks.

If a program tries to access memory that isn't in its current range of accessible memory, but nonetheless has been allocated to it, the kernel will be interrupted in the same way as it would if the program were to exceed its allocated memory. (See section on memory management.) Under UNIX this kind of interrupt is referred to as a page fault.

When the kernel detects a page fault it will generally adjust the virtual memory range of the program which triggered it, granting it access to the memory requested. This gives the kernel discretionary power over where a particular application's memory is stored, or even whether or not it has actually been allocated yet.

In modern operating systems, memory which is accessed less frequently can be temporarily stored on disk or other media to make that space available for use by other programs. This is called swapping, as an area of memory can be used by multiple programs, and what that memory area contains can be swapped or exchanged on demand.

"Virtual memory" provides the programmer or the user with the perception that there is a much larger amount of RAM in the computer than is really there.[22]

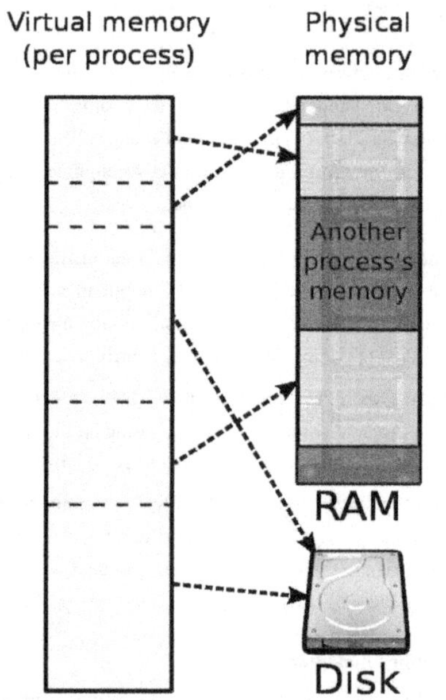

Many operating systems can "trick" programs into using memory scattered around the hard disk and RAM as if it is one continuous chunk of memory, called virtual memory.

Multitasking

Further information: Context switch, Preemptive multitasking, and Cooperative multitasking

Multitasking refers to the running of multiple independent computer programs on the same computer; giving the appearance that it is performing the tasks at the same time. Since most computers can do at most one or two things at one time, this is generally done via time-sharing, which means that each program uses a share of the computer's time to execute.

An operating system kernel contains a piece of software called a scheduler which determines how much time each program will spend executing, and in which order execution control should be passed to programs. Control is passed to a process by the kernel, which allows the program access to the CPU and memory. Later, control is returned to the kernel through some mechanism, so that another program may be allowed to use the CPU. This so-called passing of control between the kernel and applications is called a context switch.

An early model which governed the allocation of time to programs was called cooperative multitasking. In this model, when control is passed to a program by the kernel, it may execute for as long as it wants before explicitly returning control to the kernel. This means that a malicious or malfunctioning program may not only prevent any other programs from using the CPU, but it can hang the entire system if it enters an infinite loop.

Modern operating systems extend the concepts of application preemption to device drivers and kernel code, so that the operating system has preemptive control over internal run-times as well.

The philosophy governing preemptive multitasking is that of ensuring that all programs are given regular time on the CPU. This implies that all programs must be limited in how much time they are allowed to spend on the CPU without being interrupted. To accomplish this, modern operating system kernels make use of a timed interrupt. A protected mode timer is set by the kernel which triggers a return to supervisor mode after the specified time has elapsed. (See above sections on Interrupts and Dual Mode Operation.)

On many single user operating systems cooperative multitasking is perfectly adequate, as home computers generally run a small number of well tested programs. The AmigaOS is an exception, having pre-emptive multitasking from its very first version. Windows NT was the first version of Microsoft Windows which enforced preemptive multitasking, but it didn't reach the home user market until Windows XP (since Windows NT was targeted at professionals).

Disk access and file systems

Access to data stored on disks is a central feature of all operating systems. Computers store data on disks using files, which are structured in specific ways in order to allow for faster access, higher reliability, and to make better use out of the drive's available space. The specific way in which files are stored on a disk is called a file system, and enables files to have names and attributes. It also allows them to be stored in a hierarchy of directories or folders arranged in a directory tree.

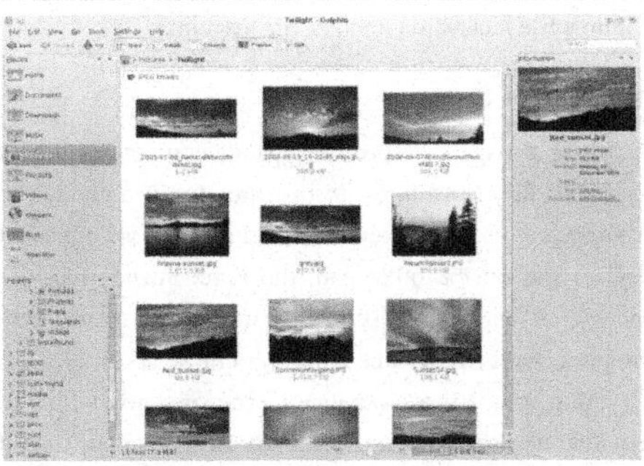

Filesystems allow users and programs to organize and sort files on a computer, often through the use of directories (or "folders")

Early operating systems generally supported a single type of disk drive and only one kind of file system. Early file systems were limited in their capacity, speed, and in the kinds of file names and directory structures they could use. These limitations often reflected limitations in the operating systems they were designed for, making it very difficult for an operating system to support more than one file system.

While many simpler operating systems support a limited range of options for accessing storage systems, operating systems like UNIX and GNU/Linux support a technology known as a virtual file system or VFS. An operating system such as UNIX supports a wide array of storage devices, regardless of their design or file systems, allowing them to be accessed through a common application programming interface (API). This makes it unnecessary for programs to have any knowledge about the device they are accessing. A VFS allows the operating system to provide programs with access to an unlimited number of devices with an infinite variety of file systems installed on them, through the use of specific device drivers and file system drivers.

A connected storage device, such as a hard drive, is accessed through a device driver. The device driver understands the specific language of the drive and is able to translate that language into a standard language used by the operating system to access all disk drives. On UNIX, this is the language of block devices.

When the kernel has an appropriate device driver in place, it can then access the contents of the disk drive in raw format, which may contain one or more file systems. A file system driver is used to translate the commands used to access each specific file system into a standard set of commands that the operating system can use to talk to all file systems. Programs can then deal with these file systems on the basis of filenames, and directories/folders, contained within a hierarchical structure. They can create, delete, open, and close files, as well as gather various information about them, including access permissions, size, free space, and creation and modification dates.

Various differences between file systems make supporting all file systems difficult. Allowed characters in file names, case sensitivity, and the presence of various kinds of file attributes makes the implementation of a single interface for every file system a daunting task. Operating systems tend to recommend using (and so support natively) file systems specifically designed for them; for example, NTFS in Windows and ext3 and ReiserFS in GNU/Linux. However, in practice, third party drives are usually available to give support for the most widely used file systems in most general-purpose operating systems (for example, NTFS is available in GNU/Linux through NTFS-3g, and ext2/3 and ReiserFS are available in Windows through FS-driver [23] and rfstool [24]).

Support for file systems is highly varied among modern operating systems, although there are several common file systems which almost all operating systems include support and drivers for. Operating systems vary on file system support and on the disk formats they may be installed on. Under Windows, each file system is usually limited in application to certain media; for example, CDs must use ISO 9660 or UDF, and as of Windows Vista, NTFS is the only file system which the operating system can be installed on. It is possible to install GNU/Linux onto many types of file systems. Unlike other operating systems, GNU/Linux and UNIX allow any file system to be used regardless of the media it is stored in, whether it is a hard drive, a disc (CD,DVD...), a USB flash drive, or even contained within a file located on another file system.

Device drivers

A device driver is a specific type of computer software developed to allow interaction with hardware devices. Typically this constitutes an interface for communicating with the device, through the specific computer bus or communications subsystem that the hardware is connected to, providing commands to and/or receiving data from the device, and on the other end, the requisite interfaces to the operating system and software applications. It is a specialized hardware-dependent computer program which is also operating system specific that enables another program, typically an operating system or applications software package or computer program running under the operating system kernel, to interact transparently with a hardware device, and usually provides the requisite interrupt handling necessary for any necessary asynchronous time-dependent hardware interfacing needs.

The key design goal of device drivers is abstraction. Every model of hardware (even within the same class of device) is different. Newer models also are released by manufacturers that provide more reliable or better performance and these newer models are often controlled differently. Computers and their operating systems cannot be expected to know how to control every device, both now and in the future. To solve this problem, operating systems essentially dictate how every type of device should be controlled. The function of the device driver is then to translate these operating system mandated function calls into device specific calls. In theory a new device, which is controlled in a new manner, should function correctly if a suitable driver is available. This new driver will ensure that the device appears to operate as usual from the operating system's point of view.

Under versions of Windows before Vista and versions of Linux before 2.6, all driver execution was co-operative, meaning that if a driver entered an infinite loop it would freeze the system. More recent revisions of these operating systems incorporate kernel preemption, where the kernel interrupts the driver to give it tasks, and then separates itself from the process until it receives a response from the device driver, or gives it more tasks to do.

Networking

Currently most operating systems support a variety of networking protocols, hardware, and applications for using them. This means that computers running dissimilar operating systems can participate in a common network for sharing resources such as computing, files, printers, and scanners using either wired or wireless connections. Networks can essentially allow a computer's operating system to access the resources of a remote computer to support the same functions as it could if those resources were connected directly to the local computer. This includes everything from simple communication, to using networked file systems or even sharing another computer's graphics or sound hardware. Some network services allow the resources of a computer to be accessed transparently, such as SSH which allows networked users direct access to a computer's command line interface.

Client/server networking allows a program on a computer, called a client, to connect via a network to another computer, called a server. Servers offer (or host) various services to other network computers and users. These services are usually provided through ports or numbered access points beyond the server's network address. Each port number is usually associated with a maximum of one running program, which is responsible for handling requests to that port. A daemon, being a user program, can in turn access the local hardware resources of that computer by passing requests to the operating system kernel.

Many operating systems support one or more vendor-specific or open networking protocols as well, for example, SNA on IBM systems, DECnet on systems from Digital Equipment Corporation, and Microsoft-specific protocols (SMB) on Windows. Specific protocols for specific tasks may also be supported such as NFS for file access. Protocols like ESound, or esd can be easily extended over the network to provide sound from local applications, on a remote system's sound hardware.

Security

A computer being secure depends on a number of technologies working properly. A modern operating system provides access to a number of resources, which are available to software running on the system, and to external devices like networks via the kernel.

The operating system must be capable of distinguishing between requests which should be allowed to be processed, and others which should not be processed. While some systems may simply distinguish between "privileged" and "non-privileged", systems commonly have a form of requester *identity*, such as a user name. To establish identity there may be a process of *authentication*. Often a username must be quoted, and each username may have a password. Other methods of authentication, such as magnetic cards or biometric data, might be used instead. In some cases, especially connections from the network, resources may be accessed with no authentication at all (such as reading files over a network share). Also covered by the concept of requester **identity** is *authorization*; the particular services and resources accessible by the requester once logged into a system are tied to either the requester's user account or to the variously configured groups of users to which the requester belongs.

In addition to the allow/disallow model of security, a system with a high level of security will also offer auditing options. These would allow tracking of requests for access to resources (such as, "who has been reading this file?"). Internal security, or security from an already running program is only possible if all possibly harmful requests must be carried out through interrupts to the operating system kernel. If programs can directly access hardware and resources, they cannot be secured.

External security involves a request from outside the computer, such as a login at a connected console or some kind of network connection. External requests are often passed through device drivers to the operating system's kernel, where they can be passed onto applications, or carried out directly. Security of operating systems has long been a concern because of highly sensitive data held on computers, both of a commercial and military nature. The United States Government Department of Defense (DoD) created the *Trusted Computer System Evaluation Criteria* (TCSEC) which is a standard that sets basic requirements for assessing the effectiveness of security. This became of vital importance to operating system makers, because the TCSEC was used to evaluate, classify and select trusted operating systems being considered for the processing, storage and retrieval of sensitive or classified information.

Network services include offerings such as file sharing, print services, email, web sites, and file transfer protocols (FTP), most of which can have compromised security. At the front line of security are hardware devices known as firewalls or intrusion detection/prevention systems. At the operating system level, there are a number of software firewalls available, as well as intrusion detection/prevention systems. Most modern operating systems include a software firewall, which is enabled by default. A software firewall can be configured to allow or deny network traffic to or from a service or application running on the operating system. Therefore, one can install and be running an insecure service, such as Telnet or FTP, and not have to be threatened by a security breach because the firewall would deny all traffic trying to connect to the service on that port.

An alternative strategy, and the only sandbox strategy available in systems that do not meet the Popek and Goldberg virtualization requirements, is the operating system not running user programs as native code, but instead either emulates a processor or provides a host for a p-code based system such as Java.

Internal security is especially relevant for multi-user systems; it allows each user of the system to have private files that the other users cannot tamper with or read. Internal security is also vital if auditing is to be of any use, since a program can potentially bypass the operating system, inclusive of bypassing auditing.

User interface

Every computer that is to be operated by an individual requires a user interface. The user interface is not actually a part of the operating system—it generally runs in a separate program usually referred to as a shell, but is essential if human interaction is to be supported. The user interface requests services from the operating system that will acquire data from input hardware devices, such as a keyboard, mouse or credit card reader, and requests operating system services to display prompts, status messages and such on output hardware devices, such as a video monitor or printer. The two most common forms of a user interface have historically been the command-line interface, where computer commands are typed out line-by-line, and the graphical user interface, where a visual environment (most commonly a WIMP) is present.

A screenshot of the Bourne Again Shell command line. Each command is typed out after the 'prompt', and then its output appears below, working its way down the screen. The current command prompt is at the bottom.

Graphical user interfaces

A screenshot of the KDE graphical user interface. Programs take the form of images on the screen, and the files, folders (directories), and applications take the form of icons and symbols. A mouse is used to navigate the computer.

Most of the modern computer systems support graphical user interfaces (GUI), and often include them. In some computer systems, such as the original implementation of Mac OS, the GUI is integrated into the kernel.

While technically a graphical user interface is not an operating system service, incorporating support for one into the operating system kernel can allow the GUI to be more responsive by reducing the number of context switches required for the GUI to perform its output functions. Other operating systems are modular, separating the graphics subsystem from the kernel and the Operating System. In the 1980s UNIX, VMS and many others had operating systems that were built this way. GNU/Linux and Mac OS X are also built this way. Modern releases of Microsoft Windows such as Windows Vista implement a graphics subsystem that is mostly in user-space; however the graphics drawing routines of versions between Windows NT 4.0 and Windows Server 2003 exist mostly in kernel space. Windows 9x had very little distinction between the interface and the kernel.

Many computer operating systems allow the user to install or create any user interface they desire. The X Window System in conjunction with GNOME or KDE is a commonly found setup on most Unix and Unix-like (BSD, GNU/Linux, Solaris) systems. A number of Windows shell replacements have been released for Microsoft Windows, which offer alternatives to the included Windows shell, but the shell itself cannot be separated from Windows.

Numerous Unix-based GUIs have existed over time, most derived from X11. Competition among the various vendors of Unix (HP, IBM, Sun) led to much fragmentation, though an effort to standardize in the 1990s to COSE and CDE failed for various reasons, and were eventually eclipsed by the widespread adoption of GNOME and KDE. Prior to free software-based toolkits and desktop environments, Motif was the prevalent toolkit/desktop combination (and was the basis upon which CDE was developed).

Graphical user interfaces evolve over time. For example, Windows has modified its user interface almost every time a new major version of Windows is released, and the Mac OS GUI changed dramatically with the introduction of Mac OS X in 1999.[25]

Real-time operating systems

A real-time operating system (RTOS) is a multitasking operating system intended for applications with fixed deadlines (real-time computing). Such applications include some small embedded systems, automobile engine controllers, industrial robots, spacecraft, industrial control, and some large-scale computing systems.

An early example of a large-scale real-time operating system was Transaction Processing Facility developed by American Airlines and IBM for the Sabre Airline Reservations System.

Embedded systems that have fixed deadlines use a real-time operating system such as VxWorks, PikeOS, eCos, QNX, MontaVista Linux and RTLinux. Windows CE is a real-time operating system that shares similar APIs to desktop Windows but shares none of desktop Windows' codebase. Symbian OS also has an RTOS kernel (EKA2) starting with version 8.0b.

Some embedded systems use operating systems such as Palm OS, BSD, and GNU/Linux, although such operating systems do not support real-time computing.

Operating system development as a hobby

Operating system development is one of the most complicated activities in which a computing hobbyist may engage. A hobby operating system may be classified as one whose code has not been directly derived from an existing operating system, and has few users and active developers. [26]

In some cases, hobby development is in support of a "homebrew" computing device, for example, a simple single-board computer powered by a 6502 microprocessor. Or, development may be for an architecture already in widespread use. Operating system development may come from entirely new concepts, or may commence by modeling an existing operating system. In either case, the hobbyist is his/her own developer, or may interact with a small and sometimes unstructured group of individuals who have like interests.

Examples of a hobby operating system include ReactOS and Syllable.

Diversity of operating systems and portability

Application software is generally written for use on a specific operating system, and sometimes even for specific hardware. When porting the application to run on another OS, the functionality required by that application may be implemented differently by that OS (the names of functions, meaning of arguments, etc.) requiring the application to be adapted, changed, or otherwise maintained.

This cost in supporting operating systems diversity can be avoided by instead writing applications against software platforms like Java, or Qt for web browsers. These abstractions have already borne the cost of adaptation to specific operating systems and their system libraries.

Another approach is for operating system vendors to adopt standards. For example, POSIX and OS abstraction layers provide commonalities that reduce porting costs.

See also

- Comparison of operating systems
- Handheld computers
- Hypervisor
- Interruptible operating system
- List of important publications in operating systems
- List of operating systems
- Microcontroller
- Network operating system
- Object-oriented operating system
- Operating System Projects
- PCjacking
- System image
- Timeline of operating systems
- Usage share of operating systems

References

[1] Stallings (2005). *Operating Systems, Internals and Design Principles*. Pearson: Prentice Hall. p. 6.

[2] Dhotre, I.A. (2009). *Operating Systems.*. Technical Publications. p. 1.

[3] "Operating System Market Share" (http://marketshare.hitslink.com/operating-system-market-share.aspx?qprid=10). Net Applications. .

[4] Hansen, Per Brinch, ed. (2001). *Classic Operating Systems* (http://books.google.com/?id=-PDPBvIPYBkC&lpg=PP1&pg=PP1#v=onepage&q). Springer. pp. 4–7. ISBN 0-387-95113-X. .

[5] http://www.apple.com/macosx/lion/

[6] Usage share of operating systems

[7] "Top 5 Operating Systems from January to April 2011" (http://gs.statcounter.com/#os-ww-monthly-201101-201104-bar). StatCounter. October 2009. . Retrieved November 5, 2009.

[8] IDC report into Server market share (http://www.idc.com/about/viewpressrelease.jsp?containerId=prUS22360110&sectionId=null&elementId=null&pageType=SYNOPSIS)

[9] GNU/Linux still top embedded OS (http://www.linuxdevices.com/news/NS4920597981.html)

[10] TOP500 List – November 2010 (1–100) | TOP500 Supercomputing Sites (http://www.top500.org/list/2010/11/100)

[11] "Global Web Stats" (http://marketshare.hitslink.com/operating-system-market-share.aspx?qprid=8). Net Market Share, Net Applications. May 2011. . Retrieved 2011-05-07.

[12] "Global Web Stats" (http://www.w3counter.com/globalstats.php). W3Counter, Awio Web Services. September 2009. . Retrieved 2009-10-24.
[13] "Operating System Market Share" (http://marketshare.hitslink.com/operating-system-market-share.aspx?qprid=8). Net Applications. October 2009. . Retrieved November 5, 2009.
[14] "w3schools.com OS Platform Statistics" (http://www.w3schools.com/browsers/browsers_os.asp). . Retrieved October 30, 2011.
[15] "Stats Count Global Stats Top Five Operating Systems" (http://gs.statcounter.com/#os-ww-monthly-201010-201110). . Retrieved October 30, 2011.
[16] "Global statistics at w3counter.com" (http://www.w3counter.com/globalstats.php). . Retrieved 23 January 2012.
[17] http://support.microsoft.com/kb/130179/EN-US
[18] http://support.microsoft.com/kb/134748/en
[19] http://support.microsoft.com/kb/163354/en
[20] "Operating System Share by Groups for Sites in All Locations January 2009" (http://news.netcraft.com/SSL-Survey/CMatch/osdv_all). .
[21] "Behind the IDC data: Windows still No. 1 in server operating systems" (http://blogs.zdnet.com/microsoft/?p=5408). ZDNet. 2010-02-26. .
[22] Stallings, William (2008). *Computer Organization & Architecture*. New Delhi: Prentice-Hall of India Private Limited. p. 267. ISBN 978-81-203-2962-1.
[23] http://www.fs-driver.org
[24] http://p-nand-q.com/download/rfstool.html
[25] Poisson, Ken. "Chronology of Personal Computer Software" (http://www.islandnet.com/~kpolsson/compsoft/soft1998.htm). Retrieved on 2008-05-07. Last checked on 2009-03-30.
[26] "My OS is less hobby than yours" (http://www.osnews.com/story/22638/My_OS_Is_Less_Hobby_than_Yours). *Osnews*. December 21, 2009. . Retrieved December 21, 2009.

Further reading

- Auslander, Marc A.; Larkin, David C.; Scherr, Allan L. (1981). *The evolution of the MVS Operating System* (http://www.research.ibm.com/journal/rd/255/auslander.pdf). IBM J. Research & Development.
- Deitel, Harvey M.; Deitel, Paul; Choffnes, David. *Operating Systems*. Pearson/Prentice Hall. ISBN 978-0-13-092641-8.
- Bic, Lubomur F.; Shaw, Alan C. (2003). *Operating Systems*. Pearson: Prentice Hall.
- Silberschatz, Avi; Galvin, Peter; Gagne, Greg (2008). *Operating Systems Concepts*. John Wiley & Sons. ISBN 0-470-12872-0.

External links

- Operating Systems (http://www.dmoz.org/Computers/Software/Operating_Systems/) at the Open Directory Project
- Multics History (http://www.cbi.umn.edu/iterations/haigh.html) and the history of operating systems
- How Stuff Works - Operating Systems (http://computer.howstuffworks.com/operating-system.htm)
- Help finding your Operating System type and version (http://whatsmyos.com)

OpenVMS

New logo

Old logo

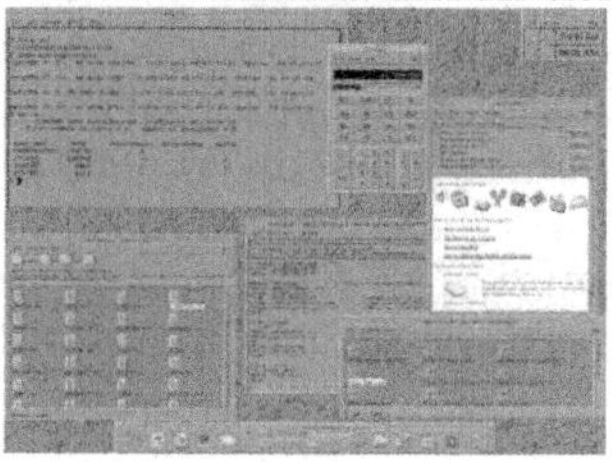

OpenVMS V7.3-1 running the CDE-based DECwindows GUI

Company / developer	Digital Equipment Corporation, Hewlett-Packard
Programmed in	BLISS, VAX Macro, C, Ada, PL/I, Fortran, UIL, SDL, Pascal, MDL, C++, DCL, Message, Document[1]
OS family	DEC OS family
Working state	Current
Source model	Closed source
Initial release	October 25, 1977
Latest stable release	OpenVMS 8.4 / June 21, 2010
Marketing target	High-end computer server
Available language(s)	English
Available programming languages(s)	Ada, BASIC, BLISS, C, C++, COBOL, DIBOL, DCL, Fortran, Lisp, MACRO32/64, Modula-2, OPS5, Pascal, Perl, Python, PL/I, Java
Update method	Concurrent Upgrades, Rolling Upgrades
Package manager	PCSI and VMSINSTAL
Supported platforms	VAX, Alpha, Itanium
Kernel type	Monolithic kernel with loadable modules

Default user interface	DCL CLI and DECwindows GUI
License	Proprietary
Official website	HP OpenVMS website [2]

OpenVMS (**Open Virtual Memory System**[3]), previously known as **VAX-11/VMS**, **VAX/VMS** or (informally) **VMS**, is a computer server operating system that runs on VAX, Alpha and Itanium-based families of computers.[4] [5] [6] Contrary to what its name suggests, OpenVMS is not open source software; however, the source listings are available for purchase.[7] Unlike many other mainframe-oriented operating systems, OpenVMS has a graphical user interface (GUI) with complete graphics support. Digital Equipment Corporation's VAX was one of the three top-selling workstations lines in the 1980s and 1990s. VMS had support for professional DTP and CAE software.[8] Software for AXP based systems was promoted by Digital's ASAP program (Association of Software and Application Partners) and could be found in the extensive "Alpha Applications Catalog".[9] AXP VMS supported OpenGL[10] and Accelerated Graphics Port (AGP) graphics adapters.

OpenVMS is a multi-user, multiprocessing virtual memory-based operating system (OS) designed for use in time sharing, batch processing, real-time (where process priorities can be set higher than OS kernel jobs), and transaction processing. It offers high system availability through clustering, or the ability to distribute the system over multiple physical machines. This allows the system to be "disaster-tolerant"[11] against disasters that may disable individual data-processing facilities. VMS also includes a process priority system that allows for real-time processes to run unhindered, while user processes get temporary priority "boosts" if necessary.[12] [13] [14]

OpenVMS commercialized many features that are now considered standard requirements for any high-end server operating system. These include:

- Integrated computer networking (originally DECnet and later, TCP/IP)[15]
- Symmetrical, asymmetrical, and NUMA multiprocessing, including clustering[16]
- A distributed file system (Files-11)[17]
- Integrated database features such as RMS[18] and layered databases including Rdb[19]
- Support for multiple computer programming languages[20] [21]
- A standardized interoperability mechanism for calls between different programming languages[22]
- An extensible shell command language (DIGITAL Command Language)[23] [24]
- Hardware partitioning of multiprocessors[25]
- High level of security[26] [27] [28] [29]

Enterprise-class environments typically select and use OpenVMS for various purposes including as a mail server, network services, manufacturing or transportation control and monitoring, critical applications and databases, and particularly environments where system uptime and data access is critical. System up-times of a decade or more[30] have been reported, and features such as Rolling Upgrades and clustering allow clustered applications and data to remain continuously accessible while operating system software and hardware maintenance and upgrades are performed, or when a whole data center is destroyed. Customers using OpenVMS include banks and financial services, hospitals and healthcare, network information services, and large-scale industrial manufacturers of various products.

History

Origin and name changes

In April 1975, Digital Equipment Corporation embarked on a hardware project, code named *Star*, to design a 32-bit virtual address extension to its PDP-11 computer line. A companion software project, code named *Starlet*, was started in June 1975 to develop a totally new operating system, based on RSX-11M, for the Star family of processors. These two projects were tightly integrated from the beginning. Gordon Bell[31] was the VP lead on the VAX hardware and its architecture. Roger Gourd was the project lead for the Starlet program, with software engineers Dave Cutler (who would later lead development of Microsoft's Windows NT), Dick Hustvedt, and Peter Lippman acting as the technical project leaders, each having responsibility for a different area of the operating system. The Star and Starlet projects culminated in the VAX 11/780 computer and the VAX-11/VMS operating system. The Starlet name survived in VMS as a name of several of the main system libraries, including STARLET.OLB and STARLET.MLB.

Over the years the name of the product has changed. In 1980 it was renamed, with version 2.0 release, to VAX/VMS (at the same time as the VAX-11 computer was renamed to simply VAX). With the introduction of the MicroVAX range such as the MicroVAX I, MicroVAX II and MicroVAX 2000 in the mid-to-late 1980s, DIGITAL released MicroVMS versions specifically targeted for these platforms which had much more limited memory and disk capacity; e.g. the smallest MicroVAX 2000 had a 40MB RD32 hard disk and a maximum of 6MB of RAM, and its CPU had to emulate some of the VAX floating point instructions in software. MicroVMS kits were released for VAX/VMS 4.4 to 4.7 on TK50 tapes and RX50 floppy disks, but discontinued with VAX/VMS 5.0. In 1991 it was renamed again to OpenVMS to indicate its support for industry standards such as POSIX and Unix compatibility, and to drop the hardware connection as the port to DIGITAL's 64-bit Alpha RISC processor was in process. The OpenVMS name first appeared after the version 5.4-2 release.

Port to DEC Alpha

The VMS port to Alpha resulted in the creation of a second and separate source code libraries (based on a source code management tool known as VDE) for the VAX 32-bit source code library and a second and new source code library for the Alpha (and the subsequent Itanium port) 64-bit architectures. 1992 saw the release of the first version of OpenVMS for Alpha AXP systems, designated *OpenVMS AXP V1.0*. The decision to use the 1.x version numbering stream for the pre-production quality releases of OpenVMS AXP caused confusion for some customers and was not repeated in the next platform port to the Itanium.

In 1994, with the release of OpenVMS version 6.1, feature (and version number) parity between the VAX and Alpha variants was achieved. This was the so-called Functional Equivalence[32] release, in the marketing materials of the time. Some features were missing however, e.g. based shareable images, which were implemented in later versions. Subsequent version numberings for the VAX and Alpha variants of the product have remained consistent through V7.3, though Alpha subsequently diverged with the availability of the V8.2 and V8.3 releases.

For general details on the port to Alpha, see the OpenVMS 20th Anniversary [33] book. For technical details on the port, see the DIGITAL Technical Journal Volume 4 Number 4 [34].

Port to Intel Itanium

In 2001, just prior to its acquisition by Hewlett-Packard, Compaq announced the port of OpenVMS to the Intel Itanium architecture.[35] This port was accomplished using source code maintained in common within the OpenVMS Alpha source code library, with conditional and additional modules where changes specific to Itanium were required. The OpenVMS Alpha pool was chosen as the basis of the port as it was significantly more portable than the original OpenVMS VAX source code, and because the Alpha source code pool was already fully 64-bit capable (unlike the VAX source code pool). With the Alpha port, many of the VAX hardware-specific dependencies had been previously moved into the Alpha SRM firmware for OpenVMS. Features necessary for OpenVMS were then moved from SRM into OpenVMS I64 as part of the Itanium port.[36]

Unlike the port from VAX to Alpha, in which a snapshot of the VAX code base circa V5.4-2[32] was used as the basis for the Alpha release and the 64-bit source code pool then diverged, the OpenVMS Alpha and I64 (Itanium) versions of OpenVMS are built and maintained using a common source code library and common tools. The core software source code control system used for OpenVMS is the VMS Development Environment (VDE); see the VDE installation kit [37] for details.

Two pre-production releases, OpenVMS I64 V8.0 and V8.1, were available on June 30, 2003 and on December 18, 2003. These releases were intended for HP organizations and third-party vendors involved with porting software packages to OpenVMS I64.

The following are recent OpenVMS I64 releases:

OpenVMS I64 V8.2, the first production-quality Itanium release, was shipped January 13, 2005. A V8.2 release is also available for Alpha platforms.

OpenVMS I64 V8.2-1, adding support for Integrity Superdome and cell based systems, was released in September 2005. V8.2-1 is available for Itanium platforms only.

OpenVMS I64 V8.3, was released for Itanium platforms in September 2006. V8.3 is also available for Alpha systems.

OpenVMS I64 V8.3-1H1, was released in October 2007. It features full c-Class Integrity BladeServer blade support. See the full announcement [38] for details. See HP BladeSystem information [39] for details on blade server products from HP.

OpenVMS I64 and Alpha V8.4, was released in June 2010. See the OpenVMS V8.4 release announcement [40] for details.

For technical details on the OpenVMS port to Itanium, see the OpenVMS Technical Journal V6 [41]. In particular, see the Porting OpenVMS to Integrity [42] article. Information on OpenVMS releases from V4.0 to current [43] is available, as are listings of upgrade paths in the OpenVMS FAQ [44] and at the HP OpenVMS site [45].

Major release timeline

Date	Version	Note
October 25, 1977	V1.0	Initial commercial release
April, 1980	V2.0	VAX-11/750
April, 1982	V3.0	VAX-11/730
September, 1984	V4.0	VAX 8600 and MicroVMS (for MicroVAX)
April, 1988	V5.0	VAX 6000
November, 1992	V1.5	first OpenVMS AXP (Alpha) specific version
June, 1993	V6.0	VAX 7000 and 10000
April/May, 1994	V6.1	merging of VAX and Alpha AXP version numbers
January, 1996	V7.0	full 64-bit virtual addressing on Alpha
1997	V7.1	
June, 2003	V8.0	limited availability eval for Integrity
February, 2005	V8.2	Common Alpha and Itanium release
September, 2006	V8.3	Alpha, Itanium dual-core support
October, 2007	V8.3-1H1	c-Class Integrity blade server support
June, 2010	V8.4	Added support for running as a virtual machine guest under HPVM Clusters over TCP/IP

Features

Graphical user interface

OpenVMS uses the DECwindows Motif user interface (based on CDE) layered on top of OpenVMS's X11 compliant windowing system.[46] [47]

Clustering

OpenVMS supports clustering (first called *VAXcluster* and later VMScluster), where multiple systems share disk storage, processing, job queues and print queues, and are connected either by specialized hardware or an industry-standard LAN (usually Ethernet). A LAN-based cluster is often called a LAVc, for Local Area Network VMScluster, and allows, among other things, bootstrapping a possibly diskless *satellite node* over the network using the system disk of a *bootnode*.

VAXcluster support was first added in VMS version 4, which was released in 1984. This version only supported clustering over CI. Later releases of version 4 supported clustering over LAN (LAVC), and support for LAVC was improved in VMS version 5, released in 1988.

Mixtures of cluster interconnects and technologies are permitted, including Gigabit (GbE) Ethernet, SCSI, FDDI, DSSI, CI and Memory Channel adapters.

OpenVMS supports up to 96 nodes in a single cluster, and allows mixed-architecture clusters, where VAX and Alpha systems, or Alpha and Itanium systems can co-exist in a single cluster (Various organizations have demonstrated triple-architecture clusters and cluster configurations with up to 150 nodes, but these configurations are not supported by HP).

Unlike many other clustering solutions, VAXcluster offers transparent and fully distributed read-write with record-level locking, which means that the same disk and even the same file can be accessed by several cluster nodes at once; the locking occurs only at the level of a single record of a file, which would usually be one line of text or a single record in a database. This allows the construction of high-availability multiply redundant database servers.

Cluster interconnections can span upwards of 500 miles, allowing member nodes to be located in different buildings on an office campus, or in different cities.

Host-based volume shadowing allows volumes (of the same or of different sizes) to be shadowed (mirrored) across multiple controllers and multiple hosts, allowing the construction of disaster-tolerant environments.

Full access into the distributed lock manager (DLM) is available to application programmers, and this allows applications to coordinate arbitrary resources and activities across all cluster nodes. This obviously includes file-level coordination, but the resources and activities and operations that can be coordinated with the DLM are completely arbitrary.

OpenVMS V8.4 offers advances in clustering technology, including the use of industry-standard TCP/IP networking to bring efficiencies to cluster interconnect technology. Cluster over TCP/IP is supported with OpenVMS version 8.4 released in 2010.

With the supported capability of rolling upgrades and with multiple system disks, cluster configurations can be maintained on-line and upgraded incrementally. This allows cluster configurations to continue to provide application and data access while a subset of the member nodes are upgraded to newer software versions.

For general details, see the OpenVMS Cluster SPD [48]. For more specific details, see the clustering-related manuals in the OpenVMS documentation set [49].

File system

OpenVMS has a very feature-rich file system, with support for stream and record-oriented IO, ACLs, and file versioning. The typical user and application interface into the file system is the RMS.

Details are in the RMS Utilities and RMS programming manuals, and in the I/O User's Reference Manual, all part of the OpenVMS documentation set [49]. Also see the available ODS2 documentation [50], and the *VMS File Systems Internals* book, by Kirby McCoy, ISBN 1-55558-056-4.

Timekeeping

OpenVMS represents system time as the 64-bit number of 100 nanosecond intervals (that is, ten million units per second; also known as a 'clunk'[51] [52]) since the epoch. The epoch of OpenVMS is midnight preceding November 17, 1858, which is the start of Modified Julian Day numbering. The clock is not necessarily updated every 100 ns; for example, systems with a 100 Hz interval timer simply add 100 000 to the value every hundredth of a second. The operating system includes a mechanism to adjust for hardware timekeeping drift; when calibrated against a known time standard, it easily achieves an accuracy better than 0.01%. All OpenVMS hardware platforms derive timekeeping from an internal clock not associated with the AC supply power frequency.

While the system is shut down, time is kept by a Time-of-Year ("TOY") hardware clock. This clock keeps time to a lower resolution (perhaps 1 second) and generally, a lower accuracy (often 0.025% versus 0.01%). When the system is restarted, the VMS 64-bit time value is recomputed based on the time kept by the TOY clock and the last recorded year (stored on the system disk).

The 100 nanosecond granularity implemented within OpenVMS and the 63-bit absolute time representation (the sign bit indicates *absolute time* when clear and *relative time* when set) should allow OpenVMS trouble-free time computations up to **31-JUL-31086 02:48:05.47**. At this instant, all clocks and time-keeping operations in OpenVMS will suddenly fail, since the counter will overflow and start from zero again.

Though the native OpenVMS time format can range far into the future, applications based on the C runtime library will likely encounter timekeeping problems beyond January 19, 2038 due to the Year 2038 problem. Many components and applications may also encounter field-length-related date problems at year 10000 (see the Year 10,000 problem).

Detailed information on time and timekeeping, and on daylight saving time and timezone differential factor operations, is contained in the OpenVMS FAQ [44].

Programming

The common language programming environment is described in the OpenVMS Calling Standard [49] and the OpenVMS Programming Concepts [49] manuals. This provides mixed-language calls, and a set of language-specific, run-time library (RTL), and system service routines. The language calls and the RTLs are implemented in user-mode shareable images, while the system services calls are generally part of the operating system, or part of privileged-mode code. This distinction between languages and RTLs and system services was once fairly clean and clear, but the implementations and specifics have become rather more murky over the years.

Various utilities and tools are integrated [49], as are various add-on languages and tools [48].

Many Programming Examples are available, see the pointers in the OpenVMS FAQ [44].

Debugging

The VMS Debugger supports all DEC compilers and many third party languages. It allows breakpoints, watchpoints and interactive runtime program debugging either using a command line or graphical user interface. OpenVMS Debugger Manual [53]

Common Language Environment

Among OpenVMS's notable features is the Common Language Environment, a strictly defined standard that specifies calling convention for functions and routines, including use of stacks, registers, etc., independently of programming language. Because of this, it is possible to call a routine written in one language (e.g. Fortran) from another (e.g. COBOL), without needing to know the implementation details of the target language. OpenVMS itself is implemented in a variety of different languages (primarily BLISS, VAX Macro and C) (per comp.os.vms newsgroup postings from members of HP OpenVMS Engineering [54]), and the common language environment and calling standard supports freely mixing these languages, and Ada, PL/I, Fortran, BASIC, and others. This is in contrast to a system such as Unix, which is implemented nearly entirely in the C language.

For details on these compilers and libraries, see the language manuals available at OpenVMS documentation [55].

Macro32 (an assembler on OpenVMS VAX, and a compiler on OpenVMS Alpha and on OpenVMS I64) is available within and integrated into OpenVMS. BLISS compilers are available for download from the OpenVMS Freeware [56], as are various ports of Perl, PHP, Ruby and other languages. Java is available from the HP Java website [57]. C, Fortran and other languages are commercial products, and are available for purchase.

Security

OpenVMS provides various security features and mechanisms, including security identifiers, resource identifiers, subsystem identifiers, ACLs, and detailed security auditing and alarms. Specific versions evaluated at DoD NCSC Class C2 and, with the SEVMS security enhanced services support, at NCSC Class B1, per the NCSC Rainbow Series. OpenVMS also holds an ITSEC E3 rating. For details on these ratings and the specific associated OpenVMS versions and ratings, see the NCSC and Common Criteria pages, and the associated product listings.

For details on the OpenVMS security mechanisms, see the HP OpenVMS Guide to System Security manual available at the OpenVMS documentation web site [49]. Also see the OpenVMS security [58] information.

Cross-platform applications

OpenVMS supports the following industry standard tools and applications:

- Samba (CIFS)
- Apache HTTP Server
- Apache Tomcat
- Diskeeper
- Zip/Unzip (Info-Zip)
- GNU Privacy Guard (gpg)[59]
- Perl[60]

Documentation

The OpenVMS operating documentation for various recent releases and for various core OpenVMS layered products is available online at the HP website http://www.hp.com/go/openvms/doc/.

Software Product Description (SPD) documents for many OpenVMS-related products (and for OpenVMS itself) are available at http://h18000.www1.hp.com/info/spd/. SPDs are introductory and legal descriptions of various products, listing the various supported capabilities and product features.

The OpenVMS Frequently Asked Questions (FAQ) contains information and pointers associated with OpenVMS, and is available in various formats at http://www.hoffmanlabs.org/vmsfaq/.

Releases, software support status

The current OpenVMS release are OpenVMS V8.4 for Alpha and Integrity servers, and OpenVMS V7.3 for VAX servers.

HP provides Current Version Support (CVS) and Prior Version Support (PVS) for various OpenVMS releases. The OpenVMS Roadmap [61] guarantees PVS status for specific releases (V5.5-2, V5.5-2H4, V6.2, V6.2-1H3, V7.3-2) until 2012, and only then ending with 24 month's prior notice. CVS is provided for the current release and for the immediately prior release.

Applicable industry standards

The following are some of the industry standards claimed in the OpenVMS Software Product Description (SPD) [48] document:

- ANSI X3.4-1986: ASCII
- ANSI X3.22-1973/FIPS 3-1: Magtape, 800 BPI NRZI
- ANSI X3.27-1987/FIPS 79: Magtape, Labels and Volume Structures
- ANSI X3.39-1986/FIPS 25: Magtape, 1600 BPI PE
- ANSI X3.40-1983: Magtape, unrecorded
- ANSI X3.41-1974: ASCII 7-bit control sequences
- ANSI X3.42-1975: Numeric values in character strings
- ANSI X3.54-1986/FIPS 50: Magtape, 6250 BPI GCR
- ANSI X3.131-1986/ISO 9316(1989): SCSI-1
- ANSI X3.131-1994/ISO 10288(1994): SCSI-2
- ANSI/IEEE 802.2-1985: logical link control
- ANSI/IEEE 802.3-1985: Ethernet CSMA/CD
- FIPS 1-2: Code for Information Interchange; includes ANSI X3.4-1977(86)/FIPS 15; ANSI X3.32-1973/FIPS 36; ANSI X3.41-1974/FIPS 35; FIPS 7
- FIPS 16-1/ANSI X3.15-1976: Serial Comms Bit Sequencing; FED STD 1010
- FIPS 22-1/ANSI X3.1-1976: Synch signaling for DTE/DCE comms; FED STD 1013
- FIPS 37/ANSI X3.36-1975: Synch High-Speed signaling for DTE/DCE comms; GIPS 1001
- FIPS 86/ANSI X3.64-1979: Additional Controls for Use with ASCII
- ISO 646: ISO 7-bit Coded Character Set for Information Exchange
- ISO 1001: Magtape, Labels and Volume Structures
- ISO 1863: Magtape, 800 BPI NRZI
- ISO 1864: Magtape, unrecorded / NRZI and PE
- ISO 2022: Code extensions for ISO 646
- ISO 3307: Time and Date Representations
- ISO 3788: Magtape, 1600 BPI PE

- ISO 4873: 8-Bit Character Codes
- ISO 5652: Magtape, 6250 BPI GCR
- ISO 6429: Control Sequences
- ISO 9660: CD-ROM volume and file structures

OpenVMS Hobbyist Program

Despite being a proprietary commercial operating system, in 1997 OpenVMS and a number of layered products were made available free of charge for hobbyist, non-commercial use as part of the OpenVMS Hobbyist Program. Since then, several companies producing OpenVMS software have made their products available under the same terms, such as Process Software [62] and MVP Systems [63].

As of 2006, the time required to obtain a hobbyist license was approximately one week from start to finish; from registration with a user group through acquisition of licenses and media. Hobbyist CD media is available for US$30, including international shipping. No anonymous FTP software downloads are available to hobbyists.

More information on the hobbyist program can be found at http:/ / www. vmshobbyist. org/ and http:/ / www. OpenVMS.org/.A number of hobbyist systems are open to the public, including the Deathrow Cluster [64].

Poetry Hacklab [65] provides telnet and ssh access (username and password is luther) to two VAX/VMS machines located at the Freaknet Computer Museum.

Central OpenVMS-related topics

OpenVMS-related terms and acronyms include:

- ACMS - Digital's transaction processing (TP) system, often used with the DECdtm distributed transaction manager system service components of OpenVMS, and with the DECforms and Rdb products in applications with transactional requirements
- Asynchronous system trap (AST)
- DECforms - Digital's successor to the Forms Management System
- DECnet - Digital's proprietary networking architecture which also includes MOP.
- DELTA and XDELTA - OpenVMS debuggers
- DIGITAL Command Language (DCL) - Digital Command Language - command line interpreter.
- DECwindows - Digital's implementation of the X Window System.
- Event flag - a simple synchronization mechanism
- Files-11 - low level filesystem
- File Description Language (FDL) - defines file record/field structure
- Forms Management System (FMS) - Digital's first generation language-independent Form driver
- Local Area Transport (LAT) - is a LAN-based non-routable communications protocol to support DEC and other Terminal Servers
- QIO Queued Input Output; the low-level I/O interface
- Oracle Rdb - An SQL compliant relational database created by DEC but now owned by Oracle
- Record Management Services (RMS) - high-level, language/device-independent Input/output
- Runtime libraries (RTL) - shared routines and functions, callable from any language
- OpenVMS Galaxy - co-habitating OpenVMS installations; a form of system partitioning
- OpenVMS Clusters - for redundancy, incremental hardware upgrades, or disaster tolerance
- System 1032 (S1032) - A high-performance database management system and application development environment designed to support the OpenVMS user community. Used at some companies in the 1980s and 90s, but, in little use today.
- XQP - the eXtended QIO Processor (XQP), which implements the Files-11 filesystem.

For information on layered products, see the Software Product Description (SPD) [48] for the product. For OpenVMS components, see the OpenVMS documentation set [49].

See also

- Comparison of operating systems
- SRM — The boot firmware required to boot OpenVMS on DEC Alpha-based computer systems [66]
- EFI — the boot firmware used by OpenVMS on Itanium platforms [67]
- FreeVMS — A software project aiming to create a GPLed clone of VMS [68]
- Paris Métro Line 14 — A notable OpenVMS client [69]
- Indian Railways — another (very) large OpenVMS client [70]
- Terry Shannon — late advocate of OpenVMS [71]

OpenVMS publications

- The Minimum You Need to Know to Be an OpenVMS Application Developer, Roland Hughes, ISBN 978097786603 [72]
- The Minimum You Need to Know About Java on OpenVMS, Roland Hughes, ISBN 978-0-9770866-1-0 [73]
- The Minimum You Need to Know About Service Oriented Architecture, Roland Hughes, ISBN 978-0-9770866-6-5 [74]
- Getting Started with OpenVMS, Michael D. Duffy, ISBN 1-55558-279-6
- Getting Started with OpenVMS System Management, 2nd Edition, David Donald Miller, Stephen Hoffman, Lawrence Baldwin, ISBN 1-55558-243-5
- Introduction to OpenVMS, 5th Edition, Lesley Ogilvie Rice, ISBN 1-55558-194-3
- Introduction to OpenVMS, David W Bynon, ISBN 1-878956-61-2
- OpenVMS Alpha Internals and Data Structures: Memory Management, Ruth Goldenberg, ISBN 1-55558-159-5
- OpenVMS Alpha Internals and Data Structures : Scheduling and Process Control : Version 7.0, Ruth Goldenberg, Saro Saravanan, Denise Dumas, ISBN 1-55558-156-0
- OpenVMS online documentation [49]
- OpenVMS Performance Management, Joginder Sethi, ISBN 1-55558-126-9
- OpenVMS System Management Guide, Lawrence Baldwin, ISBN 1-55558-143-9
- The hitchhiker's guide to VMS : an unsupported-undocumented-can-go-away-at-any-time feature of VMS, Bruce Ellis, ISBN 1-878956-00-0
- The OpenVMS User's Guide, Second Edition, Patrick Holmay, ISBN 1-55558-203-6
- Using DECwindows Motif for OpenVMS, Margie Sherlock, ISBN 1-55558-114-5
- VAX/VMS Internals and Data Structures: Version 5.2 ("IDSM"), Ruth Goldenberg, Saro Saravanan, Denise Dumas, ISBN 1-55558-059-9
- Writing OpenVMS Alpha Device Drivers in C, Margie Sherlock, Leonard Szubowicz, ISBN 1-55558-133-1
- Writing Real Programs in DCL, second edition, Stephen Hoffman, Paul Anagnostopoulos, ISBN 1-55558-191-9

References

[1] OpenVMS FAQ (http://www.openvms.compaq.com/faq/vmsfaq_002.html#vms8)
[2] http://www.hp.com/go/openvms
[3] See the OpenVMS Software Product Description (SPD) documents for OpenVMS VAX, OpenVMS Alpha, and OpenVMS I64; see the SPD repository (http://h18000.www1.hp.com/info/spd/)
[4] VAX Architecture Reference Manual (http://www.bitsavers.org/pdf/dec/vax/)
[5] DIGITAL Microprocessor and Alpha Architecture Library (http://ftp.digital.com/pub/Digital/info/semiconductor/literature/dsc-library.html)
[6] Intel Itanium documentation (http://www.intel.com/products/processor/itanium2/)
[7] OpenVMS source listing CD (http://h21007.www2.hp.com/portal/site/dspp/menuitem.863c3e4cbcdc3f3515b49c108973a801?ciid=6108078442f02110078442f02110275d6e10RCRD)
[8] http://en.wikipedia.org/wiki/VAXstation#Software
[9] Living with Alpha: Finding Help (http://technet.microsoft.com/en-us/library/cc750226.aspx)
[10] http://www.faqs.org/faqs/graphics/opengl-faq/part1/
[11] http://www.youtube.com/watch?v=qMCHpUtJnEI
[12] OpenVMS Alpha Internals and Data Structures : Scheduling and Process Control : Version 7.0, Ruth Goldenberg, Saro Saravanan, Denise Dumas, ISBN 1-55558-156-0
[13] OpenVMS Alpha Internals and Data Structures: Memory Management, Ruth Goldenberg, ISBN 1-55558-159-5
[14] VAX/VMS Internals and Data Structures: Version 5.2 ("IDSM"), Ruth Goldenberg, Saro Saravanan, Denise Dumas, ISBN 1-55558-059-9
[15] OpenVMS documentation (http://www.hp.com/go/openvms/doc/); see the DECnet and TCP/IP Services documentation, and see the User's Guide
[16] OpenVMS documentation (http://www.hp.com/go/openvms/doc); see the clustering and OpenVMS Galaxy documentation
[17] OpenVMS documentation (http://www.hp.com/go/openvms/doc/); see the RMS and XQP documentation
[18] OpenVMS documentation (http://www.hp.com/go/openvms/doc); see the RMS documentation
[19] The Oracle Rdb (http://www.oracle.com/rdb/) web site
[20] OpenVMS documentation (http://www.hp.com/go/openvms/doc/); see the language documentation
[21] OpenVMS Freeware (http://www.hp.com/go/openvms/freeware/); see the BLISS, Macro64, OPS5, Perl, PHP, Tcl/Tk and other language kits and tools
[22] OpenVMS Calling Standard (http://h71000.www7.hp.com/doc/82final/5973/aa-qsbbe-te.pdf?jumpid=reg_R1002_USEN)
[23] Writing Real Programs in DCL, second edition, Stephen Hoffman, Paul Anagnostopoulos, ISBN 1-55558-191-9
[24] OpenVMS documentation (http://www.hp.com/go/openvms/doc/); see the OpenVMS User's Guide
[25] OpenVMS documentation (http://www.hp.com/go/openvms/doc/); see the OpenVMS Galaxy documentation
[26] OpenVMS documentation (http://www.hp.com/go/openvms/doc/); see OpenVMS Guide to System Security manual
[27] NIST NCSC (http://csrc.nist.gov/checklists/repository/1080.html)
[28] National Computer Security Center (NCSC) Trusted Product Evaluation List (TPEL)
[29] OpenVMS at DEFCON9 (http://www.defcon.org/html/links/dc_press/archives/9/vmsone_writeup.htm)
[30] "The Uptimes-Project.org - Host Information: WVNETcluster" (http://www.uptimes-project.org/hosts/view/150). . Retrieved 2009-04-10.
[31] Gordon Bell Biography (http://research.microsoft.com/~gbell/bio.htm)
[32] OpenVMS VAX and Alpha Compatibility (http://h71000.www7.hp.com/DOC/73final/documentation/pdf/OVMS_COMPAT_VAX_ALPHA.pdf)
[33] http://h71000.www7.hp.com/openvms/20th/
[34] http://www.hpl.hp.com/hpjournal/dtj/vol4num4/intro.htm
[35] OvenVMS Times article (http://h71000.www7.hp.com/openvmstimes/openvmstimes.pdf)
[36] Information from various comp.os.vms newsgroup postings from OpenVMS Engineers
[37] http://h71000.www7.hp.com/freeware/
[38] http://h71000.www7.hp.com/openvms83-1h1_announce.html
[39] http://www.hp.com/go/blades/
[40] http://h71000.www7.hp.com/openvms84_announce.html
[41] http://h71000.www7.hp.com/openvms/journal/v6/index.html
[42] http://h71000.www7.hp.com/openvms/journal/v6/porting_openvms_to_integrity.pdf
[43] http://h71000.www7.hp.com/openvms/os/openvms-release-history.html
[44] http://www.hoffmanlabs.org/vmsfaq/
[45] http://h71000.www7.hp.com/openvms/os/os-upgrade-chart.html
[46] HP DECwindows Motif for OpenVMS (http://h18000.www1.hp.com/info/spd/) Software Product Description (SPD)
[47] Using DECwindows Motif for OpenVMS, Margie Sherlock, ISBN 1-55558-114-5
[48] http://h18000.www1.hp.com/info/spd/
[49] http://www.hp.com/go/openvms/doc/

[50] http://h71000.www7.hp.com/freeware/freeware40/ods2/
[51] http://www.ibiblio.org/pub/academic/computer-science/history/pdp-11/rsx/decus/rsx89b/374101/readme.clu
[52] http://www.classiccmp.org/PDP-11/RSX-11/freeware/decus/rsx86b/356030/wevol3n1.prt
[53] http://www.openvms.compaq.com:8000/73final/4538/4538PRO.HTML
[54] http://groups.google.com/group/comp.os.vms/msg/21686958ee9a195b
[55] http://www.hp.com/go/openvms/doc
[56] http://www.hp.com/go/openvms/freeware/
[57] http://www.hp.com/go/java
[58] http://www.hp.com/go/openvms/security/
[59] http://h71000.www7.hp.com/opensource/gnupg.html GnuPG, ported to OpenVMS
[60] http://h71000.www7.hp.com/openvms/products/ips/apache/csws_perl_relnotes.html Perl for OpenVMS
[61] http://h71000.www7.hp.com/openvms/roadmap/openvms_roadmaps.htm
[62] http://www.process.com/openvms/hobbyist.html
[63] http://www.mvpsi.com/hobby.aspx
[64] http://deathrow.vistech.net
[65] http://poetry.freaknet.org
[66] ftp://ftp.digital.com/pub/DEC/Alpha/firmware/index.html
[67] http://www.hoffmanlabs.com/openvms/hwi64.shtml
[68] http://www.freevms.net/
[69] http://www.adahome.com/Ammo/Success/subway.html
[70] http://h71000.www7.hp.com/openvms/brochures/indiarr/indiarr.pdf
[71] http://www.shannonknowshpc.com/
[72] http://www.theminimumyouneedtoknow.com/app_book.html
[73] http://www.theminimumyouneedtoknow.com/about_java_on_openvms.html
[74] http://www.theminimumyouneedtoknow.com/service_oriented_architecture_book.html

External links

- HP OpenVMS Systems website (http://www.hp.com/go/openvms/)
- HP OpenVMS backup with HP Data Protector (http://www.hp.com/go/dataprotector/)
- OpenVMS 20th anniversary (1997) (http://h71000.www7.hp.com/openvms/20th/), contains historical facts
- OpenVMS 30th anniversary (2007) (http://h71000.www7.hp.com/openvms/30th/), contains historical facts
- Arne Vajhøj's OpenVMS Bibliography (http://www.vajhoej.dk/arne/vms/vms_book.html)
- [news://comp.os.vms/ comp.os.vms Usenet group], archives on Google Groups (http://groups.google.com/group/comp.os.vms)
- Deathrow OpenVMS Cluster (http://deathrow.vistech.net), public access OpenVMS systems
- Hoffmanlabs.org HP OpenVMS FAQ (http://www.hoffmanlabs.org/vmsfaq/)
- Hoffmanlabs.org HP OpenVMS FAQ (http://labs.hoffmanlabs.com/node/1), new site
- OpenVMS beginner's FAQ (http://alpha.mike-r.com/VMS_beginners_faq.html)
- Introductory Info for New OpenVMS Hobbyists (http://www.hoffmanlabs.org/openvms/), at Hoffmanlabs.org
- MVP Systems (http://www.mvpsi.com)
- OpenVMS.org (http://www.openvms.org)
- OpenVMS Hobbyist Program (http://www.openvmshobbyist.com)
- OpenVMS Programmer's Corner (http://www3.sympatico.ca/n.rieck/links/openvms_demos.html), primarily HP BASIC programs
- OpenVMS Resource Center (http://www.process.com/openvms/), OpenVMS FILESERV
- OpenVMS Web Ring (http://i.webring.com/hub?ring=openvms)
- Process Software (http://www.process.com)
- Virtually Unhackable (http://www.pointsecure.com/pdf/Defconwhite.pdf), DEF CON9
- VMS Operating System Is 30 Years Old; Customers Believe It Can Last Forever (http://www.informationweek.com/news/showArticle.jhtml?articleID=202801794), InformationWeek, November 3, 2007
- OpenVMS application status report as of October, 01, 2007 (http://h71000.www7.hp.com/solutions/matrix/alphaopenvmsstatusreport.pdf) (102 pages long table of applications)

- FreeAXP (http://www.FreeAXP.com) Free Alpha hardware emulator supporting OpenVMS
- AlphaVM-free (http://emuvm.com/) freeware AlphaServer emulator supporting OpenVMS

Article Sources and Contributors

Alpha_21164 *Source*: http://en.wikipedia.org/w/index.php?title=Alpha_21164 *Contributors*: Alecv, Bwilkins, Jamelan, Kyle1278, Rich Farmbrough, Rilak, THEN WHO WAS PHONE?, 5 anonymous edits

Microprocessor *Source*: http://en.wikipedia.org/w/index.php?title=Microprocessor *Contributors*: 1111mol, 16@r, 194.230.175.xxx, 209.239.196.xxx, 7, 95jb14, A little insignificant, ActiveSelective, Adamkirkman, Adityagaur 7, Aero14, Afromayun, Ageton, Ahoerstemeier, Ahunt, Alain, Alansohn, Aldie, Alexvent, Alf Boggis, Alokchakrabarti, Altes2009, Alureiter, Aluvus, Amol.gulhane07, Andrejj, Andy Dingley, Andy M. Wang, Angelic Wraith, Anil1268, Anomalocaris, Anthony.king@westerndesigncenter.com, AnthonyQBachler, Apantomimehorse, Apyule, Arch dude, Archenzo, Arisa, Arjayay, Arnero, Arun dalvi, Asnldhln, Axeman89, BBrad31, Beerden, Beetstra, Begoon, Bender235, Berek, Berles, Bgpaulus, Bigdumbdinosaur, Biker Biker, Blainster, BobKawanaka, Bobblewik, Bongwarrior, Bookandcoffee, Brainmachine, Brandon, Brouhaha, Bubba73, C.Fred, CWY2190, Calabraxthis, Caltas, Cameltrader, Can't sleep, clown will eat me, CanadianLinuxUser, CanisRufus, Canthusus, Capricorn42, Cbturner46, Cenarium, Chankey Pathak, Cherfr, Chris the speller, Circularshift, CityOfSilver, ClanCC, Clockwork Soul, Colin99, Conskeptical, Conversion script, CoolFox, Crazysunshine, Crusadeonilliteracy, Crystallina, Cxk271, DARTH SIDIOUS 2, DMahalko, DSLITEDS, DabMachine, Damueo, DanielVonEhren, Dasarianandkumar009, Davhorn, David Gerard, David Jordan, DavidCary, Db099221, Dcljr, Deagle AP, Deor, DerHexer, Deshmukhpratik, Dgw, Dispenser, Djd1219, Donreed, Dougweller, Download, DragonHawk, Ds13, Dureo, E prosser, ENIAC, EWikist, Echo95, Edd 123, Edetic, Edunsi, Elfguy, Elipongo, Elockid, EmadIV, Endothermic, Enochhwang, Enviroboy, Epbr123, Erzahler, FatalError, Felixdakat, Ferkelparade, Figureskatingfan, Fir0002, Fnagaton, Fourohfour, Frazzydee, Fyngyrz, GVP Webmaster, Gachet, Gaius Cornelius, Galoubet, Gary King, Gcalac, Geniac, Ghettoblaster, Giftlite, GlasGhost, Glen, Glenn, Gogo Dodo, Goochelaar, Gorank4, Grafikm fr, Greenrd, Grendelkhan, Grim23, Grunt, Guy Harris, Guy Macon, Gökhan, Hadal, Haham hanuka, Hanandre, Hannes Hirzel, Hans Dunkelberg, Happysailor, Hehkuviini, Henk.muller, HenkeB, Henriok, Herbertxu, Hitchhiker89, Hooperbloob, Horsten, Hpa, IMneme, IOOI, Idleguy, Igoldste, Ilya, Inkling, Insuperable, Inswoon, Iridescent, Isacp, Island, Ixfd64, J.delanoy, JJthe13, JLaTondre, Jagged 85, Jake Wartenberg, Jamo spingal, Jaranda, Jason Michael Smithson, Jauhienij, Jcanu, Jdforrester, Jeff G., Jeffreyarcand, Jeh, Jerryobject, JiFish, Jklamo, Jo7hs2, John a s, JohnCD, JonHarder, Jonabbey, Jonathan Hall, Jondel, Jossi, Jpbowen, Jpk, Jrockley, Jsc83, Juliancolton, Junexgamer, Jusdafax, Just James, Jwy, Jóna Þórunn, KLWhitehead, Karveandhan, Kateshortforbob, Kbdank71, Kerotan, KerryVeenstra, Kingpin13, Kinu, Kjkolb, Klingoncowboy4, Kmweber, KnowledgeOfSelf, Komap, Kozuch, Krótki, Kundor, Leon7, Letdorf, Letowskie, Lexein, Liao, Lights, Lijojames, Lilg132, Lindosland, Lotje, Loul, LouScheffer, Luna Santin, MFNickster, Mac, Mack2, MafiotuL, Mahjongg, Maian, Majorly, MaltaGC, Mandarax, Mani1, Maniago, Mannafredo, Mantror, Manxarbiter, Marck69, MarkSweep, MarsRover, Mato, Matsuiny2004, Matt Britt, Matticus78, Maury Markowitz, Mav, Maxis ftw, Maxx.T, Mb3k, Mckaysalisbury, Mcleodm, Mdd4696, Mehrunes Dagon, Meldor, Melongrower, Mendiwe, Michael Hardy, Mike Van Emmerik, Mikef, Milkmandan, Minesweeper, Mintleaf, Mirror Vax, Misibacsi, Mjpieters, Moggie2002, Monowiki, MooresLaw, Moxfyre, Mr random, Mramz88, Mrwrite, Muhherfuhher, Murray Langton, Musabhusaini, Mwd, Mxn, Mysid, MysticMetal, NPalmius, Nadavspi, Nandadeep11, Nansars, NapoliRoma, Nasnema, Nate Silva, Navanee2u, Navy blue84, Neckelmann, Neelix, NellieBly, NeoPhyteRep, Netsnipe, Nihonjoe, Ninly, Norm mit, NuclearWarfare, Oknazevad, OlEnglish, Oliverdl, Olivier, OohBunnies!, Orichalque, Oystein, PCHS-NJROTC, Pankaj139, Paul23234545, Persian Poet Gal, Phil websurfer@yahoo.com, Philip Trueman, Phlar, Pingveno, Pixel8, Pmsyyz, Poppafuze, Prabodh1987, Premvvnc, Privatechef, Priyabhar, Proofreader77, Qbert203, QcRef87, Qkszkdl, Qwerty Binary, Qwerty189, RA0808, RJaguar3, Rada, RainbowOfLight, Ram-Man, Rama's Arrow, Randydeluxe, Raul654, Ray Van De Walker, Rayholt, Razorpit, RedWolf, Reisio, RexNL, Rich Farmbrough, RichardOSmith, Riki, Rilak, Rjhanson54, Rmadams, Roadrunner, RobWilloner, Roberrd, Robert Bond, RobertG, Robofish, Rror, Rubikcube, Rōnin, SMC1991, Salim Muhammad, Salvio giuliano, Sanchom, Sarenne, Sbierwagen, SchuminWeb, Scipius, Sclear02, Scootey, Search4Lancer, Seav, Senthilece19, SharpenedSkills, Sherool, Shirik, Shjacks45, Shriaunsh.sw, Shubhamthakare, Shvytejimas, Sietse Snel, SimonP, Snowolf, SoCalSuperEagle, Sp, Spacepotato, Spiff, Spitfire19, SplingyRanger, Squash Racket, Srce, SreekumarC, Srinivasasha, Stan Shebs, Stdazi, Stickee, Sunshine4921, Swtpc6800, Sylvain Mielot, TEG24601, Tarif Ezaz, Tasc, Thdremily1, The Anonymous One, The Thing That Should Not Be, The1physicist, TheGreenAc3, TheJosh, Thecheesykid, Theresa knott, Think outside the box, Thumperward, Thurinym, Tigga en, Tim Ivorson, Tinkar, Tobias Bergemann, Tomekire, Tony1, Top2Cat1, Toussaint, Toytoy, Tpbradbury, Tvdm, Twang, TyA, Uncle G, Uriel8, UtherSRG, ValC, Valery Beaud, VampWillow, Versus22, Vinnothkumar, Violetriga, Vishal5310, Viskonsas, Vivekyas, Vladmihaisima, Vmanthi, Vonfraginoff, Vrenator, Warpozio, Wavelength, Wayward, Wbm1058, Webshared, Wernher, West.andrew.g, WikiPuppies, Wikipelli, Windchaser, Wjw0111, Wknight94, WojPob, Woohookitty, Wtshymanski, Wutsje, Yamamoto Ichiro, Yarvin, Yes4us, Zajacik, Zundark, Zvika, 1006 anonymous edits

Digital_Equipment_Corporation *Source*: http://en.wikipedia.org/w/index.php?title=Digital_Equipment_Corporation *Contributors*: 62.253.64.xxx, AV3000, AdamWill, Adamantios, Aeons, After Midnight, Agentbla, Al Kossow, AlistairMcMillan, Altenmann, Amillar, Amire80, Ancheta Wis, ArnoldReinhold, Aspects, Atlant, Austinmurphy, Azikate, Badger Drink, Bbump, Bemoeial, Bender235, Bhludzin, Binarybits, Bobblewik, Bomazi, BonsaiViking, Brianski, BrokenSphere, Brouhaha, Bryanmackinnon, CWesling, CanisRufus, CarolGray, CatherineMunro, Cbh, Cbr2702, CecilWard, Cestes, Cgordonbell, Chowbok, Chris the speller, ChrisRuvolo, Christian Storm, CieloEstrellado, Cmacd123, Cminard, Cobi, Colorprobe, Computerhistory, Conversion script, Copros, Copyeditor42, Cwolfsheep, Cyanoa Crylate, DAGwyn, DMG413, DSP-user, Damian Yerrick, Daniel Pritchard, Darkguy, David spector, DavidWBrooks, Decvet, Dennis Brown, Dmsar, Dojarca, Dolovis, Don4of4, Donnymo, Dpbsmith, Dreaded Walrus, Dyl, EagleOne, Eaglizard, Edesio, Edward, Egern, Emelbee, Emperorbma, Enginear, Epbr123, Erik Corry, Evanbauer, Evil Monkey, Ewlyahoocom, Folajimi, FrankFlanagan, Funandtrvl, Gadget850, Gbuchana, Geertivp, GentlemanGhost, Gerard Czadowski, Ghettoblaster, Gihanuk, Glasnt, Greenshed, GregCutler, Guy Harris, Hairy Dude, Hansivers, Harryboyles, Hephaestos, Herostratus, Hmains, Hmich176, IMSoP, Icairns, Ideogram, IngerAlHaosului, Ingling, Ipduh, Itai, IvanLanin, JLaTondre, Jaraalbe, Jay, JayWhitney, Jedonnelley, Jerryobject, Jhobson1, Jj137, Jjzanath, Jkbw, Jll, Jnc, John Vandenberg, Jonel, Joren Six, Jp314159, Kalinrose, Kate, Ketiltrout, KnightRider, KrakatoaKatie, Lee Cremeans, Lee Daniel Crocker, Letdorf, Levin, Lightmouse, LilHelpa, Lilac Soul, Linuxlad, Litefantastic, LolaBeDen, LoopTel, Lotje, Luminifer, Lupo, M7, MITalum, ML2000, Macrakis, Maelnuneb, Martarius, Maury Markowitz, Mav, Mercurywoodrose, MichaelKirche, Mikeroetto, Mikus, Mild Bill Hiccup, Millennas, Mindmatrix, Minesweeper, Miracleworker5263, Miremare, Mirror Vax, Misternuvistor, Moink, MrDolomite, MrMichaelJKelly, Mu301, Murray Langton, Namazu-tron, NameThatWorks, Nbrouard, Neelix, NeilN, Neilc, Notheruser, NuclearWarfare, Ofiachain, Ohconfucius, One, OrgasGirl, Ortolan88, Oxymoron42, Ozga, Ozuma, Pat Berry, Paul1337, PaulLambert, Pblaauw, Peruvianllama, Peter Flass, Petr Kopač, Pinecone, Pkjohnston, PleaseStand, Pmj, Pol098, PrintStar, QTCaptain, Quadra630, Qwertyus, Qwyrxian, RTC, RageX, Raryel, Recury, RedWolf, Reify-tech, Rhe br, Rhsatrhs, Rich Farmbrough, Rilak, Riumplus, Rjwilmsi, Robinr57, Rogerd, Ronz, Roy G, RoyBoy, Rpb01r, Rwwww, Ryulong, Sam Korn, Sburke, SchuminWeb, ShadowHntr, Sheridan, Shieber, Sillybilly, Siobhanellis, Skapur, Softy, Soulpatch, Spacepotato, Starboy444, Stassats, StaticGull, Stephen, Stevestrange, StuartBrady, Supertouch, Sven, Svick, Swirsky, Tannin, TedPostol, Tedickey, Teratornis, TerrapinDundee, Thatdog, Theinfo, Time, Toresbe, TwoOneTwo, Twons, Unyoyega, Urbanrenewal, Urch9999, UtherSRG, Valtyr, Vanished user 5zariu3jisj0j4irj, Vkem, Vlad, Vt100, Wa3frp, Walin, Warpozio, Wavelength, Wayward, Wernher, Wgungfu, Wiarthurhu, WikiNickEN, Woohookitty, Woz2, Wtshymanski, Xnatedawgx, Youssefsan, Zippy, Zzedar, Δ, 344 anonymous edits

DEC_Alpha *Source*: http://en.wikipedia.org/w/index.php?title=DEC_Alpha *Contributors*: 62.253.64.xxx, Aarchiba, Aaronw, Adam Zivner, Aldie, Ali@gwc.org.uk, AlistairMcMillan, Alphaman, Arch dude, Arved, Atlant, Autiger, Bender235, Bletch, Borgx, Bovineone, BremenSaki, Brianski, Cestes, Chealer, Cmjrees, Cogiati, Conversion script, Crotalus horridus, Cuvtixo, Dan100, Darkness Productions, Ddkrahn, Delirium of disorder, Dispenser, DragonHawk, Dyl, Dysprosia, Edwin Herdman, Egern, Enatron, Enochlau, Enon, Erebus555, Ewlyahoocom, Fourohfour, Frap, Fuzheado, Gaius Cornelius, Gazpacho, Ghettoblaster, Giraffedata, Greudin, Grunt, Guy Harris, Hadal, Hellbus, Hideyuki, History2007, Hydrargyrum, Isnow, JCDenton2052, Jamo spingal, Janx Spirit, Jbalint, Jeh, Kate, Kurykh, Letdorf, Luís Felipe Braga, Macrakis, Mar5604, Marcelometal, MarkusHagenlocher, Marudubshinki, MatthewWilcox, Mattst88, Maury Markowitz, Mellum, Michael Hardy, Mild Bill Hiccup, MishMich, Morkork, Mrbill, Mtu, Myersj, NJM, Naddy, Neelix, Neilrieck, Neutrality, Norm mit, Orina, Packrat, Patcat88, Pinar, Pmj, QTCaptain, R. S. Shaw, Raven4x4x, RedWolf, Retired username, Rich257, Rilak, Rjwilmsi, Ryanaxp, Sarcastic Avenger, Sarenne, Sbisolo, Sleske, Spacepotato, Stan Shebs, Stefan B, Strangethingintheland, SunCreator, Suruena, Ta bu shi da yu, Thumperward, Thunderbird2, Timharwoodx, Tom.Reding, Toussaint, TwoOneTwo, VMS Mosaic, Vargenau, Viznut, WSF, Wernher, Whosyourjudas, Wuxb, ²¹², 169 anonymous edits

Instruction_set *Source*: http://en.wikipedia.org/w/index.php?title=Instruction_set *Contributors*: 7265, Ablonus, Adambiswanger1, Adrianwn, AdvCentral, AlphaPyro, Alriode, Andrei Stroe, Asfarer, Biblbroks, Bookmaker, Borgx, CRGreathouse, CanisRufus, CecilWard, Chaitanya lala, Chatul, Chjb, Chris the speller, Computor, Cpiral, Cyrius, Damian Yerrick, DanBishop, Davemck, David Shay, DavidCary, Dawynn, Destynova, Dicklyon, Dubious Irony, Dyl, Dysprosia, Epolk, Eumolpo, Everyking, Frap, Fyyer, GRAHAMUK, Gaius Cornelius, Goyim, Guy Harris, Hans Genten, HenkeB, HenkvD, Henriok, IanOsgood, Igodard, Jedidan747, Jiri 1984, Jkl, JonHarder, Jpbowen, Kamenraider, Kbdank71, Killdevil, Klilidiplomus, Kumioko (renamed), LaosLos, LilHelpa, LjL, Loadmaster, MER-C, Magister Mathematicae, Malcolm Farmer, Marc Mongenet, Matt Britt, Mfield, Miyagawa, Mshonle, Mudlock, Murray Langton, Music Sorter, Neelix, Neilc, Nikevich, Oliverdl, Opcode, Opelio, Orayzio, Parallelized, Pcap, PigFlu Oink, Pnm, QTCaptain, Quuxplusone, R. S. Shaw, RTC, Rachmaninoff, Raul654, Rfc1394, Riana, Rich Farmbrough, Rilak, Robert Merkel, Rotring, Sekhui, Simeon, Slowking Man, Soli1978, Solipsist, Sordomudo11, SpaceFlight89, Spinality, TakuyaMurata, That Guy, From That Show!, VampWillow, Vector4F, Vedant, Vikingstad, Wbm1058, Wdfarmer, Wengier, Wtshymanski, Yngvarr, Zetawoof, Zigger, Zink Dawg, ZyMOS, سمرقندی, 148 anonymous edits

Alpha_21064 *Source*: http://en.wikipedia.org/w/index.php?title=Alpha_21064 *Contributors*: Blaxthos, Dyl, Jamelan, Letdorf, LilHelpa, MattieTK, Oguzhan Yildiz, Rich Farmbrough, Rilak, Whitebox, 7 anonymous edits

Alpha_21264 *Source*: http://en.wikipedia.org/w/index.php?title=Alpha_21264 *Contributors*: Balloonguy, Beren, Bunnyhop11, Bwilkins, Frap, Jamelan, Lightmouse, Pavel Tkachuk, Rilak, SchreiberBike, 7 anonymous edits

Windows_NT *Source*: http://en.wikipedia.org/w/index.php?title=Windows_NT *Contributors*: 2008boy, 9258fahsflkh917fas, A Raider Like Indiana, ACupOfCoffee, AS, Adam Bishop, AgAuMoney, Agentbla, Agentlame, Akhristov, Alan Millar, Alansohn, Alerante, Alex scarfone, Alexius08, AlistairMcMillan, Amanda.da.da, An-chan, Andonic, Andyluciano, Angelbo, Antonrojo, Arch314, Arjun G. Menon, Arny, Ashley Pomeroy, Astroview120mm, Aszymanik, AussieLegend, B1atv, Bevo, Bfigura's puppy, BigNate37, Biscuittin, Blathnaid, Bobblewik, Bogdangiusca, Bomazi, Bongwarrior, Brewcrewer, Bryan Derksen, Btornado, Bwoodring, CJLL Wright, COstop, Can't sleep, clown will eat me, Ceaser, Ceyockey, Chealer, Ciphergoth, Closedmouth, CodenameCueball, Coffee, Computerdude33, Conversion script, Curlz07, DCM, Dan100, Darkhawk1591, Darrien, Delirium, Delldot, Denelson83, Dennis Brown, Denniss, Dillee1, Discospinster, Discpad, DmitTrix, Dmsar, Don Cuan, Doommaster1994, Dorsal Axe, Dysprosia, E-Magination, EagleOne, Ehurtley, Enochlau, Epbr123, FF2010, Falcon9x5, Felipe1982,

Fernvale, Fishnet37222, FleetCommand, Fragglet, Freddy011, Freebullets, Frozenport, Gary King, Gbjbaanb, Gr8ankit, Graham87, GrandDrake, Groink, Gurch, Guy Harris, HJ Mitchell, Hadal, HåeB, Hairy Dude, HairyFotr, Hammersoft, Happy Dude, HedgeHog, HolgerPollmann, I Do Care, Ibroadbent, Ichwan Palongengi, Illegal Operation, ImperfectlyInformed, Inomyabcs, Intgr, Itzraj, JStewart, Jacob.lyle1, Jamieplucinski, Jay, Jbolden1517, Jeh, Jerrysmp, JimVC3, Jlavsund, Jnc, Joffeloff, Jojit fb, Joseph Solis in Australia, Josh the Nerd, JuJube, Jutiphan, Katarighe, Kbolino, Keilana, Kesla, Kev19, Klaws, Kmanojr, Kmorozov, Kozuch, Kristof vt, KumardipSarkar, Kylegordon, Leandrod, Leoest, Letdorf, Leuk he, Linfocito B, LinkTiger, Lotje, Lowellian, Lupin, MER-C, Magnus.de, Malmckay, Malx, Marc Kupper, MarkKB, Mav, Maximus Rex, Mephiles602, Michael Angelkovich, Mike Dillon, Mikeblas, Mirror Vax, Monedula, Mr. Anon515, MtB, Mysid, N-Man, Naddy, Nanshu, Natalie Erin, NathanHawking, NawlinWiki, Nburden, NetVicious, Newportm, Newshound, Nicholas Love, Nintendude, Noypi380, Ntsimp, OSX, Ocon, Oneiros, Ortolan88, Oscarivera9, Ozzmosis, Pablo X, Patcat88, PatrikR, Paul kenneth mora, Pcuser42, Peyre, Pgan002, Piano non troppo, Pmsyyz, Poccil, Poor Yorick, Praneelreddy, Quantum Burrito, Quendus, Qwertyus, RA0808, RFBailey, Reach Out to the Truth, Rebroad, RedWolf, Resplendent, Rhobite, Rhys42, Rich Farmbrough, RichiH, Riemann Zeta, RingtailedFox, Rjwilmsi, Rl, Roadmr, Rockfang, Rodrigostrauss, Ruud Koot, Ryanaxp, SMcCandlish, Sahrin, Samlaptop85213, Samuel, Samvscat, SchmuckyTheCat, Scientus, ScottSteiner, Scottbob9, Sfan00 IMG, Shadowjams, ShaunL, Shjacks45, Slysplace, Soapfoam, SoccerMan2009, Soumyasch, SpigotMap, Sri555777, Starkiller88, Stephen Gilbert, Stephenchou0722, SteveLoughran, SteveSims, Syp, Szajd, Ta bu shi da yu, Tarquin, Tbhotch, Techkid100, Techman224, Technorob, Tedickey, Template namespace initialisation script, The Thing That Should Not Be, TheFeds, Thenerdgod, Thlump, Thumperward, Tommy2010, TonyW, Torquemada1970, Tothwolf, Tumacama, Twiek, Tyomitch, Umofomia, Uncle G, Uzume, Vanished895703, Vegaswikian, Vlad, W3bbo, WadeSimMiser, Wangowiki, Warren, Wengier, Wenli, Wiarthurhu, Wiki alf, WikiWikiPhil, Willtheoct, WinTakeAll, X-Bert, Xammer, Xpclient, Yamla, Yuhong, Yukoba, Zsinj, Zundark, שחנדופיק, 667 anonymous edits

Operating_system *Source*: http://en.wikipedia.org/w/index.php?title=Operating_system *Contributors*: 10metreh, 12.245.75.xxx, 1297, 130.64.31.xxx, 149AFK, 151.30.199.xxx, 1exec1, 1yesfan, 216.150.138.xxx, 28421u2232nfenfcenc, 2D, 2nth0nyj, 62.253.64.xxx, 789455dot38, 9258fahsflkh917fas, 9marksparks9, =Josh.Harris, A876, APH, AR bd, AVRS, AVand, Aaron north, Aaronstj, Abhik0904, Ablewisuk, Ablonus, Acerperi, Achowat, Adair2324, Adams kevin, Addshore, Adityachodya, AdjustShift, Adriaan, Ae-a, Afed, After Midnight, Agentlame, Ahoerstemeier, Ahunt, Ahy1, Aim Here, Aitias, Aladdin Sane, Alanbrowne, Alansohn, Alasdair, Ale jrb, AlefZet, Alegoo92, Alenaross07, AlexDitto, Alexei-ALXM, Alexf, Alexius08, Alexswilliams, Alextyhy, Alexwcovington, Alisha.4m, AlistairMcMillan, Alksentrs, Alll, Alsandro, Altay437, Alten, Althepal, Am088, Amicon, Amillar, Amphlett7, Anaxial, Andre Engels, Andrew Maiman, Andrewpmk, Android Mouse, Andy pyro, Andy16666, Andyzweb, Ang3lboy2001, Anna Lincoln, AnnaFrance, AnonMoos, Anouymous, Ansumang, Antandrus, Antonielly, Antonio Lopez, Applechair, Arakunem, Aranea Mortem, Arch dude, Archanamiya, Archer3, Ark, Arman Cagle, Aruton, Ashikpa, Ashish Gaikwad, Ashleypurdy, Astral, Atlant, Atomician, Attitude2000, Avenged Eightfold, Awaterl, Ayla, BMF81, Bachinchi, Bact, Badhaker, Badriram, Baron1984, Baronnet, Bastique, Bbbl67, Bbuss, Beland, Ben Webber, BenAveling, Bencherlite, Benneman, Beno1000, Betacommand, Bevo, Bhu z Crecelu, BiT, Bidgee, Big Brother 1984, BigDunc, Bigdumbdinosaur, Bijesh nair, BjörnBergman, Blainster, Bleh999, Blu Aardvark III, Bluemask, Bobo192, Boing! said Zebedee, Bonadea, Bongwarrior, Bookinvestor, Bornslippy, Branddobbe, Brianga, Brion VIBBER, Brolin Empey, Brownga, Bsadowski1, Btate, Bubba hotep, Buonoj, Burkeaj, Bwildasi, Cactus.man, Caknuck, Calabe1992, Callmejosh, Calltech, CalumH93, Camilo Sanchez, Caminoix, Can You Prove That You're Human, Can't sleep, clown will eat me, CanadianLinuxUser, Canageek, CanisRufus, Canterbury Tail, Capricorn42, Captain Goggles, Captain-n00dle, CarbonUnit, CarbonX, CardinalDan, Carlosvigopaz, Cartread, Casull, Cdills, Celebere, CesarB, Cfallin, Chairman S., Chaitanya.lala, Chamal N, ChaoticHeavens, Charles Nguyen, Charles dye, CharlotteWebb, Chase@osdev.org, Chatul, Chikoosahu, Chris1219, Chrisch, Chrislk02, Christian List, Christian75, Ck lostsword, Cleduc, Clindhartsen, Cllnk, Closedmouth, Clsin, Cncxbox, Cobi, Coffee, CommonsDelinker, Comperr, Conan, Conti, Conversion script, Cookdn, Coolcaesar, CoolingGibbon, Corpx, Courcelles, Cp111, Cpiral, Cps274203, Cpuwhiz11, Crazycomputers, Create g77, Creativename, Credema, Creidieki, Cul22dude, Cuvtixo, Cybercobra, Cybiko123, CyborgTosser, D, D6, DARTH SIDIOUS 2, DBishop1984, DJ Craig, DStoykov, DVdm, Daesotho, Damian Yerrick, Dan100, DanDoughty, Daniel C, Danieltobey, Dantheman88, Darkwind, Darth Panda, Dasnov, Daverocks, David Santos, DavidCary, DavidHalko, Davidam, Davidm617617, Dawnseeker2000, DeDroa, DeadEyeArrow, Deagle AP, Debloper, Deconstructhis, Defender of torch, Dekard, Dekisugi, Delinka, Demiurge, Demonkoryu, Denisarona, Deon, DerHexer, Desolator12, DestroyerPC, Dexter Nextnumber, Dhardik007, DiaNoCHe, DigitallyBorn, Dirkbb, DirkvdM, Discospinster, Dispenser, DivineAlpha, Djonesuk, Djsasso, Dmerrill, Dmlandfair, Doh5678, Donhoraldo, Dori, Dosman, Download, Doyley, DrDnar, DreamFieldArts, Drmies, Drummondjacob, Dsda, Dudboi, Duke56, DuncanHill, Dvn805, Dyl, Dynaflow, Dysprosia, Dzubint, E Wing, E.mammadli, ERcheck, ESkog, Eab28, Easwarno1, Echo95, EconoPhysicist, EdEColbert, Edivorce, Edward, Edwy, Eeekster, Ehheh, El C, Eleete, Elkman, Ellmist, Elockid, Elsendero, Elvenmuse, Ems2, Emurphy42, Emwave, Emx, Endothermic, Enigmar007, Enna59, Enno, Ente75, Enviroboy, Epbr123, Erickanner, Erkan Yilmaz, ErkinBatu, Escape Orbit, Ethan.hardman, Ethanhardman3, EurekaLott, Eurleif, Evercat, EwokiWiki, Excirial, Eyreland, Face, Falcon Kirtaran, Falcon8765, Favonian, Feedintm, Felyza, Ferrenrock, Fish and karate, Flewis, Flonase, Florian Blaschke, Flubbit, Fobenavi, Foot, ForrestVoight, Fram, Francis2795, Frankdushantha, Frap, Fred Gandt, FredStrauss, Fredrik, Freyr, Friecode, Fronx, Fsiler, Fubar Obfusco, Furrykef, Fvasconcellos, Fyver528, GB fan, GRAHAMUK, Gail, Gaius Cornelius, Gardar Rurak, Garlovel, Gaurav1146, Gauravdce07, Gazpacho, Gbeeker, Geekman314, GeneralChrisV, Georgia guy, Geph, Gepotto, Gerard Czadowski, Ghakko, Ghettoblaster, Ghyll, Giftlite, Glacialfox, Glen, Gogo Dodo, Gogodidi, Golfington, Golftheman, GoneAwayNowAndRetired, Goodnightmush, GorillaWarfare, Gorrister, Gortu, Grafen, Graham87, Grandscribe, GrayFullbuster, Greensburger, GrooveDog, Grosscha, Ground Zero, Grover cleveland, Grunt, Gschizas, Gscshoyru, Gtgray1948, Guess Who, Gumbos, Gurch, Guy Harris, HDrake, Hammersoft, Hanii Puppy, Hannes Hirzel, Hansfn, Harry, Harryboyles, Hashar, Hawaiian717, Hazard-SJ, Hdante, HeikoEvermann, Henriquevicente, Heron, HexaChord, Hillel, Hirzel, Hmains, Holden15, Hqb, Hrundi Bakshi, Htaccess, Huszone, Hut 8.5, Hydrogen Iodide, II MusLiM HyBRiD II, IMSoP, Iamunknown, Ian Dunster, Ian Pitchford, Ian.thomson, Icefirearceus, Ida Shaw, Ideogram, Idleguy, Ilmari Karonen, Indon, Inferno, Lord of Penguins, Ino5hiro, Insanity Incarnate, Integralexplora, Intgr, Ioeth, Iridescent, IronGargoyle, Ishanjand, Iswariya.r, It Is Me Here, ItsMeowAnywhere, Ixfd64, J Milburn, J.delanoy, J00tel, JForget, JHunterJ, JLaTondre, JSpudeman, Jaan513, Jackfork, Jackmiles2006, James pic, JamesAM, JamesBWatson, Janitor Starr, Jarble, Jasper Deng, Jatkins, Javierito92, Jaxl, Jaysweet, Jbarta, Jclemens, Jdm64, Jdrowlands, Jebus989, Jedikaiti, Jeff G., Jeffwang, Jeltz, JeremyA, Jerome Charles Potts, Jeronimo, Jerry, Jerryobject, Jerrysmp, Jesse V., JetBlast, Jfg284, Jfmantis, Jh51681, Jhonsrid, Jijojohnpj, Jim1138, JimPlamondon, Jimmi Hugh, Jjk, Jjupiter100, Jkl4201, JoanneB, Jobrad, JoeSmack, Joecoolatjunkmaildotcom, Joemaza, Joffeloff, John Nevard, Johnnaylor, Johnny039, Johnuniq, JonHarder, Jonathan Hall, Jordi Burguet Castell, Jorge.guillen, JorgePeixoto, Josef.94, Josepsbd, Josh the Nerd, Joshlk, Joshua Gyamfi, Joy, Jpeeling, Jstirling, Jsysinc, Julepalme, Jumbuck, Jusdafax, K7jeb, KAtremer, KDesk, KGasso, Ka Faraq Gatri, Kagredon, Kajasudhakarababu, Kamanleodickson, Karabulutis252, Karimarie, Karnesky, Karol Langner, Karolinski, Kashmiri, Katalaveno, Kathleen.wright5, Katieh5584, Kaustubh.singh, Kaypoh, Kbdank71, Kbrose, Kcordina, Ke5crz, KenBest, Kenny sh, KenshinWithNoise, Kenyon, Kerowhack, Kev19, Kevin586, Kgoetz, Khoikhoi, Kidde, Kim Bruning, Kimdino, Kjaleshire, Kjetil r, Kjkolb, Kku, Klungel, Knokej, Knownot, Kokamomi, Kotiwalo, KrakatoaKatie, Krauss, Kubanczyk, Kuru, Kushalbiswas777, Kusma, Kusunose, Kwiki, Kyle1278, Kyng, Kyuuseishu, L Kensington, LFaraone, La Pianista, Lambiam, Landroo, Latka, Law, Leaflord, LeaveSleaves, Lejarrag, LeoNomis, Letdorf, Leuko, Lifemaestro, Lightedbulb, Lindert, Linkspamremover, Linnell, Littlegeisha, Livajo, Lkatkinsmith, Lmmaaaoooo, Loadmaster, Logan, Logixoul, Lordmarlineo, Lost.goblin, Love manjeet kumar singh, Lovelac7, Lowellian, Lradrama, Lt monu, Ltomuta, Lucid, Lucy-seline, Lucyin, Luk, Lumos3, Luna Santin, Lvken7, Lysander89, Lyt701, M.r santosh kumar., M2Ys4U, M4gnum0n, MBisanz, MC MasterChef, MER-C, MONGO, Mabdul, Macintosh User, Macintosh123, Magnus Manske, Maitchy, Makeemlighter, Manassehkatz, Mandarax, Manickam001, Manmohan Brahma, Manojbp07, Manticore, March23.1999, Marek69, MarioRadev, MarkSG, Markaci, Marko75, MarmotteNZ, Martarius, Martin smith 637, Martinwguy, Masonkinyon, Materialscientist, MattGiuca, Mattbr, Matthardingu, Matthuxtable, MattieTK, Mav, Max Naylor, Maxim, Maximus Rex, Maziotis, Mbalamuruga, Mblumber, Mc hammerutime, McDutchie, McLovin34, Mcloud91, Mdd, Mdikici, Meaghan, Medovina, Meegs, Melab-1, Melsaran, Memset, Mendalus, Meneth, Meowmeow8956, Merlion444, MetaEntropy, Miaers, Michael B. Trausch, MichaelR., Michaelas10, Mickyfitz13, Mike33, Mike92591, MikeLynch, Mikeblas, Milan Keršláger, Mild Bill Hiccup, Minesweeper, Minghong, Miquonranger03, Mirror Vax, Miss Madeline, MisterCharlie, Mistman123, MithrandirAgain, Mmxx, Mnemoc, Mononomic, Monz, Moondyne, Mortus Est, MovGP0, Mppl3z, Mptb3, Mr.Z-man, MrOllie, MrPaul84, Mrankur, Mthomp1998, Mualif02, Muehlburger, Mufka, Mujz1, Muralihbh, Murderbike, Musiphil, Mwanner, Mwheatland, Mwtoews, Mxn, Müslimix, N sharma000, N419BH, N5iln, NNLauron, Nakon, Nanshu, Naohiro19 revertvandal, NapoliRoma, Nasnema, NawlinWiki, Nayak143, Nayvik, Ndavidow, NellieBly, Nergaal, Neversay.misher, Ngch89, Ngien, Ngyikp, Nick, Nikai, Ninuxpdb, Nixeagle, Njuuton, Nk, Nlu, No Guru, Nobody Ent, Noldoaran, Nono64, Norm, Northamerica1000, NotAnonymous0, Nothingisoftensomething, Notinasnaid, Nrabinowitz, Nsaa, Numlockfishy, Nvt, Nwusr123log, O.Koslowski, OKtosiTe, Ocolon, Oda Mari, Odell421, Odie5533, Ohnoitsjamie, Olathe, Oliverdl, Olivier, OllieWilliamson, OlurotimiO, Omicronpersei8, Omniplex, Ondertitel, Onorem, Oosoom, Optimisticrizwan, OrgasGirl, Orrs, Oxymoron83, P.Marlow, Papadopa, Parasti, Patato, Patrick, Paul E T, Paul1337, Pcbsder, Pepper, PeterStJohn, Petrb, PhJ, PhantomS, Phgao, Phil websurfer@yahoo.com, Philip Howard, Philip Trueman, Photonik UK, Piano non troppo, Pierre Monteux, Pinethicket, Pinkadelica, Pithree, Plasticup, PlutosGeek, Pmlineditor, Polluks, Polyamorph, Pontiacsunfire08, Posix memalign, Prashanthomesh, PrestonH, Programming geek, Prolog, Prophile, Pruefer, Public Menace, Puffin, Qaanol, Quarkuar, Qwerty0, Qwyrxian, R'n'B, R. S. Shaw, RA0808, RB972, RTC, Raanoo, Rabi Javed, Raffaele Megabyte, RainbowOfLight, Rainsak, Rami R, Ramif 47, Random Hippopotamus, RandomAct, RaseaC, Ratnadeepm, RattusMaximus, RavenXtra, Rayngwf, Raysonho, Raywil, RazorICE, Rbakels, Rbanzai, Rdsmith4, Reach Out to the Truth, RedWolf, Reedy, Rektide, Remixsoft10, Rettetast, RexNL, Rfc1394, Rhyswynne, Riana, Rich Farmbrough, Rilak, Rjgarr, Rjwilmsi, Rlinfinity, Rmere, Rmhermen, Robert K S, Robert Merkel, RobertG, Robertwharvey, RockMaster, Rockstone35, Rodri316, RogierBrussee, Rokfaith, Rolandg, Romanm, Ronark, Ronhjones, RossPatterson, Rotem Dan, RoyBoy, Rrelf, Rror, Rubena, Rubicon, Rzelnik, S.borchers, S10462, SF007, SNIyer12, SPQRobin, Safinaskar, Sainath468, Sakariyerirash, Sam Vimes, SampigeVenkatesh, Sander123, Sanfranman59, Sango123, Sardanaphalus, Sarikaanand, Scherr, SchmuckyTheCat, SchuminWeb, Schwallex, Schzmo, Sdfisher, Sean William, Seba5618, Sedmic, Senator Palpatine, Sewing, Shadowjams, Sharanbngr, Sharkert, SheikYerBooty, Shizhao, Shreevatsa, Shreshth91, Shriram, Sidious1741, Sigma 7, Signalhead, Silas S. Brown, Simon the Dragon, SimonP, Simxp, Sir Nicholas de Mimsy-Porpington, SirGrant, SirGre, SivaKumar, Skarebo, Skomes, Slgrandson, Slogan621, Slon02, SmackEater, Smadge1, Snowmanradio, Snowolf, Socalaaron, Socrates2008, SocratesJedi, SolKarma, SolarisBigot, Sommers, Sophus Bie, South Bay, Sp, Spanglegluppet, Sparkle24, SpooK, SpuriousQ, Squash, Sridip, Staffwaterboy, Stealthmartin, Stephen Gilbert, Stephen Turner, Stephenb, Stephenchou0722, SteveSims, Stevenj, Stewartadcock, Stickee, Stormie, SudoGhost, SunCountryGuy01, SunCreator, Sunay419, Super Mac Gamer, SuperLuigi31, Superswade, SusanLesch, Susheel verma, Sven Manguard, Sven nestle, Sweet blueberry pie, Synchronism, Syzygy, THEN WHO WAS PHONE?, THeReDragOn, Ta bu shi da yu, Tannin, TarkusAB, Tarmo Tanilsoo, Tarquin, Tasting boob, Tatrgel, Tdrtdr, Tdscanuck, TempestSA, TexasAndroid, Texture, Tgeairn, Tgnome, The Anome, The Random Editor, The Thing That Should Not Be, The undertow, The1DB, TheAMmollusc, TheNewPhobia, TheWorld, Thecomputist, Theda, Thedjatclubrock, TheguX, Themoose8, Theshibboleth, Thingg, Thorpe, Thumperward, Tide rolls, TigerShark, Timir Saxa, Titoxd, Tnxman307, Tobias Bergemann, Toddst1, Tokai, Tom Hek, Tom harrison, Tomcool, Tommy2010, TommyB7973, Tompsci, Tony1, Tothwolf, Touch Of Light, Tpbradbury, Tpk5010, Traroth, Travelbird, Trevj, Trevjs, Trimaine, Triona, Trisweb, Triwbe, TurboForce, Twas Now, Twistedkevin, Twitty666, Twsx, Tyler, Tyomitch, Typhoon, Tyrel, Ultimus, Umofomia, Unbreakable MJ, Uncle Dick, Unixguy, Unknown-xyz, Uogl, Upthegro, Ursu17, Urvashi.iyogi, Useight, User A1, Utahraptor ostrommaysi, Utilitytrack, VampWillow, Vanessaezekowitz, Vanished user 39948282, Vbigdeli, VegaDark, Verrai, Vicenarian, Vikrant manore, Vincenzo.romano, Viriditas, Vorosgy, Vox Humana 8', Vrenator, W163, WJetChao, Wapcaplet, Wareh, Warren, Warut, Wasted Sapience, Waterjuice, Wavelength, Wayward, Wbm1058, Wdfarmer, Wdflake, Weedwhacker128, WellHowdyDoo, White Shadows, Who.was.phone, Widefox, WikHead, Wiki Wikardo, Wiki alf, WikiDan61, WikiPuppies, WikiTome, Wikievil666, Wikiloop, Wikipelli, WilyD, Winchelsea, Wingnutamj, Winhunter, Winston365, Wisconsinsurfer, Wk muriithi, Wknight94, Wluka, Woohookitty, World-os.com, WorldBrains, Wormsgoat, Wtmitchell, Wtshymanski, Wwagner, X42bn6, Xdenizen, Yaronf, Yellowdesk, Yes-minister, Yidisheryid, Yoink23, Youwillnevergetthis, Yunshui, Yworo, Zephyrus67, Zfr, Zidonuke, Zigger, Ziiike, Zlemming, Zondor, Zotel, Zx-man, Zzuuzz, 212, Ævar

Arnfjörð Bjarmason, Милан Јелисавчић, نوری سارای, පසිඳු කාවින්ද, , 3140 anonymous edits

OpenVMS *Source*: http://en.wikipedia.org/w/index.php?title=OpenVMS *Contributors*: Adamantios, AlexKarpman, AlistairMcMillan, Alphaman, Amire80, Andrés Santiago Pérez-Bergquist, Anilocra, Arch dude, Armistej, Arthena, Atlant, Atrivo, BB98uk, BBCWatcher, Bachcell, Batpox, Bclaremont, Betacommand, Billposer, Bk0, Bkil, Bovineone, Brian McNeil, CWesling, Causa sui, CecilWard, Cestes, Citizensmith, Conversion script, Cpiral, Crusadeonilliteracy, Cwhii, DNewhall, Damian Yerrick, Danakil, Daniel.Cardenas, David Gerard, Dbeorn, Deeahbz, Denimadept, Deville, Dojarca, DrMemory, DragonHawk, Druiloor, Eagleamn, Edward, Egern, El C, ElBenevolente, Enatron, EncMstr, ErkinBatu, EugeneZelenko, Evice, Ewlyahoocom, FatalError, Floyd Flemmingsworth, Frap, Garion96, Geertivp, Gerard Czadowski, Ghettoblaster, Gndjaldod, Graham87, Greenrd, Grstain, Gurch, Guy Harris, Hairy Dude, Helpsloose, Hornlo, Hroðulf, IEdML, Iamcamiel, Intgr, JC Chu, JaGa, Jdcope, Jerryobject, Joe Sewell, Joffeloff, John of Reading, Jonabbey, Jonlandrum, Kate, Kbrose, Kellyprice, Kku, Kubanczyk, Ldo, Leofric1, Leotohill, Letdorf, Loadmaster, LolaBeDen, Lopifalko, Lunchdoes, Lupin, Magnus.de, Mardus, Mark Foskey, Mark Renier, MarkusHagenlocher, Marudubshinki, Maxbe, Methem, Mikko J. Putkonen, Mirror Vax, Mkrajenke, NapoliRoma, NawlinWiki, Neilrieck, Oneiros, Ortolan88, PGSONIC, Paddles, PanTarkan, Pauli133, PauloCalipari, Pavel Tkachuk, PeteVerdon, Phatphilosopher, PkerUNO, Pocopocopocopoco, Polluks, Portnadler, Qwertyus, RTC, Rajeevgm, Raul654, Ravenswing, Reub2000, Rfc1394, Rich Farmbrough, Rilak, Ringbang, Rjwilmsi, Royhills, Rwwww, Ryanaxp, Scotth1, Seashorewiki, Seasoned geek, Sgould, SirPavlova ♥, Sjorford, Slathering, Smallpond, Softy, Solak, Soulpatch, Ste4k, Stilroc, StormWillLaugh, Stormie, Strongbow, Surv1v4l1st, Swaq, Teeschmid, Thalakan, The Anome, The Thing That Should Not Be, TimBentley, Tobias Bergemann, Towopedia, Ummit, VMS Mosaic, Vanished user 34958, Viznut, VoxLuna, W2bh, Warren, Warren.sander@hp.com, Wavelength, Weimanm, Wereon, Wernher, WikiNickEN, WojPob, Yworo, 229 anonymous edits

Image Sources, Licenses and Contributors

Image:Processor board cray-2 hg.jpg *Source*: http://en.wikipedia.org/w/index.php?title=File:Processor_board_cray-2_hg.jpg *License*: unknown *Contributors*: User:Hgrobe

Image:DEC Alpha 21164.jpg *Source*: http://en.wikipedia.org/w/index.php?title=File:DEC_Alpha_21164.jpg *License*: unknown *Contributors*: User:Appaloosa

File:Intel 4004.jpg *Source*: http://en.wikipedia.org/w/index.php?title=File:Intel_4004.jpg *License*: unknown *Contributors*: Original uploader was LucaDetomi at it.wikipedia

File:Z80 arch.svg *Source*: http://en.wikipedia.org/w/index.php?title=File:Z80_arch.svg *License*: unknown *Contributors*: User:Appaloosa

File:C4004.JPG.jpg *Source*: http://en.wikipedia.org/w/index.php?title=File:C4004.JPG.jpg *License*: unknown *Contributors*: Photo by John Pilge.

File:Gl250 PICO1 die photo.jpg *Source*: http://en.wikipedia.org/w/index.php?title=File:Gl250_PICO1_die_photo.jpg *License*: unknown *Contributors*: User:Jamo spingal

File:80486DX2 200x.png *Source*: http://en.wikipedia.org/w/index.php?title=File:80486DX2_200x.png *License*: unknown *Contributors*: User:Uberpenguin

File:Digital 556-flattened4.svg *Source*: http://en.wikipedia.org/w/index.php?title=File:Digital_556-flattened4.svg *License*: unknown *Contributors*: User:Brianski

File:Maynard MA Clock Tower Place.jpg *Source*: http://en.wikipedia.org/w/index.php?title=File:Maynard_MA_Clock_Tower_Place.jpg *License*: unknown *Contributors*: self

File:Dec SYSTEM BUILDING BLOCKS 1103.jpg *Source*: http://en.wikipedia.org/w/index.php?title=File:Dec_SYSTEM_BUILDING_BLOCKS_1103.jpg *License*: unknown *Contributors*: Original uploader was RTC at en.wikipedia Later version(s) were uploaded by Dpbsmith at en.wikipedia.

File:Steve Russell and PDP-1 - Vintage Computer Fair 2006.jpg *Source*: http://en.wikipedia.org/w/index.php?title=File:Steve_Russell_and_PDP-1_-_Vintage_Computer_Fair_2006.jpg *License*: unknown *Contributors*: Alex Handy

File:PDP-8.jpg *Source*: http://en.wikipedia.org/w/index.php?title=File:PDP-8.jpg *License*: unknown *Contributors*: ArnoldReinhold, Bayo, EugeneZelenko, Hellisp, Methem, 1 anonymous edits

file:KA10 mod end.jpg *Source*: http://en.wikipedia.org/w/index.php?title=File:KA10_mod_end.jpg *License*: unknown *Contributors*: User:Jnc

File:AlphaServer-2100-guts.jpg *Source*: http://en.wikipedia.org/w/index.php?title=File:AlphaServer-2100-guts.jpg *License*: unknown *Contributors*: Adamantios

File:Digital Equipment Corporation 1993 logo.png *Source*: http://en.wikipedia.org/w/index.php?title=File:Digital_Equipment_Corporation_1993_logo.png *License*: unknown *Contributors*: Original uploader was Geertivp at en.wikipedia

Image:Alpha AXP 21064 diephoto1.jpg *Source*: http://en.wikipedia.org/w/index.php?title=File:Alpha_AXP_21064_diephoto1.jpg *License*: unknown *Contributors*: User:Dyl

Image:DEC Alpha 21-35023-13 J40793-28 top.jpg *Source*: http://en.wikipedia.org/w/index.php?title=File:DEC_Alpha_21-35023-13_J40793-28_top.jpg *License*: unknown *Contributors*: Cookie, EugeneZelenko, GreyCat, Morkork, 1 anonymous edits

Image:Alpha AXP 21064 card1.jpg *Source*: http://en.wikipedia.org/w/index.php?title=File:Alpha_AXP_21064_card1.jpg *License*: unknown *Contributors*: User:Dyl

Image:KL Compaq DEC ALPHA 21264C.jpg *Source*: http://en.wikipedia.org/w/index.php?title=File:KL_Compaq_DEC_ALPHA_21264C.jpg *License*: unknown *Contributors*: Konstantin Lanzet

File:Dec alpha small.JPG *Source*: http://en.wikipedia.org/w/index.php?title=File:Dec_alpha_small.JPG *License*: unknown *Contributors*: User:Jamo spingal

File:Mips32 addi.svg *Source*: http://en.wikipedia.org/w/index.php?title=File:Mips32_addi.svg *License*: unknown *Contributors*: German, JMCC1, Nachcommonsverschieber

Image:KL_DEC_Alpha_21066.jpg *Source*: http://en.wikipedia.org/w/index.php?title=File:KL_DEC_Alpha_21066.jpg *License*: unknown *Contributors*: User:Adrignola

File:Alpha 21264.png *Source*: http://en.wikipedia.org/w/index.php?title=File:Alpha_21264.png *License*: unknown *Contributors*: Hellisp

File:Windows NT logo.svg *Source*: http://en.wikipedia.org/w/index.php?title=File:Windows_NT_logo.svg *License*: unknown *Contributors*: Artem Karimov, Dedalus, J.delanoy, Jjupiter100, Mads Ren`ai, Mike.lifeguard

Image:IBM360-65-1.corestore.jpg *Source*: http://en.wikipedia.org/w/index.php?title=File:IBM360-65-1.corestore.jpg *License*: unknown *Contributors*: Original uploader was ArnoldReinhold at en.wikipedia

Image:PC-DOS 1.10 screenshot.png *Source*: http://en.wikipedia.org/w/index.php?title=File:PC-DOS_1.10_screenshot.png *License*: unknown *Contributors*: Remember the dot at en.wikipedia (PNG)

Image:Apple Macintosh Desktop.png *Source*: http://en.wikipedia.org/w/index.php?title=File:Apple_Macintosh_Desktop.png *License*: unknown *Contributors*: A104375, Akhilsnair, AlistairMcMillan, BorgQueen, Chmod007, Ctachme, Diego Moya, EdC, Ferrenrock, Grm wnr, HereToHelp, N. Harmonik, Ricardo Cancho Niemietz, 4 anonymous edits

File:Unix history-simple.png *Source*: http://en.wikipedia.org/w/index.php?title=File:Unix_history-simple.png *License*: unknown *Contributors*: User:Eraserhead1

Image:First Web Server.jpg *Source*: http://en.wikipedia.org/w/index.php?title=File:First_Web_Server.jpg *License*: unknown *Contributors*: User:Coolcaesar at en.wikipedia

File:Mac OSX Lion screen.png *Source*: http://en.wikipedia.org/w/index.php?title=File:Mac_OSX_Lion_screen.png *License*: unknown *Contributors*: User:JohnHWiki

File:Ubuntu 11.10 Final.png *Source*: http://en.wikipedia.org/w/index.php?title=File:Ubuntu_11.10_Final.png *License*: unknown *Contributors*: Hydriz, KAMiKAZOW, Michael Barera, 1 anonymous edits

File:Android 4.0.png *Source*: http://en.wikipedia.org/w/index.php?title=File:Android_4.0.png *License*: unknown *Contributors*: Android Open Source project

File:Windows To Go USB Drive.png *Source*: http://en.wikipedia.org/w/index.php?title=File:Windows_To_Go_USB_Drive.png *License*: unknown *Contributors*: Adrignola, SF007, 2 anonymous edits

File:Windows 7.png *Source*: http://en.wikipedia.org/w/index.php?title=File:Windows_7.png *License*: unknown *Contributors*: Addihockey10, Althepal, AnOddName, Anakin101, Andyso, Anomie, AussieLegend, Bkell, Captaincollect1970, Crazlunatic, Drilnoth, Feinoha, FleetCommand, GSK, Grayshi, Jan Hofmann, JetBlast, Jjupiter100, Josh the Nerd, Koman90, LOL, LobStoR, Mephiles602, Ngyikp, Nicholas Love, OriginalGamer, PhilKnight, RegularBreaker, Roscelese, S0aasdf2sf, SF007, SchuminWeb, Sdrtirs, Seaphoto, Sonicdude558, Sotcr, SpaceFlight89, The 888th Avatar, Warren, Wtshymanski, 35 anonymous edits

Image:Kernel Layout.svg *Source*: http://en.wikipedia.org/w/index.php?title=File:Kernel_Layout.svg *License*: unknown *Contributors*: User:Bobbo

Image:Priv rings.svg *Source*: http://en.wikipedia.org/w/index.php?title=File:Priv_rings.svg *License*: unknown *Contributors*: Hertzsprung, 6 anonymous edits

File:Virtual memory.svg *Source*: http://en.wikipedia.org/w/index.php?title=File:Virtual_memory.svg *License*: unknown *Contributors*: User:Ehamberg

File:Dolphin FileManager.png *Source*: http://en.wikipedia.org/w/index.php?title=File:Dolphin_FileManager.png *License*: unknown *Contributors*: KDE

File:Command line.png *Source*: http://en.wikipedia.org/w/index.php?title=File:Command_line.png *License*: unknown *Contributors*: The GNU Dev team, and the Arch Linux Dev team (for the Pacman command in the example)

File:KDE 4.png *Source*: http://en.wikipedia.org/w/index.php?title=File:KDE_4.png *License*: unknown *Contributors*: KDE

Image:OpenVMS logo Swoosh 30 lg.jpg *Source*: http://en.wikipedia.org/w/index.php?title=File:OpenVMS_logo_Swoosh_30_lg.jpg *License*: unknown *Contributors*: Geertivp

Image:Vms shark hp.png *Source*: http://en.wikipedia.org/w/index.php?title=File:Vms_shark_hp.png *License*: unknown *Contributors*: CWesling, McLoaf

Image:DECwindows-openvms-v7.3-1.png *Source*: http://en.wikipedia.org/w/index.php?title=File:DECwindows-openvms-v7.3-1.png *License*: unknown *Contributors*: User:Lady Lysine Ikinsile

Made in United States
Orlando, FL
04 November 2026

90200177R00069